UNFLINCHING GAZE

Unflinching Gaze

Morrison and Faulkner Re-Envisioned

Edited by

Carol A. Kolmerten,

Stephen M. Ross, and

Judith Bryant Wittenberg

University Press of Mississippi/*Jackson*

Copyright © 1997 by the University Press of Mississippi
All rights reserved
Manufactured in the United States of America
00 99 98 97   4 3 2 1
The paper in this book meets the guidelines for permanence and
durability of the Committee on Production Guidelines for Book
Longevity of the Council on Library Resources.

Library of Congress Cataloging-in-Publication Data
Unflinching gaze : Morrison and Faulkner re-envisioned / edited by
    Carol A. Kolmerten, Stephen M. Ross, Judith Bryant
    Wittenberg.
        p.   cm.
    Includes bibliographical references and index.
    ISBN 0-87805-955-5 (cloth : alk. paper).—ISBN 0-87805-956-3
(paper : alk. paper)
    1. Morrison, Toni—Criticism and interpretation.   2. Literature
and society—United States—History—20th century.   3. American
fiction—20th century—History and criticism.   4. Faulkner, William,
1897–1962—Influence.   5. Afro-Americans in literature.   6. Race
relations in literature.   7. Sex role in literature.   8. Women in
literature.   I. Kolmerten, Carol A., 1946–   .   II. Ross, Stephen
M.   III. Wittenberg, Judith Bryant, 1938–   .
    PS3563.O8749Z93   1997
    813'.54—dc20   96-35243
                                                                        CIP

British Library Cataloging-in-Publication data available

CONTENTS

ACKNOWLEDGMENTS

This book owes a great debt to its intended audience: students. The questions that our students at Hood College and Simmons College have raised, their refusal to "look away," their insistence upon confronting literary, racial, and cultural issues without backing off have been an ongoing source of inspiration. We would like to thank the students in English 341 at Hood College in the spring of 1995: Carol Dorsey, Erin Franklin, Elisha Fridley, Lisa Jaronsinski, Tanya Miller, Beth Patrinicola, and Christie Spencer. Their final project for the class was to advise us in selecting the essays for this volume and to help shape them into a coherent whole. Their abilities astounded both them and us.

To Beth Patrinicola, we owe a special debt. Throughout the 1995–96 academic year, Beth was our research assistant and "jargon monitor." Beth read every essay many times, helping us clarify the issues and ensuring that an undergraduate student could follow and appreciate the arguments. Her comments to our contributors resulted in clearer, cleaner prose.

We also owe special thanks to the people and resources of Hood College and Simmons College. Specifically, we thank Grace Sheffield at Hood for all her efforts to help make this an exceptional collection. We also appreciate having the technology available to us—fax machines, laptop computers, e-mail—that make possible a collaboration when one of us lives and works in Boston, another of us works in Washington, D.C., and the other works in Frederick, Maryland.

We value the support of the University Press of Mississippi. Seetha A-Srinivasan was enthusiastic about the collection from first hearing about it; the efficient press staff helped to make the book a reality. The anonymous reader for the Press offered us immensely valuable suggestions for revisions.

Finally, we thank our contributors, who became our collaborators. Their willingness to reconsider ideas, to accept (or resist gracefully) our editorial suggestions, and to meet deadlines made the anthology a pleasure to prepare. More important, it is their insights, their analyses, their specific examples that bring into sharp relief the profound ways that Morrison's and Faulkner's fictions illuminate each other.

INTRODUCTION
Refusing to Look Away

Carol A. Kolmerten, Stephen M. Ross,
Judith Bryant Wittenberg

The idea for this collection of original essays grew out of a classroom experience when two of us team-taught "Faulkner and Morrison" to undergraduates in the spring of 1991. Our organization of the course was relatively simple: we paired four sets of texts, one by Faulkner and the other by Morrison, and then sat back and let the texts and the students speak to each other. Our readings of both authors were enriched in ways we had not quite expected. Preconceptions—ours and the students'—began to burst like soap bubbles. The first to go was any naive version of "influence." Quite soon we were reading Faulkner as much through Morrison as we were reading Morrison through Faulkner.

Notions of race and gender were challenged by the course as well. The women's college where we taught had in many ways prepared our students for frank discussions of gender, but nowhere had they (or we) been prepared for the explosive discussions of race that followed our readings of the paired Faulkner and Morrison texts. Students wept openly; one ran out of the room. White students felt threatened; black students felt threatened; *we* felt threatened; but we kept returning to our discussions from different angles, brought back by Morrison's and Faulkner's own refusal to look away, to let us fall back on easy stereotypes or conventional plot structures. Unsettled, we asked unsettling questions of each other that we had never asked before: can the white members of the class "appropriate" Toni Morrison, on the authority of a canonical Faulkner, into a "dominant" cultural discourse? Can the black members of a class "appropriate" Morrison, on the authority of a discredited canon, as spokesperson for racialized culture? Do we respond to this literature in racial ways? Is race a credential for the authority to speak about either author? Is gender? If so, how can one learn? How can our students become authorized by their education to step, intellectually or emotionally, across cultural, racial, or gender lines—in either direction?

Our often painful but always stimulating classes led our students to the library to seek what others had written about these two mutually compelling authors. They were surprised and unhappy when they found very few essays and no monographs that paired Faulkner and Morrison or that explored the kinds of issues we were raising in class. At some moment toward the end of the semester, in discussions among the three of us about the class experience, we decided that we needed to provide our students with just what they had not found. This collection is intended for our students and for all readers of Faulkner and Morrison, to keep the discussion alive.[1]

These original essays, then, explore the resonant intertextual relationship between the fiction of William Faulkner and that of Toni Morrison. Although the two writers are separated by a generation as well as by differences of race, gender, and regional origin, a close critical examination of the creative dialogue between their oeuvres is both timely and appropriate. Until now, the enormous body of critical writing on Faulkner and Morrison has included little that considers the profound interconnections between their works.[2] This volume, with its provocative contributions by 15 scholars of American literature, is the first collection to undertake an extensive examination of this interrelationship.

Toni Morrison's brilliant and powerful novels of the past two decades have accorded her a position in the front ranks of American writers, and like Faulkner before her, she has been awarded the Nobel Prize for literature. Morrison has publicly acknowledged her artistic indebtedness to Faulkner on a number of occasions. Certainly her 1955 M.A. thesis at Cornell demonstrates her preoccupation with Faulkner at a critical stage in her intellectual development. She has said that she had "spent a great deal of time thinking about Mr. Faulkner" and that he had "an enormous effect on me, an enormous effect" ("Faulkner and Women" 295, 296). At another moment Morrison admitted her desire to emulate Faulkner in focusing on a specific region, saying that the literature which resulted is both "good—and universal—because it is specifically about a particular world. That's what I wish to do" ("Language"; rpt. Taylor-Guthrie 124). Morrison's admiration for Faulkner in itself provides a rationale for exploring similarities in their fiction.

But, as a number of our contributors point out, Morrison also resists the Faulknerian heritage in profound ways. In her best-known repudiation, Morrison said, "I am not *like* James Joyce; I am not *like* Thomas Hardy; I am not *like* Faulkner" (Interview with Nellie McKay; rpt. Taylor-Guthrie 152). This resistance is certainly, in part at least, the natural reluctance of any highly original artist to be regarded as the product of her predecessors' influence ("I am not *like* in that sense"). The resistance, too, is also related to the inevitable differences in perspective between that of a white male novelist from Mississippi writing in the early to mid-twentieth century and that of an African-American[3] female novelist from Ohio writing in the waning years of the century. One major source of the critical energy exhibited in this collection is Morrison's complexly ambiguous response to the Faulknerian heritage, which oscillates between admiration and intense ambivalence.

The essays in this collection respond to the energy that emanates so powerfully from the interplay of Faulkner's and Morrison's literary discourses. Each of our contributors, whether addressing broad, general issues in both writers or whether detailing similarities and differences in particular works, finds that the authors illuminate each other. Not only does Morrison respond to Faulkner—"signify" on Faulkner, to use Henry Louis Gates's term—but no reader of Faulkner will ever read him in the same way after encountering the works of Morrison. The critical comparison of Morrison and Faulkner by this group of insightful critics enhances our understanding of individual texts and pairs of texts; it also explores a complex thematic and aesthetic dialogue that is one of the most compelling in American literary history.

But our reasons for jointly considering the work of these two distinguished American novelists go beyond formalistic matters or problems of literary "influence" and intertextuality. Read together, the fiction of Faulkner and Morrison offers a richly varied and profoundly moving meditation on racial, cultural, and gender issues in twentieth-century America. Both authors' fiction illuminates many of the most significant aspects of twentieth-century American culture and the past two centuries of American social history. Central to both their oeuvres are questions of, and about, "difference." These questions are often painful to explore but imperative to confront. Their work is memorable for what Morrison described as a characteristic of Faulkner's—a "refusal to look away." That refusal to look away applies, of course, as much to Morrison as it does to Faulkner. That their unflinching gaze creates profound discomfort in readers such as our students is unquestionable. That this discomfort and the reflections it provokes are of crucial importance in this particular historical moment is equally unquestionable.

This collection, assembled from a gratifyingly large number of responses to a call for papers, begins with a group of four essays that discuss broadly defined topics central to both authors and to the relationship between them. In "Toni Morrison and the Anxiety of Faulknerian Influence," John Duvall explores the fundamental and problematic question of what "influence" means when we consider Morrison's works in terms of Faulkner's. At stake explicitly in this lead essay and implicitly in all the essays is the nature of intertextuality itself: the issue of whether we can acknowledge and explore the significance of an intertextual relationship between Faulkner's and Morrison's texts without, even inadvertently, granting Faulkner's the status of "master text" or Morrison's the status of "corrective revisionary text." Duvall approaches this basic question in two ways, first by charting Morrison's own "decided ambivalence" toward Faulkner, evident in her conflicting statements about Faulkner's effect on her work, and second by defining some exemplary features of these two novelists' fictions that cause readers to see connections between them. Carolyn Denard, in "The Long, High Gaze: The Mythical Consciousness of Toni Morrison and William Faulkner," asks perhaps a more fundamental question: Why are we putting these two authors side by side? After (like Duvall) rejecting any answer reliant on influence, her answer is a refreshingly positive look at both writers. She finds that Morrison and Faulkner share a "mythical consciousness," a "redemptive gaze," that looks upon our human condition and refuses to look away from even the most discredited of humankind. In the worlds of these great authors, Denard concludes, we confront the possibility of grace through suffering.

Andrea Dimino's essay, "Toni Morrison and William Faulkner: Remapping Culture," places the two writers in a more explicitly cultural arena by examining how Morrison has rewritten Faulkner's canonical texts into her fiction in such a way as to allow us to see the changes in the cultural role and identity of the American artist in the twentieth century. Canvassing a wide range of the two authors' oeuvres, both fictional and nonfictional, Dimino examines the powerful doubleness of Morrison's "re-vision" of Faulkner, which pays tribute to his artistry while it combats some of his cultural affiliations and values. Whereas Faulkner persisted in trying, with mixed success, to separate his artist self from his role within society, Morrison's strategy reflects a complex, "nonreified" conception of artistic identity interweaving her perspectives as a fiction writer, a black woman, an American citizen, and a member of the academic community. Philip Weinstein's essay, "David and Solomon: Fathering in Faulkner and Morrison," looks specifically at one crucial theme that cuts across all the works of both authors, the concept of "fathering." He illustrates how Faulknerian tragedy, centered on the pathos of outraged sons, is grounded in the failure of the Oedipal norm of Western patriarchy, while Morrison has written her way beyond tragedy by reconceiving black manhood outside these norms.

The next seven essays juxtapose individual texts more explicitly and, through these pairings, explore a variety of thematic and methodological questions. Nancy Batty, in "Riff, Refrain, Reframe: Toni Morrison's Song of Absalom," looks specifically at musical forms such as gospel, blues, and jazz in Morrison's *Song of Solomon* and Faulkner's *Absalom, Absalom!*. In doing so she returns us to questions of influence by proposing an "intertextual practice" on Morrison's part that defines a cultural space shared but inhabited very differently by the two authors. In her evocative talk (originally given at the American Literature Association in 1994), "Narrative Time/Spiritual Text: *Beloved* and *As I Lay Dying*," Karla Holloway explores another kind of intertextuality, deriving from spirituality of place and narrative in novels of the dead and mourned. Lucinda MacKethan takes a different approach from either Weinstein or Holloway in looking at legacies of the past in Faulkner and Morrison. In her essay "The Grandfather Clause: Reading the Legacy from 'The Bear' to *Song of Solomon*," she demonstrates how both stories can be read as about making and reading texts of the past. MacKethan suggests that Morrison creatively misreads the signs that determine Ike McCaslin's experience, allowing Morrison to reconfigure these signs so as to challenge the power of language to exert control of the past over the present. Like MacKethan, Theresa Towner illustrates how Morrison recasts a Faulknerian mold. In "Black Matters on the Dixie Limited: *As I Lay Dying* and *The Bluest Eye*," Towner shows how Morrison's novel "signifies" on—plays upon, revisits, and rewrites—Faulkner's by repeating and modifying nearly every major thematic and structural component of the two novels. In her examinations of sibling relationships, generational conflicts, gender constraints, repressed sexuality, cathartic violence, and insanity, Morrison re-envisions Faulkner's Bundren family as pre-World War II African-Americans struggling to find a way to live in a culture that shuns them.

Both Keith Byerman and Doreen Fowler turn our attention to women in Morrison and Faulkner. In "Untold Stories: Black Daughters in *Absalom, Absalom!* and *The Bluest Eye*," Byerman analyzes how Morrison revisits the status of the black daughter, placing her at the center of her text to probe the meanings and implications of marginality and dehumanization. What

Faulkner writes as "inscrutability," Morrison rewrites as violence and victimization. Whereas Denard describes as "mythic" the consciousness Morrison and Faulkner share, and Weinstein examines a male-oriented version of the Oedipal, Fowler explicitly focuses on a realm of the unconscious where two females attempt to thwart, through infanticide, the terrible effects of patriarchal Oedipal strictures. In "Reading for the 'Other Side': *Beloved* and *Requiem for a Nun*," she uses a Lacanian lens to view how in both novels a mother or mother-surrogate uses infanticide as a means of reasserting female power. Concluding the second section, Roberta Rubenstein's essay "History and Story, Sign and Design: Faulknerian and Postmodern Voices in *Jazz*" discusses how both Faulkner and Morrison explore the unstable intersections of "history" and "story," disrupt linear chronology, and shape their narratives through multiple narrators. However, says Rubenstein, Morrison—more explicitly than Faulkner and from a position more reflective of postmodern assumptions—calls attention to the irreducible provisionality and artifice of narrative.

In the third section, three essays focus closely—and with intriguing similarities and differences—on the two writers' acknowledged masterpieces, *Absalom, Absalom!* and *Beloved*. All the essays note the striking similarities between the texts: both are concerned with constructing monuments to the past; both are ghost stories; both use a family catastrophe as a synecdoche for a larger social drama; both narratives must work through a repressed memory of an interfamilial murder. Michael Hogan, in "Built on the Ashes: The Fall of the House of Sutpen and the Rise of the House of Sethe," reads Faulkner's and Morrison's fictional houses as significant sites of narrative action. Using Abraham Lincoln's famed 1858 speech "A house divided against itself cannot stand" as a basis, Hogan's essay considers Sutpen's mansion and 124 Bluestone Road as fictional manifestations of Lincoln's American "house," and he reads the dwellings as spaces defined by gender as well as individual and community identity. Next, in her essay "A Postmodern *Absalom, Absalom!*, a Modern *Beloved*: The Dialectic of Form," Catherine Gunther Kodat discusses Morrison's use of the formalistic conventions of high modernism in order to "remaster" Faulkner's texts. Both novels, she asserts, are wedded to a common technical concern: making fragmentation work simultaneously as both method and theme. At the same time, comparing the two texts serves to explore the larger question of the relationship between modernism and postmodernism. The concluding essay in this section offers a dialogic re-reading of the subject of Kodat's essay: in "Signifying Silences: Morrison's Soundings in the Faulknerian Void," Phillip Novak asserts that both novels are designed to produce or represent a series of marked absences—the absence of narratable meaning. For Faulkner, this technique is associated with the concept of universal human suffering, while in Morrison the technique is deployed to validate a suppressed cultural tradition.

The concluding essay, a coda for the collection, turns the notion of "influence" on its head. Patrick O'Donnell, in "Faulkner in Light of Morrison," finds a theory of intertextuality in Morrison's *Playing in the Dark* that forces us to read Faulkner in terms of his figurations of shadow and absence and his representations of presumably black bodies. Reading through *Playing in the Dark* in this way allows us to understand Faulknerian tropes as they have been revised and transformed by Morrison's fiction; O'Donnell thus suggests that we study the degree to which Faulkner is "influenced" by Morrison, that is, how our reading of Faulkner has been—must be—profoundly changed by our reading of Morrison.

Notes

1. A recent session at the American Literature Association reinforces how important these discussions are. In May of 1996 the three co-editors along with nine of the contributors of this collection conducted a workshop on "Reading Faulkner/Morrison." In the discussion period following the presentations, a number of people in the audience brought up many of the same questions our students continue to bring up: can white scholars appropriate Morrison; should black scholars read Faulkner? The passionate discussion that ensued both at the session and among individuals later that day and in following days illustrates how important it is to foreground issues of race (and gender). We hope this volume will contribute to the discussion.

2. Two of the earliest to compare Morrison and Faulkner in any extensive way were David Cowart and John Duvall ("Authentic" and "Doe Hunting"). The fullest treatment is Philip Weinstein's *What Else But Love*. The American Literature Association conferences in 1994 and 1996 included panels on Faulkner and Morrison.

3. Even editorial style can be implicated in issues of race, gender, or ethnicity. Although common usage (see, for example, the *Chicago Manual of Style*, 14th edition) leaves the term "African-American" un-hyphenated, we are following Toni Morrison's usage in *Playing in the Dark* (see, for example, 4, 5). Morrison discusses the hypen as a symbol of dual identity (*Playing* 47–48), and Patrick O'Donnell elaborates on this issue in the Coda to this volume.

I INTERTEXTUALITY

1. TONI MORRISON AND THE ANXIETY OF FAULKNERIAN INFLUENCE

John N. Duvall

I am not like *Faulkner.*
  —*Toni Morrison*

. . . *all texts Signify upon other texts, in motivated and unmotivated ways.*
  —*Henry Louis Gates, Jr.* [1]

Any discussion of Toni Morrison's work in relation to modernism (or post-modernism) in general or to William Faulkner in particular is fraught with the possibility of misunderstanding. To speak of a possible Faulknerian influence on Morrison's work runs the risk of calling up memories of racial and sexual abuse in the American past. Does not positing such an influence imply that, without a white Southern man's seminal texts, those of the African-American woman would never have come to fruition? But arguing for an intertextual relationship between Morrison's and Faulkner's fiction does not require granting Faulkner's the status of master text. In fact, my purpose here is less a discussion of Faulkner's influence on Morrison than it is an examination of Morrison's apparent anxiety that Faulkner may have influenced her writing. [1]

The point of examining the relation between Morrison and Faulkner certainly should not be to measure Morrison on the yardstick of a Faulkner but rather

3

to understand how her texts reclaim those of the modernists.[2] The notion of intertextuality, with its emphasis on the infinitely resonating signification of language, means that one can validly read not only Faulkner's influence on Morrison, but also Morrison's influence on Faulkner—how her fiction and literary criticism may cause one to rethink Faulkner in a fundamental way. To the extent that language is self-referential, any set of literary or non-literary texts may be juxtaposed, since every text participates in the Borgesian library of intertextuality, pointing in myriad ways to an infinite regress of prior representations. The only question of validity becomes one of utility: What do such acts of mutual framing reveal?

African-American literary theory and criticism, however, make problematic the issue of intertextuality through an appropriately politicized urge to focus solely on African-American texts, a part of the aesthetic past that historically has not received equal status or attention. Taking their cue from Morrison herself, some of Morrison's critics argue that the most appropriate frame for assessing her literary work is an African-American folk and oral tradition.[3] In his work on the theory of African-American literature, Henry Louis Gates, Jr., does acknowledge that African-American writers revise texts by white writers with "a sense of difference based on the black vernacular" (*Signifying* xxii). His project, however, is to understand the "web of filiation" created when black writers reinvent the tropes of other black writers (xxii). In her recent book on Morrison, Denise Heinze follows Gates's position on what texts should be read as the intertext of African-American fiction. Using W. E. B. Du Bois's famous discussion of black American "identity" in *The Souls of Black Folk* as an always divided "double-consciousness," Heinze notes that double-consciousness may intersect with Bakhtin's double-voicedness, the Russian theorist's trope for intertextuality. Still, for Heinze, the issue is quite clear: "Morrison's double-consciousness cannot ultimately be explained in terms of her relationship to the dominant culture" (10). She turns to Michael Awkward's reading of *The Bluest Eye* to support this claim; for Awkward, Morrison's novel needs to be understood in relation to other African-American texts that represent Du Bois's notion of double-consciousness, particularly Hurston's *Their Eyes Were Watching God*. Despite Morrison's claim never to have read Hurston, Heinze concurs with Awkward's thesis that Morrison's novels function as refigurations of the African-American aesthetic past (Heinze 10–11). Awkward's linking of Morrison and Hurston does not need to depend on Morrison's reading of Hurston, since such a reading strategy is already legitimated by theories of intertextuality, whether eurocentric (Bakhtin's double-voicedness, Kristeva's semiotic, Barthes's authorless text) or afrocentric (Gates's Signifyin(g)).

While not wishing to gainsay the value of Heinze's insights, I would nevertheless contend that the converse of her claim also has a legitimacy: the double-
consciousness of Toni Morrison's work cannot ultimately be understood without
some consideration of its relation to the dominant culture. A brief example may
help illuminate my point. When Morrison titles her third novel *Song of Solomon*,
she directs the reader to a biblical intertext as clearly as Joyce signals his mythic
intertext in *Ulysses*.[4] Both "The Song of Solomon" and the song Milkman
discovers that sings his family's African genealogy detail sexual suffering. The
dialogue between the lovers in the biblical text speaks to Milkman's relationship
with Hagar, just as Morrison's meditation on American culture's reification of
color makes the woman's assertion, "I am very dark, but comely" (Song Sol. 1.5),
resonate in a new way, both historically and culturally.

Less overtly than the previous example, Toni Morrison's fiction nevertheless
contains a good deal of compelling evidence that suggests particular resonances
between her writing and that of William Faulkner, a writer whose canonical
status clearly marks him as a part of the dominant culture. Before considering
some of these fictional resonances, however, I would like to examine a different
sort of evidence. Morrison herself in a number of forums has commented
upon Faulkner's fiction. Morrison's remarks about the relation of her work
to Faulkner's show a decided ambivalence. His influence is at times affirmed,
at times denied, at times simultaneously affirmed and denied. That she has
read Faulkner closely and carefully is undeniable, so the question of Morrison's
relation to Faulkner in some sense turns on what it means that a writer is always
inescapably also a reader.

In 1955, as a master's student at Cornell, Morrison completed her thesis,
"Virginia Woolf's and William Faulkner's Treatment of the Alienated." Her
sixteen-page chapter on Faulkner focuses primarily on Thomas Sutpen and
Quentin Compson. In *Absalom, Absalom!* and *The Sound and the Fury*, Morrison
sees "elements of Greek tragedy," such as "the fall of a once great house" and
"old family guilts inherited by an heir"; moreover, "the fact that incest plays
such an important part . . . is evidence that Faulkner patterns these histories
after the Greeks" ("Virginia" 24). What these comments point to, I believe,
is that any piece of writing (even the academic prose of a master's thesis)
is always unavoidably a form of intellectual autobiography, no matter how
little the autobiographical impulse forms part of the writer's intentions. We
might say, for example, that Morrison's previous work on the classics as an
undergraduate at Howard University prepared her to make the kinds of claims
she does in her master's thesis about Faulkner. So that when one sees incest and
family history as elements of Morrison's fictional matter in, say, *The Bluest*

Eye or *Song of Solomon*, one need not attribute this presence to Faulkner *per se* nor even to Greek tragedy. The relation between Morrison's texts and those of the aesthetic past, therefore, is not determined but overdetermined. What this means from a reader's perspective is that numerous cultural texts examine incest and that this whole matrix of prior representations becomes available for a critical examination of what and how incest might mean in Morrison's work.

In the first published interview in which Morrison mentions Faulkner, she fairly bristles at Thomas LeClair's suggestion that some readers—white readers—will not understand a certain scene in *Sula*; says Morrison:

> There is a level of appreciation that might be available only to people who understand the context of the language. The analogy that occurs to me is jazz: it is open on the one hand and both complicated and inaccessible on the other. I never asked Tolstoy to write for me, a little colored girl in Lorain, Ohio. I never asked Joyce not to mention Catholicism or the world of Dublin. Never. And I don't know why I should be asked to explain your life to you. We have splendid writers to do that, but I am not one of them. It is that business of being universal, a word hopelessly stripped of meaning for me. Faulkner wrote what I suppose could be called regional literature and had it published all over the world. It is good—and universal—because it is specifically about a particular world. That's what I wish to do. ("Language"; rpt. Taylor-Guthrie 124)

Her mild approval of Faulkner's fiction—its goodness depends on its representation of particularity—nevertheless signals her desire to put distance between herself and Faulkner, as well as other canonical novelists, and to position herself specifically as an African-American woman author writing the specificity of African-American experience. At the same time, the particular authors Morrison mentions (Tolstoy, Joyce, and Faulkner) reveal the scope of her ambition as a writer.

Morrison reiterates her difference more forcefully in an interview with Nellie McKay in 1983:

> Our—black women's—job is a particularly complex one. . . . We have no systematic mode of criticism that has yet evolved from us, but it will. I am not *like* James Joyce; I am not *like* Thomas Hardy; I am not *like* Faulkner. I am not *like* in that sense. I do not have objections to being compared to such extraordinarily gifted and facile writers, but it does leave me sort of hanging there when I know that my effort is to be *like* something that has probably only been fully expressed perhaps in music, or in some other culture-gen that survives almost in isolation because the community manages to hold on to it. (Rpt. Taylor-Guthrie 152)

In distinguishing herself from Faulkner, Hardy, and Joyce, Morrison stresses the particularity of African-American experience, from its aurality to its investment in the supernatural (152–53).

Both the LeClair and the McKay interviews, however, serve as a prelude to Morrison's much fuller treatments of the ways Faulkner may have influenced her. Morrison's remarks framing her reading from her then work-in-progress *Beloved* at the 1985 Faulkner and Yoknapatawpha Conference serve as one of the clearest instances of her ambivalence toward Faulkner. Prior to her reading she said, "there was for me not only an academic interest in Faulkner, but in a very, very personal way, in a very personal way as a reader, William Faulkner had an enormous effect on me, an enormous effect" ("Faulkner and Women" 296). But after her reading, in answer to the first question put to her regarding the effect Faulkner had on her literary career, Morrison responds:

> Well, I'm not sure that he had any effect on my work. I am typical, I think, of all writers who are convinced that they are wholly original and that if they recognized an influence they would abandon it as quickly as possible. . . . My reasons, I think, for being interested and deeply moved by all his subjects had something to do with my desire to find out something about this country and that artistic articulation of its past that was not available in history, which is what art and fiction can do but sometimes history refuses to do. . . . And there was something else about Faulkner which I can only call "gaze." He had a gaze that was different. It appeared, at that time, to be similar to a look, even a sort of staring, a refusal-to-look-away approach in his writing that I found admirable. At that time, in the 50's or the 60's, it never crossed my mind to write books. But then I did it, and I was very surprised myself that I was doing it, and I knew that I was doing it for some reasons that are not writerly ones. I don't really find strong connections between my work and Faulkner's. (296–97)

Morrison's attempt here to make Faulkner a "was"—to relegate his influence to her pre-writerly past—seems (especially in light of her subsequent comments about him) as unreliable as Faulkner's frequent claim to those who did not know better that he had never read Joyce, a claim undercut by others who heard Faulkner recite long passages of Joyce's work from memory (Blotner, rev. ed. 287).

Still, in *Playing in the Dark: Whiteness and the Literary Imagination*, Morrison's discussion of racial figuration in canonical literature by white authors—Cather, Poe, Twain, and Hemingway—appears to give some credence to her claim that Faulkner has receded from her consciousness. His work is mentioned twice in passing, with only a brief elaboration in the conclusion of her discussion of *The Narrative of Arthur Gordon Pym* and *Huckleberry Finn*: "We are reminded of other images at the end of literary journeys into the forbidden space of blackness. Does Faulkner's *Absalom! Absalom!* [sic], after its protracted search for the telling African blood, leave us with just such an image of snow and the eradication of race? Not quite. Shreve sees himself as the inheritor of the blood of African kings; the snow apparently is the wasteland of unmeaning, unfathomable whiteness" (58). This general omission of Faulkner's texts in *Playing in the Dark*, however, does not mean that Faulkner has fallen away from her field of vision; indeed at another level Faulkner reappears in Morrison's critical text through her reading of Faulkner criticism. Her development of "the common linguistic strategies employed in fiction to engage the serious consequences of blacks," draws liberally on James A. Snead's book on Faulkner, *Figures of Division* (*Playing* 66–69).

If Faulkner belongs only to Morrison's past, then what does one make of her comments regarding her experiences teaching *Absalom, Absalom!* from a 1993 interview in *The Paris Review*?

> Faulkner in *Absalom, Absalom!* spends the entire book tracing race, and you can't find it. No one can see it, even the character who *is* black can't see it. I did this lecture for my students that took me forever, which was tracking all the moments of withheld, partial or disinformation, when a racial fact or clue *sort* of comes out but doesn't quite arrive. I just wanted to chart it. I listed its appearance, disguise and disappearance on every page, I mean every phrase! . . . Do you know how hard it is to withhold that kind of information but hinting, pointing all of the time? And then to reveal it in order to say that it is *not* the point anyway? It is technically just astonishing. As a reader you have been forced to hunt for a drop of black blood that means everything and nothing. The insanity of racism. So the structure is the argument. . . . No one has done anything quite like that ever. So, when I critique, what I am saying is, I don't care if Faulkner was a racist or not; I don't personally care, but I am fascinated by what it means to write like this. ("Art" 101)

Morrison, as this quotation makes clear, still reads Faulkner. And if she still turns to Faulkner's texts, how is she to contain that "very personal" and "enormous effect" ("Faulkner and Women" 296)? Does Faulkner exist for her as a reader, as a teacher, as a critic, but not as writer? This writerly desire to deny influence leads Morrison to a compartmentalizing of self and identity that belies her portrayals of characters who overcome such fragmentation. Indeed, Morrison's denial of Faulkner's influence on her as a writer contradicts one of the central enabling claims of her critical project in *Playing in the Dark*. She contends that she developed the ability to see moments of racial figuration that literary critics cannot only after she stopped "reading as a reader and began to read as a writer" (*Playing* 15). It is this fundamental difference, she believes, that allows her, as "a writer reading," to understand that "the subject of the dream is the dreamer"; her insistence on a special understanding of "how language arrives" for a writer produces insightful speculations regarding how Cather may have struggled over her representation of Till in *Sapphira and the Slave Girl* or what writerly conflict Hemingway might have experienced by silencing an African-American character in *To Have and Have Not* (*Playing* 17). If one removes the burden of authorial consciousness from these two moments, Morrison's insights still stand, perhaps more clearly, as instances of the way racial ideology functions both in Cather's and Hemingway's texts and more broadly in their particular cultural moment. My point is, simply, that when Morrison claims, as she does in *The Paris Review* interview, that her classroom critique of Faulkner proceeds from being "fascinated by what it means to write like" Faulkner, she is reading the same way she reads Cather and Hemingway—as a writer reading. It may be a useful and enabling fiction for Morrison to see her novels as unmarked by Faulkner. Nevertheless, the rhetorical separation between reader and writer that Morrison wishes to maintain in her critical discourse largely collapses.

Having examined the various and conflicting ways that Morrison has thought about (and perhaps misinterpreted) her relation to Faulkner, I would like to turn to some specific features of these two novelists' fiction that—against Morrison's wishes—might cause readers to see connections. I acknowledge that positing such connections also serves as a misreading in the sense that looking at Morrison through the lens of Faulkner (or Faulkner through the lens of Morrison) will bring to the foreground only certain features of the textuality of each. But this is a misreading that I am willing to risk on pedagogical grounds. Teaching at a Southern urban institution, The University of Memphis, I find that Faulkner's and Morrison's examinations of race speak to the lived experience of my students. Such a pairing, therefore, makes sense ethically as well as aesthetically. My teaching has taught me that placing Morrison against Faulkner is useful, not just for understanding Morrison, but for gaining a different critical purchase on Faulkner.

The utility of pairing Morrison and Faulkner occurs, in large part, because of the way both novelists portray the individual's relation to the community. It is hardly surprising that Roberta Rubenstein several years ago titled a book chapter on Toni Morrison "Pariahs and Community," a moment of naming that echoes the title of Cleanth Brooks's famous reading of *Light in August*, "The Community and the Pariah." Without much difficulty one can construct a long list of characters who stand convicted of difference in the eyes of Morrison's and Faulkner's respective communities. Pecola Breedlove, Sula, Pilate, Sethe, and Violet Trace are some of the more obvious of Morrison's outsiders, while Darl, Joe Christmas, Joanna Burden, Popeye, Thomas Sutpen all stand as Faulknerian pariahs.

What is less immediately obvious, however, is that both authors employ recurring structures that suggest that the individual never stands alone for very long. One might be inclined at first to identify these recurring social groupings as deviant or abnormal, since so often the members who comprise these alternative formations are the ones whom the community has shunned. A few years ago I pointed out that in Faulkner the outsiders repeatedly come together in pairs—a woman marked by the cultural masculine and man marked by the cultural feminine.[5] In *Light in August*, Joe Christmas and Joanna Burden find each other, as do Byron Bunch and Lena Grove. In *The Wild Palms* Harry Wilbourne and Charlotte Rittenmeyer and the tall convict and the hill woman repeat the pairings of *Light in August*. The gender ambiguity in these recurring formations provides a purchase for thinking about the supposedly normal family and the agrarian community comprised by those families. This recurring structure is not monolithically positive; sometimes these alternative couples, such as Joe Christmas and Joanna Burden, end up reproducing racial ideology, even as they challenge gender ideology. At other times the pairings are so grotesque that the notion of any alternative seems to disappear. In *Sanctuary*, Popeye and Temple Drake, for example, by themselves are horrific as rapist and victim, yet Popeye's place in the ironic "family" of the Old Frenchman place ultimately reveals how incest defines the supposedly normal family of Judge Drake.[6]

Morrison's symbolic meditations on African-American community also have a recurring structure that poses an alternative to the nuclear family. Susan Willis first noted the repetition of what she calls Morrison's "three-woman utopian households" (41). In *The Bluest Eye* one sees the earliest articulation of this formation in the three prostitutes—China, Poland, and Miss Marie—who live together. This pattern recurs in *Sula* (Eva, Hannah, and Sula Peace), in *Song of Solomon* (Pilate, Reba, and Hagar Dead), and in *Beloved* (Sethe, Denver, and Beloved). "Utopian," however, may be too strong a term to apply to these trios, since they have a certain fragility, despite the strong women who comprise these alternative families. Because these three-women households are not dependent upon men for their economic survival, they serve as a space for meditation on the sexual politics of the community. Like Faulkner's marginal couples, Morrison's alternative formations are not always unproblematically represented as positive. Pilate and Reba, for example, are unable to provide Hagar with an identity stable enough to withstand the onslaught of consumer culture. Perhaps Sethe's household most clearly suggests the problem of a radical isolation. This three-woman household, in some ways the site of Morrison's most intense meditation on an alternative spirituality of the maternal body, needs the intervention of a larger community of women to reintegrate that spirituality so that it may serve as a counterforce to the patriarchal Word of Christianity. Whatever their limitations, these recurring three-woman households create a dialectic, an oppositional point from which Morrison is able to question the value of the traditional nuclear family. The dysfunction of the nuclear family is particularly freighted for Morrison, since she sees African-Americans who attempt to live within its frame as inauthentically trying to assimilate to the values of white culture. By repeatedly presenting the spiritual possibilities of a non-Western form of social organization, Morrison suggests that African-Americans can recover their West African origins, a thematic that helps us better understand why Heinze sees Morrison's fiction "as an articulation of Black Cultural Nationalism" (8).

One important effect, finally, of these alternative formations in both Morrison's and Faulkner's work is quite similar. The ability of those in some larger community to identify themselves as normal is made problematic; the proliferation of difference becomes so great that the very concept of "normal" begins to dissolve.

It might be objected that Morrison writes of African-American community, while Faulkner was concerned with white Southern agrarian community. But such an urge to mark difference is complicated by complex cultural interaction. The diverse ways in which cultures mix point to the need for a broader cultural poetics, one that acknowledges that cultures themselves—not just texts—are inescapably mulattoes (Gates, *Signifying* xxiii). Even if Faulkner had wished to repudiate completely African-American culture, such a gesture would have been futile. An African-American oral tradition in narrative and music (the blues, spirituals) surrounded Faulkner throughout his life and undoubtedly marked him in ways he could not have articulated. But clearly Faulkner did not wish to repudiate black culture, as his dedication of *Go Down, Moses* to Caroline Barr (Mammy Callie) indicates. The title of this novel, along with stories such as "That Evening Sun," reveal Faulkner's awareness of African-American culture. So that even though Faulkner's portrayal of black characters in a number of instances seems stereotypical, the kinds of figurations that ultimately confirm white identity (as Morrison argues in her discussion of Hemingway [*Playing* 69–90]), he nevertheless was attempting a cultural synthesis. Perhaps the aurality of Faulkner's fiction—the quality of voice—that so many critics have commented upon will only be fully understood when there is a fuller acknowledgment by

Faulkner critics of the Africanism of Southern culture in general and the white Southern community in particular.

Morrison's African-American community almost always bears traces of the rural black Southern community. The Bottom of *Sula* reproduces elements of an agrarian community by blacks who have moved to Ohio from the South. In *Song of Solomon*, Milkman may grow up in Flint, Michigan, but in retracing his family's migration from rural Pennsylvania to Shalimar, Virginia, he comes to understand how agrarian his origins are. Even in *Jazz*, set primarily in Harlem, the two central characters, Joe and Violet Trace, are shaped by an agrarian beginning that illustrates that a central reason for the Northern migration itself was the virulent racism of the white Southern community. So that in a crucial sense, the oral, blues, and folk traditions that Morrison wishes to employ to define her difference from white modernist writers are all legitimate gestures of self-definition; yet, from a slightly different perspective, one might argue that these same traditions have inescapably marked Faulkner's texts. Perhaps to follow through the mixed genealogy of Southern community—black and white—one needs turn to the Caribbean where finally one discovers that the attempt to understand cultures as discrete is as doomed to failure as Thomas Sutpen's desire to keep his white bloodline pure, all the while he fathers children by black women.

To invoke the mulatto as a metaphor of intertextuality suggests another possible way to conceive a relation between Morrison's and Faulkner's portrayal of community—the presence and effects of miscegenation. I noted earlier that Morrison uses a book of Faulkner criticism as a starting point in the development of her list of linguistic strategies white writers employ when attempting to represent black characters. Fetishization, the fourth item on her list, is elaborated as follows: "Blood, for example, is a pervasive fetish: black blood, white blood, the purity of blood; the purity of white female sexuality, the pollution of African blood and sex" (*Playing* 67–68). Faulkner is not mentioned at this moment in Morrison's text, yet his recurring treatment of miscegenation places him as present in Morrison's remark nevertheless.

For Faulkner, the matter of miscegenation allows his novels to perform a kind of anatomy of racism and prejudice in his white agrarian community. The pernicious effects of racial division are intensely foregrounded in *Absalom, Absalom!*, *Go Down, Moses*, and *Intruder in the Dust*. In *Light in August* the mere possibility of a parent who might have mixed blood renders Joe Christmas unable to bond with either the white or black community, making him one of the most alienated figures of twentieth-century literature. Miscegenation is also a subject matter in Morrison's fiction. From the African-American community's preference for the "high yellow" Maureen Peal over dark-complected Pecola Breedlove in *The Bluest Eye* to Dr. Foster's obsessive concern for the color of his granddaughters' skin in *Song of Solomon*, miscegenation allows Morrison to scrutinize colorism in her community.[7] Colorism in Morrison at times seems almost an obverse reflection of racism in Faulkner, so that the act of mutually enframing the work of these two authors can help readers—teachers and students—think the issue of race further.

The matter of miscegenation for these two novelists comes into sharper relief in the way *Jazz* comments upon an apparent intertext, *Absalom, Absalom!* Given the attention Morrison has paid to this particular Faulkner novel, I am tempted to say that she has in *Jazz* performed a tour-de-force reclamation of "what it means to write like" Faulkner ("Art" 101). Particularly in the unnumbered "chapters" six and seven, Morrison seems to have produced a pastiche of Faulknerian style and matter in her delineation of the racially mixed Golden Gray. In *Absalom*, Faulkner creates a complicated genealogy, where bloodlines are crossed and recrossed to the point that the very rationale of the white Southern community is continuously threatened. But the moments of miscegenation in *Absalom* always occur when black (mulatto, quadroon, octoroon) women have children by white fathers. Still, Faulkner employs a racial brinkmanship to tease out and maximize the cultural horror of his white Southern community to raise this specter: what if a black man slept with a white woman? This question of course is central to Quentin and Shreve's construction of Henry Sutpen's motive for murdering Charles Bon. Henry could accept the incest but not the miscegenation, in Shreve and Quentin's narration, and they imagine this exchange between Henry and Bon:

> —*You are my brother.*
> —*No I'm not. I'm the nigger that's going to sleep with your sister. Unless you stop me, Henry.* (286)

Charles Bon, seductive and charming, serves as the white Southern community's repressed ideological horror in Faulkner's ghost story: if white men can father black men who appear white, then these same "white" black men can beget children on white women. This is the precipice Faulkner continually leads up to and dares his white reader to peep over. And this is precisely the precipice Morrison flies over in *Jazz*'s signifyin(g) relation to *Absalom, Absalom!*

Like Charles Bon, Golden Gray is the product of miscegenation, yet Morrison reverses Faulknerian genealogy: Gray is the son of a privileged white woman, Vera Louise Gray, and a dark-skinned slave, Henry LesTroy (or Lestory). Colonel Gray, who like Colonel Sutpen has fathered mixed-race children, experiences

Sutpen's worst nightmare when he learns what his daughter has done; he gives her a large amount of money to go away. Banished from her home, Vera Louise and her servant True Belle move to Baltimore to raise Golden Gray in opulence as a gentleman. Golden Gray's maturation serves simultaneously to comment upon and recast two situations in *Absalom*. On the one hand, Morrison's scenario recalls Sutpen's denial of Bon, the child of his marriage to the daughter of a Haitian planter. Repudiating her for having a mixed bloodline, Sutpen nevertheless gives her a large settlement and she is able to raise Bon as a gentleman. On the other hand, Golden Gray's situation reverses that of Charles Bon's son, Charles Etienne de Saint Valery Bon, the product of Bon's relation with his octoroon mistress in New Orleans. Etienne Bon, born in luxury, is taken after his mother's death to live in the privation of the post-Civil War Sutpen home, where he is raised by Judith and Clytie, Judith's servant and half-sister.

Structurally, then, Golden Gray's upbringing parallels Etienne Bon's, but in Gray's desire to confront his father, he more closely recalls Charles Bon's obsession, though with a difference: Bon seeks Sutpen for recognition; Gray, at least initially, seeks LesTroy to kill him, since LesTroy is indeed the black man who has slept with Gray's mother. When he enters LesTroy's cabin and sits on his father's bed, Golden Gray's response reveals why "Faulknerian pastiche" may be an appropriate way to term Morrison's prose:

> Only now, he thought, now that I know I have a father, do I feel his absence: the place where he should have been and was not. Before, I thought everybody was one-armed, like me. Now I feel the surgery. The crunch of bone when it is sundered, the sliced flesh and the tubes of blood cut through, shocking the bloodrun and disturbing the nerves. They dangle and writhe. Singing pain. Waking me with the sound of itself, thrumming when I sleep so deeply it strangles my dreams away. There is nothing for it but to go away from where he is not to where he used to be and might be still. Let the dangle and the writhe see what it is missing; let the pain sing to the dirt where he stepped in the place where he used to be and might be still. I am not going to be healed, or to find the arm that was removed from me. I am going to freshen the pain, point it, so we both know what it is for. (158)

This rhetorical flight of Gray's, so close to naming Bon's agony,[8] is grounded, however, when LesTroy returns home. He tells Gray that he will accept the young man as a son if he can act like a son but warns, "don't bring me no whiteboy sass" (173), an expression that seems to deflate Gray's "Faulknerian" tragic rhetoric.

Metaphorically—though obviously not literally—Golden Gray is the "father" of Joe Trace, for if Gray had not stopped to bring Wild to shelter, she would not have lived to give birth to Joe. Joe Trace's quest for identity, therefore, continues the dialogue with *Absalom*. Paternity for Joe is out of the question, since his mother cannot name a putative father. What, finally, is Joe Trace's desire for recognition from his mother but a moment of narratological signifyin(g) that plays on Charles Bon's desire for Sutpen's recognition? Wild, who is outside language, serves as the antipatriarchal antithesis of Faulkner's Thomas Sutpen, who believes in the ability of language to designate absolutely the order of social relations.

I would defend my examination of the way *Jazz* comments on *Absalom, Absalom!* even if Toni Morrison explicitly said she never intended such. The voices of their respective (though always already mixed) cultures that Morrison and Faulkner embody ensure that such analysis has a legitimacy in the production of literary history. William Faulkner is not the source of Morrison's work, and if that is what one hopes to say by identifying influence, then Morrison is undoubtedly right—she is not *like* Faulkner. William Faulkner's textuality, however, considered as intertextual possibility, becomes one frame among many that can provide insights into the polyvalent and multicultural textuality of America's most recent Nobel Laureate.

Notes

1. I of course am invoking Harold Bloom's well-known version of intertextuality, first articulated in *The Anxiety of Influence*. Bloom's sense of poetic misprision easily translates to fiction, so that the strong novelist (Morrison, for example) will inevitably misread her own work's relation to the aesthetic past. Bloom's point is simple, but fraught with significance in the inevitably racialized context of thinking about Morrison and Faulkner together: to overidentify with one's aesthetic precursors is slavery, while reading one's difference is creatively liberating.

2. David Cowart judges Morrison's fiction a success inasmuch as it performs "meaningful variations on [Joyce's and Faulkner's] themes—freedom, identity, history" (89).

3. For example, in her interview with Nellie McKay, Morrison claims: "Black people have a story, and that story has to be heard. There was an articulate literature before there was print. There were griots. They memorized it. People heard it. It is important that there is sound in my books—that you can hear it, that I can hear it. . . . That oral quality is deliberate" (rpt. Taylor-Guthrie 152). Trudier Harris's "study of the influence of oral traditions upon" (1) Morrison's fiction is the fullest treatment to date on this topic.

4. Although the biblical intertext is unquestionably marked, it does not provide an explicit narrative scaffold that *The Odyssey* provides Joyce. In this regard, Morrison's act of titling her novel *Song of Solomon* is more akin to E. L. Doctorow's titling his fictive reexamination of the Rosenberg executions *The Book of Daniel*.

5. See particularly Chapter 1 of *Faulkner's Marginal Couple*.

6. John T. Matthews draws out these parallels in considerable detail ("Elliptical" 256–258).

7. See Heinze's useful discussion of this topic (16–24).

8. Charles Bon desires from Sutpen "the living touch of that flesh warmed before he was born by the same blood which it had bequeathed him to warm his own flesh with, to be bequeathed by him in turn to run hot and loud in veins and limbs after that first flesh and then his own were dead" (*Absalom* 255).

2. THE LONG, HIGH GAZE
The Mythical Consciousness of Toni Morrison and William Faulkner

Carolyn Denard

Their voices bespeak civilizations gone and yet to be; the precipice from which their imaginations gaze will rivet us; they do not blink or turn away.
—*Toni Morrison*

In biographical profile and historical time, Toni Morrison and William Faulkner have few similarities. Faulkner, a white male of southern, upperclass ancestry, was born in New Albany, Mississippi, in 1897. Morrison, a black woman descendant of sharecroppers, was born more than a generation later in 1931 in Lorain, Ohio. Faulkner wrote mostly of white southerners in a defeated post-slavery, post-Civil-War South. Morrison writes of blacks mostly, living in a post-migration full-of-promise-and-disappointment North. In the context of American social and cultural history, these differences of race, gender, place, and time alone are enough to create an uncloseable gulf.

But increasingly since Morrison began her writing career in 1970, Morrison and Faulkner have become the subject of literary comparisons. On what basis we can compare two writers who seem to come from such divergent poles of experience in the United States and what their similarities mean for us as readers of American literature are the questions this essay seeks to answer.

Perhaps more than anyone else it is Morrison herself who initiated critics' interest in what we may call now the "Faulkner-Morrison" comparison. In 1955, she wrote her Master's thesis on William Faulkner and Virginia Woolf at Cornell University. In 1985, at the Yoknapatawpha Conference at the University of Mississippi, Morrison explained her early attraction to Faulkner: "I have to say, even before I began to read [for the thesis], that there was for me not only an academic interest in Faulkner, but in a very, very personal way as a reader, William Faulkner had an enormous effect on me, an enormous effect. . . . My reasons, I think, for being interested and deeply moved by all his subjects had something to do with my desire to find out something about this country and that articulation of its past that was not available in history" ("Faulkner and Women" 296).

Early critics and reviewers of Morrison's novels praised her work and offered approval often on the basis that Morrison's work was *like* Faulkner's. Harold Bloom's observations are representative: "Part of appreciating Morrison's command here of sensation and perception involves attending to the genealogy of her art. It is not a question of allusion or of echoing but of style, stance, tone, prose rhythm, and mimetic mode, and these do stem from an amalgam of Faulkner and Woolf, the father and mother of Morrison's art as it were" (*Toni Morrison* 4). Morrison, herself, and many Morrison scholars, however, have rejected the kind of generative association Bloom suggests here because it diminishes Morrison's own genius. The comparisons seem to suggest that Morrison's skill is imitative rather than original, she a mimicking protégé rather than an innovative artist in her own right. As she told Nellie McKay in an interview in 1978, "Critics of my work have often left something to be desired, in my mind, because they don't always evolve out of the culture, the world, the given quality out of which I write. . . . I am not *like* James Joyce; I am not *like* Thomas Hardy; I am not *like* Faulkner. I am not *like* in that sense" (rpt. Taylor-Guthrie 151–52). And while Morrison, by her own admission, was certainly affected as a student-reader by William Faulkner and drawn to his work, there is no simple generative, imitative relationship between Morrison and Faulkner. It is more probable, in fact, that Morrison's early interest in Faulkner as a subject for her Master's thesis in 1955 had more to do with an early resonance she found in Faulkner with *her* long-held world view—although hers was yet to be articulated in her imaginative writing. Faulkner was one of the few white southern male writers who took neither a dismissive, condescending posture regarding black characters nor a simplistic, purely sympathetic view of southern white characters. For many black readers of American literature, he was one of the first white southern writers to offer a complex view of the lives of whites and blacks in the South. His works suggested, in a way that seemed uncharacteristic for its time, that blacks had inherited the moral high ground from the legacy of slavery and that whites, with a typical Faulknerian lament, were the disinherited. It is not surprising that Morrison, as did many black readers of her generation, found Faulkner appealing.

Morrison did not, however, have her imaginative world view and hence her artistry, "shaped" by Faulkner as Bloom and others have suggested. Her rich family history, her early reflective personality as a child, her individual genius, and the nearly forty years of black life she had lived before she began writing were certainly more influential factors in shaping her world view. That she and Faulkner assume a similar creative stance, or a similar writing style, is testimony more, I believe, to their individual and extraordinarily keen sensitivity to the highs and lows of the human spirit—a sense that most often has been considered the singular domain of women in general if not black women in particular. Certainly, then, it is more remarkable that Faulkner ends up with a sensibility shared by Morrison than the other way around. Morrison is an independent artist, not a protégé, a literary master of equal merit, not a borrowing novice. Morrison and Faulkner are literary prophets in succession, with their own unique and prophetic vision for their own time and place. Theirs is the relationship of Abraham and Moses rather than that of Abraham and Isaac as Bloom and others suggest.

If we move, then, from the generative, hierarchical nature of these earlier comparisons between Morrison and Faulkner—and we must—there is still, I believe, a large space in which to establish a basis for common consideration of Faulkner and Morrison. There are, for example, their similar achievements in American literary history. They have been prolific in their writing careers, creating a repertoire of increasingly powerful novels that meditate on the most piercing issues of American culture: class, race, and history. Both writers share a distinguished, unsurpassed command of language in their fiction, writing prose so richly charged that readers consider their novels to be "poetry in prose." Both have been honored for their works on the world stage as Nobel Laureates.

There is something more, however, than their language, their interest in race and history, or their shared literary esteem that has us seeing Morrison and Faulkner in a comparative way. The larger, more important basis for the common critical consideration of Faulkner and Morrison, I believe, is what Ernst Cassirer and other myth critics call a "mythical consciousness."[1] Mythical consciousness creates an awareness in these writers of the role that imaginative narratives may serve in providing a cognitive, unbroken connection of the present with the past and with the future, an awareness that it is the writer's obligation to tell an essential, unchanging truth, to make life make sense to his or her readers. The mythical consciousness creates a particular angle of vision. It is as if Faulkner and Morrison sit perched above our present reality with an expansive, aerial view able to see the points at which the present situates itself in the procession of time, complete with a knowledge of its repetitions and its intersections with the past and the future. It is a mode of thought that raises to cosmic, epic levels the daily choices and events of our lives. It allows a longer, lingering vision that penetrates outer layers of individual behavior and personality and seeks to find meaning in lives that goes beyond what we see and observe on the surface. As such, while not myths themselves, the stories of Faulkner and Morrison serve what myth critic Bronislaw Malinowski calls the *function* of myth: "Myth supplies a retrospective pattern of moral values, sociological order and magical belief. . . . It fulfills a function *sui generis* closely connected with the nature of tradition, and the continuity of culture, with the relation between age and youth, and with the human attitude towards the past. The function of myth . . . is to strengthen tradition and endow it with a greater value and prestige by tracing it back to a higher better more supernatural reality of initial events" (194).

The imaginative vision that results from this mythic consciousness, this expansive look at the present that equates it with primeval and historical pasts, this deep look at the human individual that sees both defeats and triumphs as part of the universal human design, Morrison calls the writer's "gaze." It was the term she first used when she described, at the Faulkner Conference in Mississippi in 1985, what attracted her to Faulkner's writing: "There was something about Faulkner which I can only call gaze. He had a gaze that was different. It appeared at that time to be similar to a look, even a sort of staring, a refusal-to-look-away approach in his writing that I found admirable" ("Faulkner and Women" 297). Later, in her 1993 Nobel Prize acceptance speech, Morrison would again invoke the writer's "gaze" as the nature of the imaginative vision that she believed would be the defining characteristic of the best writers yet to come: they "bespeak civilizations gone and yet to be; the precipice from which their imaginations gaze will rivet us; they do not blink or turn away" (33).

The "gaze" that Morrison first noticed in Faulkner, and which she believes necessary for the best writing to come, is what she also possesses. And it is this imaginative posture, this "writer's gaze," that is hauntingly and strikingly common to the fiction of both Faulkner and Morrison. This gaze from the precipice is a vision high enough to see the broad expanse and connectedness of history, and it is long and deep enough to elevate daily life to the level of epic, to visualize it as something far larger and with more impact than we can at first see. The gaze merges mythical and historical time and transforms the dismissed, the lowly, the not-seen into complex entities with connected, meaningful roles in the human drama.

Every part of their creations, of these imaginative and transforming narratives by Faulkner and Morrison, are fashioned with the desire to connect time, to lift up, to enhance our understanding of that part of the world we have learned to dismiss or ignore because it is past, or alien, defeated, ordinary, shallow, or, seemingly, cultureless. In the works of Morrison and Faulkner, there is no miniature now, no gone-forever then, no diminutive them—no maid or master, idiot or vagabond, bear or robin, marigold or wisteria that is not part of the grand design of the universe. Time, character, and situation are strengthened and heightened in their stories, connected with the past and pointing toward the future. The awareness of Faulkner and Morrison of this mythical role of the writer and their willingness to imbue their subjects with its import and still to question, transform, and enlarge the mythical tradition to which they believe all history is connected constitute the great merit of their work.

Many writers have taken what we may call a mythical posture in their writing. Indeed, it is the perennial measure by which we judge most of the writers we consider "great." It is a consciousness certainly as old as the ancient writers of Africa, Asia, and southern Europe. In American literature, nineteenth-century writers such as Whitman, Hawthorne, Dickinson, and Douglass forged an early mythical consciousness in American literature. Twentieth-century American writers such as T. S. Eliot, Hemingway, Fitzgerald, Du Bois, Faulkner, Baldwin, and Ellison also employed what Eliot called in 1923 "the mythical method" in their fiction.[2] It is one thing to put the pattern of innocence, hope, and rebirth of immigrants coming to these shores in the great cycle of the discovery and the loss of "virgin land," as did many of these writers. It is yet another, however, to place the dejected and defeated, those who historically have been written out of the "national myth," into a mythical paradigm as well—a paradigm of sacred, religious underpinnings that is older and larger than the national myth and which is capable of revealing its often limited and exclusive nature. What is unique to Morrison and Faulkner, then, is the people they place within their mythical paradigm, the individuals they cast their "gaze" upon. For both Morrison and Faulkner, their long, high gaze rests upon those "other" Americans, those whom Morrison calls the "discredited."[3]

For Faulkner, the discredited are the defeated southern whites who after the Civil War were silenced by being from a region which had seceded from the Union, lost the war, and lived with the scarred legacy of the sin of slavery. After the Civil War, the South became the national stepchild. It was written out of the great American myth of innocence, progress, and liberalism that characterized so much of early twentieth-century America. Faulkner looks long at this South, his region and its people: the slaveholding Sutpens and McCaslins, the poor white Bundrens and Snopeses, the black domestics and those of mixed blood like Dilsey Gibson and Joe Christmas. He gives voice also to the "discredited" within the South—the alienated, the insane, the idiosyncratic—Ike, Benjy, Darl. These nationally and locally discredited get Faulkner's gaze, and it allows him to tell their stories in their own voices. In so doing, Faulkner is at once able to raise the action of their lives to epic proportions, and he is also able to advance his own artistic purposes as well. He does not simply praise these characters—the gaze is not applause; it is a sincere, lingering consideration of their place in the universe—how they fail and how they triumph, but always how they matter.

Artistically for Faulkner, the language of these "discredited"—poor whites and aristocrats, insane and alienated—becomes a way of accessing a language that matches what Walter Brylowski calls the "mythic mode of thought." "Several critics," Brylowski recalls, "have remarked the dissatisfaction Faulkner expresses in his early novels with 'talk, talk, talk,' and I believe it is his felt need to discover a mode of communication which carries an aura of meaning beyond the bounds of what might be recognized as a scientifically rational mode of knowledge that leads him to employ the perceptions of irrational characters, characters whose truth is a configuration of the mythic mode of thought" (15). Here we may remember Vardaman's agonized explanations of his mother's death in *As I lay Dying:* "My mother is a fish" (84), " 'Jewel's mother is a horse' " (101), or Darl's interior monologues in search of self: "I don't know what I am. I don't know if I am or not. Jewel knows he is, because he does not know that he does not know whether he is or not" (80), or Benjy's disjointed storytelling in *The Sound and the Fury:* "I wasn't crying, but I couldn't stop. I wasn't crying, but the ground wasn't still, and then I was crying. The ground kept sloping up and the cows ran up the hill. . . . Then the barn wasn't there and we had to wait until it came back" (20–21). Through the irrational language of the child, the introvert, the idiot, Faulkner is able to access what becomes his characteristically idiosyncratic prose style. The deep thoughts of the characters, their primeval realities, become Faulkner's narrative language.

Morrison's discredited are American blacks, with slave and sharecropper pasts, who were summarily disenfranchised and dehumanized by slavery and racism. Morrison's narrative posture, her imaginative gaze, includes a desire to look long and sensitively at blacks generally and more specifically at those who have been discredited even within the black community in order to make them visible and credible, to give them a kind of human validity that the world has taken away: the

Pecola Breedloves, the Eva Peaces, the Shadracks, the Pilates, the Yardmans, the Thérèses, the Paul Ds, the Violets and Joe Traces of the world. "I have to make the reader look at people he may not wish to look at," Morrison explains. "You don't look at Pilate. You don't really look at a person like Cholly in *The Bluest Eye*. They are always backdrops, stage props, not the main character in their own stories. In order to look at them in fiction you have to . . . strike a certain posture as narrator" ("Language"; rpt. Taylor-Guthrie 123). This "posture" is the from-the-precipice look, the long stare, the imaginative gaze that Morrison claims is the signature of the best writers. For Cholly Breedlove, the father whose life of dejection leads to the rape of his daughter in *The Bluest Eye*, it is a chapter-long devotion to his growth from infancy to adulthood—who loved him, who did not, his favorite color, his favorite food, his humiliation, his alienation. We cannot look away or dismiss the humanity of Cholly Breedlove because Morrison does not look away. Under Morrison's gaze, Cholly Breedlove becomes as much a victim of alienation as does his daughter Pecola.

Morrison also gives this same penetrating gaze to "discredited" black women domestics—the silent steady women who have been so perennially present yet invisible in American society. Of these women, discredited by society and often by their communities, Morrison writes: "Everybody in the world was in a position to give them orders. White women said, 'Do this.' White children said, 'Give me that.' White men said, 'Come here.' Black men said, 'Lay down.' The only people they need not take orders from were black children and each other. But they took all that and recreated it in their own image. . . . The hands that felled trees also cut umbilical cords; the hands that wrung the necks of chickens and butchered hogs also nudged African violets into bloom; the arms that loaded sheaves, bales, and sacks rocked babies into sleep" (*Bluest* 138). By the time we stop our gaze on the black women Morrison describes here, the hierarchy of human values, heavily weighted in most societies toward class, is turned upside down. These unprivileged in society become in Morrison's novels, with a closer, longer look, the privileged.

The impetus for her two most recent novels, in fact, came from just this kind of posture, this willingness to look long and through surface representations. She read the newspaper story of Margaret Garner, a Kentucky slave woman who was caught after she escaped from slavery with her three children. Morrison saw the ink drawings of her calm face after she tried to kill her children rather than have them returned to slavery, and, instead of dismissing Garner as a crazed woman, Morrison's long look created the complicated archetype of motherhood that Sethe in *Beloved* comes to represent. In a 1920s photo by James Van der Zee of a young dead woman who reportedly refused to reveal the name of the lover that shot her, Morrison sees a deep haunting love unlike what she sees as the superficial, conditional romance of today. Under Morrison's gaze, that woman of unconditional love becomes Dorcas, the symbolic centerpiece of the deep and difficult love she explores in *Jazz*. In addition to getting her thematic, ethical message across in this long look at the discredited, Morrison, in the same way as Faulkner, is able to give value to the language of the discredited— to have their unspoken languages become the spoken in her novels. Nowhere is this more beautifully made clear than in the three-woman chant in *Beloved* that begins: "Beloved/ You are my sister/You are my daughter . . . /You are my face; I am you. Why did you leave me who am you?" (216), incantations that are irrational, non-linear, but echo a deep sense of connected consciousness between these three women.

Both Faulkner and Morrison look directly in an unblinking way at those believed not worthy of our gaze and suggest that no matter their difference or their faults, there is an equalizing value in their being. We find a redemptive possibility in Morrison's and Faulkner's focus on the discredited—a focus not just intended to make heroes out of their characters but to affirm their connectedness to the universe despite their failures and shortcomings.

Awareness of the mythic potential of the people and the places they write about is not only made manifest in the depth of Faulkner's and Morrison's gaze but also in its breadth. In addition to *whom* they stare upon, it is also *what* they see as a result of their angle of vision that is important in their gaze. The long, deep look at characters is one part of their gaze; their high, expansive look at history and its connection to mythical time, the present, and the future is the other part.

The expanse of the mythical gaze in the works of both Faulkner and Morrison is perhaps most clearly evident in their use of allusions and analogies from ancient mythologies—African, Hebrew, Greek, and northern European. There are the biblical references in the titles of the novels; *Go Down, Moses, Song of Solomon, Absalom, Absalom!,* and *Beloved*. There are also the biblical echoes of character names: Hagar, Rebecca, Mary Magdalene, and First Corinthians; there are motifs from biblical myths: the prodigal son, the Eden story, the Christ figure; there are also the many references to European myths in Faulkner and Morrison, and Morrison's extension of the use of myth to African and African-American motifs in the story of the Tar Baby and the Flying African. Faulkner extends his mythological sources also to "Southern mythology," where we see a lingering sense of the Confederate dead that continues to haunt his characters.

There are also the title-page epigraphs in Morrison's work from books of the Bible: "For it hath been declared unto me of you, my brethren, by them which are of the house of Chole, that there are contentions among you" (I Corinthians 1.11) in *Tar Baby*; from Romans in *Beloved*: "I will call them my people who are not my people; and her beloved which was not beloved" (Romans 9.25). And finally in Morrison there is the epigraph at the beginning of *Jazz* from the gnostic holy book the *The Nag Hamadi* in "I am the name of the sound/and the sound of the name. I am the sign of the letter and the designation of the division" (see "Thunder, Perfect Mind" 296–303). All of these suggest an association of the action of the novels within long and sacred mythical traditions.

The characters in Morrison's and Faulkner's novels are another "chosen people," their lives becoming the ever-new testament of humankind's engagement with the universe and its continued construction of good and evil. When juxtaposed to their mythical contexts, they are no longer the dejected or the insignificant, as Richard Adams concludes: "When a character is made to look like Christ, or when, in *The Hamlet*, Eula Varner is characterized as the Helen of Frenchman's Bend and the idiot Ike Snopes falls gallantly in love with Houston's cow, [or when Milkman becomes the Flying African or Jadine has a haunting encounter with the swamp women made of tar], . . . the resulting intrusion of the Biblical, the classical, the feudal, [the African,] or the American legendary past into the modern situation contradicts the flow of time and provides an artificially static moment into which Faulkner [and Morrison] can compress great quantities of life" (11).

The mythical allusions and analogies, the mythic plots, the epigraphs are all important manifestations of the "high" gaze that Morrison and Faulkner cast on their subjects, of the aerial view that allows them to see down the long corridor of history and make the connections between the myths and the characters of their novels. The most overwhelming and convincing manifestation of the high-gazed posture of Morrison and Faulkner, however, is in their long view of history which they chronicle in the extensive narrative commentaries that introduce and close so many sections of their novels. There is the opening of the fourth section of "The Bear" from *Go Down, Moses* when Ike McCaslin, in the context of time that begins with Eden, decides that he cannot accept "ownership" of the land:

> 'I cant repudiate it. It was never mine to repudiate. It was never Father's and Uncle Buddy's to bequeath me to repudiate because it was never Grandfather's to bequeath Ikkemotubbe to sell to Grandfather for bequeathment and repudiation. . . . Because He told in the Book how He created the earth, made it and looked at it and said it was all right, and then He made man. He made the earth first and peopled it with dumb creatures, and then He created man to be His overseer on the earth and

to hold suzerainty over the earth and the animals on it in His name, not
to hold for himself and his descendants inviolable title forever, generation
after generation, to the oblongs and squares of the earth, but to hold the
earth mutual and intact in the communal anonymity of brotherhood, and
all the fee He asked was pity and humility and sufferance and endurance
and the sweat of his face for bread.' (245–46)

Faulkner's expansive view of history here, a view that allows a 21 year old to
make a decision to repudiate the land in terms of a before-time sense of history,
is the view that enchants and "rivets" us and causes us to look back long at
the import and the impact of decisions in our own lives. This similar long
view, this dawn-of-time connection to the present, is the same way Morrison
introduces and shapes our perception of the island wealth of Valerian Street,
who has taken the money he has made and purchased a summer house off the
Caribbean on the Isle des Chevaliers:

> The end of the world, as it turned out, was nothing more than a
> collection of magnificent winter houses on Isle des Chevaliers. When
> laborers imported from Haiti came to clear the land, clouds and fish were
> convinced that the world was over, that the sea-green of the sea and the
> sky-blue sky of the sky were no longer permanent. Wild parrots that had
> escaped the stones of hungry children in Queen of France agreed and
> raised havoc as they flew away to look for yet another refuge. Only the
> champion daisy trees were serene. After all, they were part of a rain forest
> already two thousand years old and scheduled for eternity, so they ignored
> the men and continued to rock the diamondbacks that slept in their arms.
> It took the river to persuade them that indeed the world was altered. That
> never again would the rain be equal, and by the time they realized it and
> had run their roots deeper, clutching the earth like lost boys found, it was
> too late. The men had already folded the earth where there had been no
> fold and hollowed her where there had been no hollow. . . . (*Tar Baby* 9)

After this introduction in Chapter One of *Tar Baby*, when we get to the now
time of the novel, to the houses "wide and breezy and full of light," Morrison
has already set an against-nature mood for whatever happens in these houses.
As this mythical introduction indicates, things got off course a long time ago
and thus there can be no expectations of good to go on in the real time of
the novel. There is only the exploration of why it happened or how we can
make it right again. This is Morrison's lament in *Tar Baby*, and it is Faulkner's
lament in "The Bear" and in *Absalom Absalom!*: humankind has moved away
from the mythical course established in the Bible (for Faulkner) and from the
primeval course of the natural world (for Morrison). They look down from
the precipice with the long mythical view of history assured in the knowledge

that either someone makes a drastic turn back to the sacredness, the conviction of the time before now, or we are doomed. Invoking the mythical is a way to validate a world before humans were enslaved, before land was bought and sold, before land investors changed a forest in harmony to a strip of foreign and invading summer homes. Morrison and Faulkner engage, if not enchant, us with such passages. We can never focus just on the details of the lives of the characters or the impact of their actions on each other. All behavior now is connected, according to Morrison and Faulkner, and so we read these novels aware of a kind of signifying going on constantly between the specific group they represent (southerners and blacks or planter class slaveowners and invading land developers) and humankind generally and the larger, mythical movement of time.

This aerial view of history is also made manifest in the "shorter" view of history—a view that includes the recent and distant historical if not mythical past. Still, the imaginative gaze comes from afar and situates present moments in such a way that they become charged with history—we absorb them as something more than immediate instances. The aligning with nature, the recalling of events now past as a continuous stream of memory—shape how we view the present. In Quentin Compson's after-dinner talk with his father, the present time of *Absalom, Absalom!* becomes only a small pivot around which the land, the past and the future constantly circle:

> It was a summer of wisteria. The twilight was full of it and of the smell of his father's cigar . . . the odor, the scent, which five months later Mr. Compson's letter would carry up from Mississippi and over the long iron New England snow and into Quentin's sitting-room at Harvard. It was a day of listening too—the listening, the hearing in 1909 mostly about that which he already knew, since he had been born in and still breathed the same air in which the church bells had rung on that Sunday morning in 1833 and, on Sundays, heard even one of the original three bells in the same steeple where descendants of the same pigeons strutted and crooned or wheeled, in short courses resembling soft fluid paint-smears on the soft summer sky. (23)

In the opening of *Sula*, Morrison laments the loss of the "sameness," the connectedness that Faulkner affirms in *Absalom, Absalom!*. The destruction of an all-black neighborhood in Medallion, Ohio, by the "razing forces of urban renewal" breaks the sustaining cultural continuity for the people who lived there and their descendants. The writer must provide the history that the present generation of readers does not know. The novel becomes for Morrison a necessary conduit, a way to connect, to see again the land and the people that

were displaced by progress. Even as the novel laments the loss of a past way of
life, it encodes in its recall that past life upon the present:

> In that place where they tore the nightshade and blackberry patches
> from their roots to make room for the Medallion city golf course, there
> was once a neighborhood. It stood in the hills above the valley town of
> Medallion and spread all the way to the river. It is called the suburbs now,
> but when black people lived there it was called the Bottom. One road,
> shaded by beeches, oaks, maples and chestnuts, connected it to the valley.
> The beeches are gone now, and so are the pear trees where children sat
> and yelled down through the blooms to passers by. Generous funds have
> been allotted to level the stripped and faded buildings that clutter the road
> from Medallion up to the golf course. They are going to raze the Time and
> a Half Pool Hall, where feet in long tan shoes once pointed down from
> chair rungs. A steel ball will knock to dust Irene's Palace of Cosmetology,
> where women used to lean their heads back on sink trays and doze while
> Irene lathered Nu Nile into their hair. Men in khaki work clothes will pry
> loose the slats of Reba's Grill, where the owner cooked in her hat because
> she couldn't remember the ingredients without it. (3)

While Faulkner insists on the still-connectedness of the past and the present,
and Morrison laments the past's destruction by the present, both writers share
an overarching view of the necessity of the connection. Whether the novel
project becomes one of declaring affirmation or loss, the view, the writers' gaze
on their setting, is one that keeps the past as a necessary part of the present in
focus. Morrison and Faulkner never lose sight of, they do not miss or forget
the historical moments that affect the present, nor the future moments that the
present will affect.

The high gaze of history makes possible not only the ability to see the
unbroken connections with the past, but it also allows prophecy, an ability
to see far ahead and predict the future. Morrison's mythical predictions are
more abstract than Faulkner's. In *Song of Solomon*, Milkman's embrace (and
by extension his generation's embrace) of the mythical possibilities of flight—
however he imagines it—are predicted in the novel's closing paragraph: "As fleet
and bright as a lodestar he wheeled toward Guitar and it did not matter which
one of them would give up his ghost in the killing arms of his brother. For now
he knew what Shalimar knew, if you surrender to the air you can ride it" (337).

In Shreve's last conversation with Quentin in *Absalom, Absalom!*, Faulkner
offers a bold, more tangible prediction of the future of the South, but it, too, is
laced with broad historical import that indicates a knowledge of the movement
of time and its outcome, however bleak that outcome might be for the people
represented in the present time of the novel: " 'I think that in time the Jim
Bonds are going to conquer the western hemisphere. Of course it wont quite be

in our time and of course as they spread toward the poles they will bleach out again like the rabbits and the birds do, so they won't show up so sharp against the snow. But it will still be Jim Bond; and so in a few thousand years, I who regard you will also have sprung from the loins of African kings' " (302).

It is hard to read a novel by Morrison or Faulkner and not somehow feel a part of the progression of history. They are "seers" in that way, literary prophets— unblinking in their gaze—seeing life and the world and the humans in it whole, as cause *and* effect, as the ebb *and* flow of decisions and movements begun long before the present and which will extend long into the future.

We are drawn to Faulkner and Morrison because of this mythical conscious- ness, because of the connecting, probing, deliberate, redemptive nature of their gaze. The imaginative posture of their works says as much about the individual genius of Morrison and Faulkner as it does about our own inner, continued longings as human readers: the desire to see ourselves as connected to something larger than our present reality, as meaning something more than what we can see and interpret with the physical eye. Through a vision informed by a knowledge of the mythical connection of the universe, Morrison and Faulkner help readers achieve this desired end. Mythical connections appeal to us, as noted myth critic Mircea Eliade concludes, because myth "is a vital ingredient of human civilisation . . . it satisfies deep religious wants, moral cravings, social submissions, assertions and practical requirements" (20).

Morrison and Faulkner are blessed with a kind of "sixth sense," a mind's eye, that gives them a vantage point not shared by all of us. And it is their position as writers, *the way* that they look at the world and all of those who people it, that attracts us. It is their gaze, their high-up place, their long unblinking look, their ability to see the mythical drama of life in the unexpected places (in small Mississippi towns and countrysides, in Ohio bottoms and segregated, forgotten communities) and among unexpected people and events (the slaves and the masters, the aristocrats and the commoners, in bear hunts and homecomings, in births and in deaths) that "rivets" us. For under their gaze, it is made clear to us that if there is the possibility for grace, redemption, and justice for the Breedloves and the Sutpens, for the Snopeses and the Deads, for Ike McCaslin and Sethe, then perhaps grace, redemption, and justice are available to us all.

Notes

1. See Ernst Cassirer's discussion of "mythical consciousness" in *The Philosophy of Symbolic Form* (vol. II, 11–13). See also Walter Brylowski's discussion in the conclusion of his study, *Faulkner's Olympian Laugh* (220–223).

2. See T. S. Eliot's essay "Ulysses, Order, and Myth" (483). He recommended to American writers the "mythical method" after reading Joyce's *Ulysses*.

3. See Morrison's discussion of the "discredited" in "Rootedness" (342). She also discusses the discredited in her interview with Thomas LeClair ("Language"; rpt. Taylor-Guthrie 123–27).

3. Toni Morrison and William Faulkner
Remapping Culture

Andrea Dimino

As two of America's most gifted novelists, as Nobel Prize winners from different generations, as writers from different cultural groups, and as public commentators on literature, culture, and political issues, Toni Morrison and William Faulkner help us to understand the changes in the cultural role and identity of the American artist in the twentieth century. These changes are highlighted all the more strongly because of an exceptional relation: for forty years Morrison has had a sustained, intense engagement with Faulkner's work. One aspect of this engagement, which will be examined in the first part of this essay, challenges us to reformulate our ideas of cultural interchange and intertextuality. Neither Kenneth Burke's image of the complex, dynamic "conversation" of American culture, nor even Adrienne Rich's more highly charged and activist concept of "re-vision" will do justice to the tenacity and depth of Morrison's involvement with Faulkner in her novels (Burke 110–11). For Rich as a feminist, "re-vision" is "the act of . . . seeing with fresh eyes, of entering an old text from a new critical direction . . ." (Rich 35). Implicit in Morrison's cultural activity as a black woman is a sharing of Rich's urgent belief that "re-vision" is "more than a chapter in cultural history: it is an act of survival" (35). For Morrison, however, this "re-vision" takes the form not simply of new perceptions, but of *literal* revision, the rewriting of canonical texts in her own fiction.

31

Moreover, as it does for Rich, the "re-vision" has a second aspect. In order to help change the dynamics of American culture, to shape a different cultural consensus, Morrison engages in overt canonical politics. Since the 1950s, when she wrote a Cornell master's thesis that dealt in part with alienation in Faulkner, Morrison has been engaged with the established canon not only as a writer of fiction but as a critic, an editor, and a teacher of literature (Blake 189). Morrison's multiple roles help to direct us beyond a conception of literary history as an agon between individual great artists (as depicted in Harold Bloom's well-known *Anxiety of Influence*); in her nonfiction writing and public statements, Morrison insists that we perceive literature in relation to its wider culture. This essay will thus have two movements. After outlining Morrison's "re-vision" of Faulkner in her fiction, in the last two sections I shall compare Morrison's and Faulkner's involvement with academic and public culture, which largely parallels the shift in literature departments from the traditional humanities to the study of culture.

Morrison herself, in opening her book on whiteness and the American literary imagination, provides a suggestive image of her work: we can see it as an ambitious project of cultural remapping. She wants to extend "the study of American literature into what I hope will be a wider landscape. I want to draw a map, so to speak, of a critical geography and use that map to open as much space for discovery, intellectual adventure, and close exploration as did the original charting of the New World—without the mandate for conquest" (*Playing* 3). Informing this activity is Morrison's firm belief that the artist's life is "both solitary and representative" at the same time: "If anything I do, in the way of writing novels (or whatever I write) isn't about the village or the community or about you, then it is not about anything. I am not interested in indulging myself in some private, closed exercise of my imagination that fulfills only the obligation of my personal dreams. . . . [T]he best art is political and you ought to be able to make it unquestionably political and irrevocably beautiful at the same time" ("Rootedness" 340, 344).

Such statements stand as a challenge to Faulkner's proud memories of creating "a cosmos of my own" as he laid the foundation for the Yoknapatawpha novels in *Sartoris* (*Lion* 255). Faulkner's well-known and vivid statement should not obscure the fact that both in his writing of fiction and in his other cultural activities he develops some alternative conceptions and images of the artist's relation to the wider culture. As I shall argue in the last two sections of this essay, however, this exploration of the artist's cultural work remains scattered and contradictory for Faulkner, whereas for Morrison it has been carried out in a more conscious and deliberate way, in contexts that reaffirm the communal nature of the enterprise.

Faulkner as Ancestor: Morrison's Fiction

As a part of her cultural remapping, Morrison's "re-vision" of Faulkner is stimulating because it is intensely double. Her revisiting of his works in much of her own fiction could be seen as a tribute to his imagination and artistry and to his engagement with important cultural issues. But this revisiting also represents a continuing combat with Faulkner, a foregrounding of certain elements in his work in order to reveal problematic cultural affiliations and values. Morrison's relation to Faulkner thus reiterates the basic tension expressed in her image of cultural remapping, since she insists that a second charting of the New World must occur "without the mandate for conquest."

Morrison's double relation to Faulkner sheds a new light on the statement that begins her Nobel Prize Acceptance Speech: "I entered this hall pleasantly haunted by those who have entered it before me" (*Nobel* 31). As the essays in this volume show, Morrison's novels have been powerfully, strangely, sometimes uncannily haunted by Faulkner's writing, but I wonder how often this haunting was merely "pleasant." In fact, as a recurrent presence in Morrison's novels, Faulkner could even be said to mirror in a disturbing, often negative way a specific positive figure identified by Morrison—the black "ancestor" that she sees as a "distinctive" feature of African-American writing: "these ancestors . . . are sort of timeless people whose relationships to the characters are benevolent, instructive, and protective, and they provide a certain kind of wisdom" ("Rootedness" 343).

The doubleness in Morrison's response to Faulkner can be linked to a doubleness in Faulkner himself. When recent critics look at Faulkner's own depiction of race and gender, for example, they see not only the official divisions that the people of Yoknapatawpha County try to impose, but also a tissue of contradictions in Faulkner's texts. In general the "self" for Faulkner is a white male, and women and black people are seen as the other—their voices are muted or erased.[1] Nevertheless we find in his novels, instead of binary differences, countless examples of the merging or mirroring of self and other.[2] When a contemporary writer like Morrison, as part of her own cultural project, actually expands and alters for her characters the voice of the Faulknerian other, she could be seen as continuing a process begun in his works: to assert against the voices of the past a narrative of the present.

One of the broadest affinities between Morrison and Faulkner appears in the scope of their fictional projects. Both writers have aimed at nothing less than a large-scale mapping of culture, a journeying in book after book to new social, psychological, and historical territories, all partaking in a complex way in a common vision and goal. Their readers, once alerted to the ambitiousness of these careers, are primed to set each foray in relation to the others.

By concentrating on such areas of affiliation between Morrison and Faulkner, I do not, of course, mean to suggest that Morrison is always working consciously in relation to Faulkner; although some affiliations are direct responses, others may simply be shared cultural ground. Nor am I suggesting that Faulkner provides the only important, or the most important, literary or cultural context for Morrison's work. Her engagement with American, and especially African-American, culture and history has been studied by many scholars, and Morrison has also spoken of her interest in African culture. In the following brief overview of Morrison's novels, one of my goals is to show the complexity and diversity of Morrison's relation to Faulkner in her fiction; I seek to highlight important social and cultural issues that impelled both writers to expand the field of their work to nonfiction writing and public appearances—a topic that I shall later develop at length.

Some general links to Faulkner, involving common interests and similarities of fictional technique, appear in Morrison's first novel, *The Bluest Eye* (1970). Like Faulkner, Morrison depicts troubled families, especially from the child's perspective, and she portrays disturbing and extreme psychological states in some characters, at times using the familiar Faulknerian technique of flashback to create sympathy for them.

Morrison's *Sula* (1973) engages with Faulkner largely on the level of character. Above all, Sula recalls Joe Christmas in *Light in August*, who rebels against the attempt of other characters to define and domesticate him, and who calls into question communal standards of morality. Sula too wants to live an "experimental life" (*Sula* 118). When her grandmother tells her that it's time to get married and have babies, Sula answers " 'I don't want to make somebody else. I want to make myself' " (92). This is a strong echo of Joe Christmas's ultimate rejection of Joanna Burden's offer of marriage and security: " 'No. If I give in now, I will deny all the thirty years that I have lived to make me what I chose to be' " (Faulkner, *Light* 265). But in contrast to Faulkner, who emphasizes Joe's rootlessness, Morrison makes Sula more radically double, an insider/outsider; she builds on Faulkner to probe more deeply the interrelations of the community and the maverick. Sula cannot live without her community, the Bottom, no matter how different she may be, no matter how many cities she has lived in; and the community needs her to define itself.

In Morrison's 1977 novel *Song of Solomon* the double relation to Faulkner becomes more sharply etched. The novel starts with some striking similarities and moves to an assertive rewriting of Faulkner and a questioning of the values played out in his fiction, particularly in *Absalom, Absalom!* and "The Bear" in *Go Down, Moses.* These works all depict young men undergoing initiations into adulthood by way of a quest to understand the past: Milkman Dead and Guitar Bains in *Song of Solomon*, and Quentin Compson, Shreve McCannon, and Isaac McCaslin in Faulkner's works. Morrison and Faulkner also share an engagement with the problem of human time; most of their characters find it impossible to live creatively in the present moment, to have an energizing and fruitful orientation toward the future, and to come to terms with a tragic or troublesome past.

In terms of its depiction of race and gender, however, *Song of Solomon* presents us with a significant restructuring of the cultural and psychological issues that Faulkner portrays. The range of intertextual links that accompany the Faulknerian strain in Morrison's novel undercuts Faulkner's ringing rhetoric of "a cosmos of my own" and his labeling (partly humorous, of course) of the Yoknapatawpha map that appears after the text of *Absalom, Absalom!*, "William Faulkner, sole owner and proprietor." Faulkner's proprietorship is called into question as Morrison incorporates in her text diverse voices from her own family history and from African-American culture, including canonical works like Du Bois's *The Souls of Black Folk* and noncanonical ones like folk tales about flying Africans. Morrison's creation of her fictional voices is, moreover, grounded in African-American culture as a whole: language is "the thing that black people love so much—the saying of words, holding them on the tongue, experimenting with them. It's a love, a passion. Its function is like a preacher's: to make you stand up out of your seat, make you lose yourself and hear yourself" (Blake 198). Thus Morrison's textual practice brings a greater range of voices into dialogue, refutes Faulkner's understanding of the basic relation between the individual writer and the wider culture, and, as I shall show, meshes with the heightened dialogic practice of her nonfiction writing.

The character of Circe, for example, who in *Song of Solomon* teaches Milkman the powerful lesson of black people's love and suffering, revises the inscrutable and all but silent Clytie, who in *Absalom, Absalom!* presides over the near-total destruction of Sutpen's legacy. For Morrison, Clytie's silence is symptomatic of the role that black people play in the classics of American literature: as she once said, they "don't speak for themselves" (Interview with Bill Moyers 262). It is vital, then, that in *Song of Solomon* Morrison gives Circe a voice of her own with which to recount the history of both blacks and whites.[3]

Morrison's engagement with *Absalom, Absalom!* extends into her next novel, *Tar Baby* (1981). At first glance this story of Jadine, a sophisticated, well-educated black model, the wanderer Son with whom she falls in love, a wealthy white couple on a Caribbean island, and their black domestic workers (the aunt and uncle of the young woman) may seem to be light years away from Yoknapatawpha County. But on the level of symbolic setting, and as a meditation on the dynamics of power in relation to race, the novel evokes *Absalom, Absalom!* strongly. The wealthy white man, Valerian Street, whose power makes him the center of existence for most of the novel's characters, recalls the patriarch Thomas Sutpen, and the Isle des Chevaliers has a double symbolic meaning. It stands first of all as Morrison's version of the Haitian "heart of darkness" where Thomas Sutpen asserts his strength and gains a fortune derived from sugar cane. Ironically, sugar is also the basis of Valerian Street's power, since he has inherited a candy factory.

The Isle des Chevaliers also functions in *Tar Baby* as a version of Sutpen's Hundred itself, the hundred square miles that Thomas Sutpen has coerced out of the wilderness. Sutpen's children Henry and Judith have been marked by the solitude of their powerful father's domain; similarly, we see in Valerian Street's greenhouse a vivid image of his need to exert absolute power: "he built the greenhouse as a place of controlled ever-flowering life to greet death in" (53). Morrison's engagement with Faulkner in creating this character and these symbolic settings becomes more explicit and sharply focused when Valerian begins to analyze himself in terms of "innocence." Faulkner, of course, uses the term "innocence" to describe the rigid, inhumane quality of Sutpen's morality; Sutpen rejects Charles Bon with cold and ruthless legalism because a son with black blood will not fit into his dynastic design. Valerian's innocence lies in his ignorance of the actual lives of his wife and son. Only as an old man does he learn from his black cook that his beauty-queen wife took pleasure in wounding their little boy.[4]

As Faulkner does with Shreve in *Absalom, Absalom!*, Morrison includes in this novel some non-American characters who both participate in and observe the story. Morrison chooses black Caribbean characters, Gideon and Thérèse, and portrays them as more distant and critical in relation to white American culture than Shreve is; Thérèse actually precipitates Son's choice of his black heritage. As voices of the black diaspora, these characters thus help create a more complex cultural mediation in *Tar Baby*.

Given the power and variety of Faulknerian elements in Morrison's *Song of Solomon* and *Tar Baby*, it may be surprising that *Beloved* (1987), which reveals her growing mastery, could also replay the involvement with Faulkner in a new key. Like *Song of Solomon*, and like Faulkner's *Absalom, Absalom!*, *Beloved* involves the reader in the excavation of a haunting, sometimes terrible past; but compared to *Song of Solomon* the novel develops its subject on a larger scale and conveys greater historical depth and emotional power. The tensions of the historical situation are, for Morrison as for Faulkner, fully realized in the tortured passion of primary human relationships: hunted by her owner, Sethe kills her child, her " 'best thing' " (*Beloved* 272), just as Sutpen rejects his own son Charles Bon because of his black blood, and Henry Sutpen kills his beloved brother.

When we look at *Beloved* through a Faulknerian lens, there are a number of fruitful comparisons, and many are developed in other essays in this volume. Morrison's greater stylistic exuberance in this novel reminds us of Faulkner's masterful interweaving in his best novels of an elevated rhetoric and strong vernacular elements. Moreover, Morrison has created an intricate and very powerful narrative structure, as Faulkner does above all in *Absalom, Absalom!*. If the striking monologues of Sethe, Denver, and Beloved recall Faulkner's experiments in first-person narration in *The Sound and the Fury* and *As I Lay Dying*, the intermingling of voices in the fourth monologue evokes instead the highly indeterminate chapter 5 of *Absalom, Absalom!*, where the voice of Miss Rosa Coldfield blends with other narrative voices (*Beloved* 200–217).[5] And in terms of plot and theme, Morrison is able to envision for her characters some psychological and social victories that notably evade Faulkner's characters: at the end of the novel Paul D reaffirms his love for Sethe, and Denver, in contrast to Quentin Compson, has won her maturity by reaching out to a community that nurtures her and that does battle with the ghost.

Faulknerian elements also reappear in the highly distinctive New York City setting of *Jazz* (1992). In general, we see Morrison returning to Faulkner in *Jazz* when her black protagonists need to deepen their relation to the past, to different social and economic systems, and to the wilderness as well; at crucial points her urban twentieth-century narrative plunges back into the rural nineteenth-century South. Above all, we are reminded of young people's troubled relations with their parents, especially Charles Bon's urgent quest for recognition from Sutpen in *Absalom, Absalom!*. So important is this quest for a parent that Morrison deploys the theme twice in the novel. Though she strikingly echoes Faulknerian language in both episodes, she transforms the relation between Bon and Sutpen with a racial reversal, in Golden Gray's journey to find his black father, Henry Lestory. Since Lestory (with the wilderness skills of Faulkner's Isaac Mc-Caslin) is called "Hunters Hunter," Morrison is also claiming the complex values of the Faulknerian hunt and the Faulknerian wilderness for black people (168).[6]

Morrison achieves another "re-vision" of Faulkner by bringing women characters into the foreground of these Faulknerian scenes; Joe Trace yearns for a mother, not for a father, and it is Violet Trace, not a young man like Quentin

Compson, whose past is shadowed by the story of Golden Gray. The importance of gender extends to the novel's narrator as well, who sometimes seems to be an individual voice reflecting the collective consciousness of Harlem women, but may also be of indeterminate gender.

That Morrison returns to Faulkner in the context of a setting and period so strongly linked to African-American culture, the Harlem Renaissance, suggests more insistently that as her career progresses she is using Faulkner's work as a key cultural referent, emphasizing various aspects of his fiction in different novels. As she revisits Faulkner in her vibrant and tenacious project of cultural remapping, Morrison brings into visibility points of view that are buried or erased in her predecessor's fiction, with the constant aim of revealing a much broader scope of cultural relations. Like her character Baby Suggs in *Beloved*, whose house serves as a center of interchange for her community, Morrison develops an art of fiction as cultural mediation. Building on Faulkner's own practice of mediation, but critiquing it and going beyond it, she brings into relation black and white, "high" and mass culture, the canonical and the noncanonical, the past and the present, and American and foreign perspectives.

"We Are Not 'Other'": The Artist in Culture

Morrison's engagement with the established canon is not, of course, limited to rewriting it in her own works. She is deeply involved in cultural politics on many fronts, carrying forward a parallel project of cultural mediation that complements and nourishes her writing of fiction. Unlike Faulkner, who came to play a stronger public role after he had largely filled in the fictional map of Yoknapatawpha County, Morrison has worked in different fields while at the height of her powers as a novelist, and like many other writers of her generation, has had a longstanding involvement with the academic world.

We can see an especially complex and provocative cultural remapping in Morrison's 1989 essay "Unspeakable Things Unspoken: The Afro-American Presence in American Literature." Identifying the traditional literary canon as a "protected preserve" of the works of "whitemen" (in other words, writers like Faulkner), Morrison enters an academic debate in which the combatants seek to defend the canon or to transform it ("Unspeakable"; rpt. Bloom 202). As proof that the cultural stakes are high, this canonical warfare is not limited to "gun-slinging cowboy-scholars," but has "spilled out of the academy into the popular press" (204). Of special interest is the expository strategy of this essay, in which Morrison plays three successive roles. She appears first as a participant in a wide-ranging interdisciplinary debate; then as a reader of American fiction, as she puts forward a "re-vision" of *Moby-Dick*; and finally as a critic of her own fiction and as a black writer interrogating the nature of her blackness.

Our attention to these shifts is heightened by related changes in voice and in discourse. We know from the outset that this is not a typical scholarly essay; the first word is "I," and the first paragraph is a joke about her original plan to call the paper "Canon Fodder" (201). Morrison then shifts to more standard academic discourse, but seamlessly embedded in the second paragraph is a reference to "whitemale" definitions of value, without a space between the two words: a condensed explosive charge in a decorous package (201). Throughout the essay we find strategic shifts to more colloquial diction, including sardonic jabs at conservative academics, whose "guns are very big . . ." (204). As a joining of two realms of discourse that usually remain separate, one of Morrison's rhetorical moves is particularly electrifying: "the present turbulence seems not to be about the flexibility of a canon . . . but about its miscegenation" (205). With the use of one surprising word, the emotionally charged field of social discourse about miscegenation erupts into a discourse about—books.

At the end of the essay's first section Morrison jolts the reader into an awareness of the overall distancing effect of academic writing. Right after referring to "the Afro-American artistic presence" and to "their meaningful place in . . . American culture," she reminds us about the human subject who is writing: "it is no longer acceptable merely to imagine us and imagine for us. . . . We are the subjects of our own narrative. . . . We are not, in fact, 'other'" (208). The essayistic/academic "I" has shifted its identity, and now speaks as part of a collective African-American voice. Morrison also insists on connecting "voice" in writing with living speech, brought very close to home: "It could never have occurred to Edgar Allan Poe in 1848 that I, for example, might read 'The Gold Bug' and watch his efforts to render my grandfather's speech to something as close to braying as possible . . ." (212).

Morrison's project in this essay is multi-dimensional, for she needs not only to convey her understanding of the "contemporary battle plain" in literary studies but also to contextualize the canon debate in historical and political terms (201). This includes articulating the historical moment of her own essay, which is nothing less than the moment at which something unspeakable can begin to be spoken: "it is to my great relief that such terms as 'white' and 'race' can enter serious discussion of literature. Although still a swift and swiftly obeyed call to arms, their use is no longer forbidden" (202). Morrison also reminds us of earlier cultural upheavals that can shed light on our own. Though in sections of the essay her statements are so tightly packed that the argument is not always clear, she is successful overall in calling our attention to the vested interests and political motives at play in a clash of cultures. Writers, as she says, can transform politics into "intelligible, accessible, yet artistic modes of discourse" (213). Like literary and cultural critic Edward Said, whose work she admires, Morrison seeks to reveal cultural links between "canon building" and "Empire building" (207).

In a sense Morrison is criticizing academic culture for not being academic enough, for failing to undertake the "hard work of analysis" of African-American art and applying instead "lazy, easy, brand-name" labels—thus ironically mimicking the commodity culture that many literary critics censure (209). To combat this laziness, Morrison proposes three related projects in literary study: to develop "a theory of literature that truly accommodates Afro-American literature"; to re-interpret the traditional American canon in order to see in what ways the presence of African-Americans in our culture has shaped it; and to examine contemporary and non-canonical works with the same goal (210).

Morrison carries out the last two inquiries in the essay itself. Drawing on the work of Michael Rogin and other scholars, she proposes a reading of Melville's *Moby-Dick* that maps a new possibility in contemporary culture, that says to her audience, "this can now be spoken." To see Melville's white whale as the ideology of race, and Ahab as "the only white male American heroic enough to try to slay the monster . . . ," is to make the book become "luminous in a completely new way" (215). In the last, and strongest, section of her essay, Morrison turns to her own novels in order to understand the specific elements that make her a black writer. Her spirit of questioning and her careful scrutiny of minute textual details provide a model for new critical work. We are invited to use Morrison's practice of language itself as a map: for example, in order to transfigure the "wealth of Afro-American culture into a language worthy of the culture," she makes particular choices of the colloquial, relies "on codes embedded in black culture," and parodies other writing styles (221). One of her choices is especially revealing: we learn that the abrupt first sentence of *Beloved*, "124 was spiteful," snatches the reader into a foreign environment "just as the slaves were," creating a shared experience between us and "the novel's population" (228). Such a map enables us to enter this text, like *Moby-Dick*, in a luminous new way.

Morrison has returned more recently to the second critical project outlined in this essay, that of reinterpreting the traditional canon. In an important series of lectures at Harvard in 1990, which became her 1992 book *Playing in the Dark: Whiteness and the Literary Imagination*, she challenges the academic world, with a metaphor quoted earlier, to develop a new "critical geography" (3).[7] In order to link *Playing in the Dark* with Morrison's other nonfiction writing, I want only to note her expository strategy, which again makes us sharply aware of her multiple roles. The book begins with the assertion that "I do not bring to these matters solely or even principally the tools of a literary critic. As a reader (before becoming a writer) I read as I had been taught to do. But books revealed themselves rather differently to me as a writer" (3).

Morrison's thesis is nothing less than this: that the new American identity created in our literature, or rather "the construction of the American as a new white man," was achieved in relation to the Africanist presence in this country (39). She develops this view in readings of texts by Cather, Poe, Twain, and Hemingway. Though Morrison's book outlines four main topics that need critical investigation, the aim of the book goes beyond her proposal of an agenda for research. Like "Unspeakable Things Unspoken," *Playing in the Dark* is an impassioned, often sardonic critique of the blindness of some of the people who help to make the canon, the critics and literary historians who hold that "traditional canonical American literature is . . . unshaped by the four-hundred-year-old presence of, first, Africans and then African-Americans in the United States" (4–5). For Morrison, only the urgent work of *critical* remapping will enable us to stop "playing in the dark," and let us see the canonical texts that we have been reading for so long.

Morrison's expository strategies in "Unspeakable Things Unspoken" and *Playing in the Dark* show that she is probing the nature of her connection to the academic world. As a further move toward developing a public voice in the wider culture, she integrates the roles of writer, literary and cultural scholar, and politically concerned citizen in the introduction to her 1992 collection of essays, *Race-ing Justice, En-gendering Power: Essays on Anita Hill, Clarence Thomas, and the Construction of Social Reality*. Again, the shifting roles that Morrison plays in her expository strategy are significant. In "Introduction: Friday on the Potomac," she begins by evoking two different groups of black people: one prays in front of the White House that Thomas will not be barred from the Supreme Court, but the other, watching television, deplores his unfitness for the position. She then moves quickly to a broad view of American culture, with race no longer highlighted: during the confirmation hearings for Thomas, "There are passionate, sometimes acrimonious discussions between mothers and daughters, fathers and sons, husbands and wives, siblings, friends. . . . Sophisticated legal debates merge with locker-room guffaws . . ." (*Race-ing* viii). As the essay progresses, Morrison sharpens her focus on different groups of Americans, who bring to the debate perspectives that are problematic or insightful: she contrasts the "visual and print media," who engage in a typical "summing-up process" that fosters a quiescent attitude of " 'business as usual,' " with the "seismic reactions of women and men in the workplace" (x). Given this conflicting activity of two groups, Morrison asserts the value of a third cultural force, the academic world, which can provide "contextualized and intellectually focused insights" (xi). As the editor of the volume, Morrison has carefully shaped a context for her own essay. It appears as the introduction to a joint enterprise of people with strong academic credentials in a variety of fields; many, like Morrison herself, have been affiliated with Princeton University. Here her situation contrasts with that of Faulkner, who functioned in the academic world as an honored but relatively marginal figure.

Soon after her comment about the academic world, in examining Senator Danforth's comment about Thomas's laugh and identifying it as a "metonym for racial accommodation," Morrison shifts from her role as a member of the academic community to her identity as a black American: "Every black person who heard [Danforth's words] understood. How necessary, how reassuring were both [Thomas's] grin and its being summoned for display" (xiii). In such quick changes of perspective, Morrison asserts the complementarity, the seamlessness of the cultural roles and identities of an individual observer.

For Morrison's general readers, an unexpected shift takes place at the end of the essay, where her analysis of Defoe's *Robinson Crusoe* resoundingly confirms the relevance of literary study to a wide range of political and historical questions. For academic readers, the novel is a familiar landmark in discussions of postcolonial culture. Morrison sees Clarence Thomas as a Friday in contemporary America, someone who has internalized the master's language, but she is encouraged by the vigor of the dialogue that has surrounded his appointment: "In matters of race and gender, it is now possible and necessary, as it seemed never to have been before, to speak about these matters without the barriers, the silences, the embarrassing gaps in discourse" (xxx). She also welcomes the evidence that the participants in the debate are not playing unitary cultural roles: "Nor is it as easy as it used to be to split along racial lines, as the alliances and coalitions between white and black women, and the conflicts among black women, and among black men . . . prove" (xxx). Thus Morrison's own attempt to move beyond a "reified" concept of identity in her nonfiction writing comes to be seen as representative of a movement in her culture, complementing her challenge to reified identity in her fictional "re-vision" of Faulknerian characters with reversals of gender and race and with expansions of voice. Like *Playing in the Dark*, *Race-ing Justice* combines an energetic strain of critique with a sense of newly widened cultural perspectives.

The World and the Carpenter: Faulkner in Virginia

In order to bring into sharper focus the scope and urgency of Morrison's current project, it is revealing to compare Faulkner's venturing into a more public role after winning the Nobel Prize in 1950, as he channeled more of his energy into speeches, interviews, public appearances, and public letters. In this new kind of work, Faulkner tended to separate his cultural and social roles from one another. His tenure as Writer-in-Residence at the University of Virginia in 1957–58 is of particular interest, for this association repeatedly brought him into contact not only with literature students and professors but with journalists, psychiatrists, law school wives, students at other Virginia colleges, and the Charlottesville public, for a total of 37 group conferences and many individual ones. In spite of his lifelong reluctance to present himself as a public figure, Faulkner was forced to confront the varied literary, cultural, and social preoccupations of his audiences. Sometimes he responded in a formulaic way; but in other sessions, quickly seeing problems in his statements, Faulkner had to think on his feet. Eloquent and groping in turn, he worked through the perennial problem of the American artist seeking orientation in a complex culture and trying to provide that orientation for others. We can thus read Faulkner's year at Virginia as an activity of cultural mapping in which he considers American life in the 1950s in relation to his vision of the artist.

For the reader of the 1990s, it is striking to see how Faulkner acknowledges (at least minimally) but keeps in discrete compartments of discourse some key cultural and political issues that current literary critics and cultural theorists are working to link together. Not surprisingly, Faulkner builds his public persona on a core role as the artist with a transcendent vocation, depicting the "universal verities" of the human heart in conflict with itself and with other human hearts (*Faulkner in the University* 197). As an ultimate goal, this godlike and demon-driven artist seeks to create "one perfect book. . . . It's one single urn or shape that you have to do" (65). And since the passions of the human heart are universal, "there's no such thing as a regional writer . . ." (197). The literary canon exists for Faulkner as a clearcut map of greatness, whose terrain he may convey confidently to his audiences while revealing very little about the actual process of evaluation: Homer, Cervantes, Dickens, Flaubert, Balzac, Melville, Tolstoy, Conrad, Joyce, Mann, Ben Jonson, Marlowe, Burns, Keats, Whitman ("now and then"), Laforgue, Goethe (61, 145, 280). These great precursors have a special identity as a group, forming part of a "myriad company" who function "in individuality," pursuing the truths of the human heart (244).

In response to the audience's questions, however, Faulkner finds himself shifting from a universal context to that of modern America. Inevitably he develops images in tension with the one that he wants to keep central. Asked to explain some aspects of his fiction, including its locale, Faulkner refers to the writer as a "carpenter" who uses "the material which he knows, the tools which are at hand"—not universal elements, but his "environment," the concrete details of his culture and society (3, 57). The questioning thus stretches Faulkner from an emphasis on the creative imagination of the master artist to the now-familiar concern with the reader and with the study of culture.

In general, though, Faulkner's map inserts a large distance between writing and intellectual life; "there's a great difference," he remarks, between writers and "literary people that have no impulse to create at all, that simply . . . love to talk about books and ideas" (15). Exalting the artist's depiction of the human heart, Faulkner tells his audience, "I don't have much confidence in the mind. . . . [T]he mind lets you down sooner or later" (6). As for critics, "I don't know that I ever listened to one, ever read one" (13); Morrison, in contrast, reads all her reviews " 'twice' " ("All" 285).

Finally, Faulkner invests the canon with a historical sweep that dwarfs the cultural activity of the present: "I think that a writer wants to make something that he knows that a hundred or two hundred or five hundred, a thousand years later will make people feel what they feel when they read Homer, or read Dickens or Balzac, Tolstoy, that's probably his goal" (61). Since they are unlikely to be budding Homers, your coevals only threaten to distort your own gifts: "Only an individualist can be a first-rate artist," Faulkner asserts. "He can't belong to a group or a school and be a first-rate writer" (33). The emphasis on individualism persists in spite of Faulkner's statement that the talented writer "robs and steals from everything he ever wrote or read or saw" (115).[8] What we could call the "canonical imperative" transmutes this activity, however, so that the writer "ain't too interested in what the contemporary world thinks about him" (64).

Fortified by his vision of the Western canon, Faulkner needs to confront an alternative, and inimical, system of mapping: "the artist has . . . almost no place at all in our American culture and economy," which he associates with buying Cadillacs and deep freezes on the installment plan, and with the invention of "atom and hydrogen bombs" (34). In common with what John Matthews (in "Faulkner and the Culture Industry") calls the "myth advanced by modernist aesthetics," Faulkner does not probe the relation of his own art to commodity culture, in spite of his tours of duty as a Hollywood screenwriter (70).

In America, as in the modern world in general, "there's too much pressure against being an individualist. . . . Maybe to belong to a gang, you might escape the atom bomb" (33). In Europe, the "old culture," however, the canonical map and the contemporary social map are more in harmony: "In Europe it is taken as a matter of course that anyone who is first in his own craft or his media in the arts will also be socially conscious enough to have a voice in the economy and the culture and also anyone who is wise enough to be first in his own art will also be wise in the condition of the state" (164). Though cut off from this kind of cultural power, Faulkner is nevertheless in touch with "the people": "I like to listen to them, the way they talk or the things they talk about. . . . I have known them in farming and in dealing with horses and hunting . . ." (233). One hundred years after Whitman, he is still connected to the poet's expansive catalogue-maps of America.

In venturing beyond the clear chart of the canon to consider the role of the artist in American culture, Faulkner must hold in tension the realm of universal truth and value with evidence of cultural relativism and difference. Though he believes that the "human spirit" can communicate across cultures, when he recalls his trip to Japan as a cultural ambassador for the State Department, Faulkner admits, "I never did touch the Japanese. They all spoke English, but it was like two people running at top speed on opposite sides of a plate-glass window . . ." (153, 89).

Faulkner's mapping is most severely strained when he has to confront American regional differences. His identity as a southerner inevitably involves him in speaking about the longstanding racial problems of the South and the civil rights controversy of the late 1950s. In fact, racial issues define the basic difference between the northerner and the southerner. Asked if his characters are derived from Mississippi, Faulkner says, "I think there is not a great deal of difference between Southerners and Northerners . . ." (87). But in response to a question from a foreigner about regional divisions, Faulkner replies that "we are not going to confederate on the problem of segregation, that's the only issue that we balk at, but everything else is ephemeral"—in other respects, Americans are united (227).

Faulkner's regional discourse changes in different contexts. Asked if he is picturing the South in his novels, Faulkner protests: "I was trying to talk about people. . . . I wasn't . . . writing sociologically at all" (10). But when he thinks about the southern literary renaissance and about his readers, ideas of regional difference come into play: "The Northerner, the outlander, had a queer and erroneous idea of what Southern people were. It may be that that was an instinctive desire in Southerners to tell the outlander just what we were . . ." (136). When the conversation switches to law and social change, Faulkner condemns racism as a "basic human wrong," but at the same time emphasizes regional identity and autonomy: "the South has got to work that curse [of slavery] out and it will, if it's let alone" (46, 79).

Faulkner's images of black people, a key factor in his regional identity, also change in the course of his appearances in Virginia.[9] During the first session in February 1957, answering a question on *The Sound and the Fury* that evokes the humanist discourse of his Nobel Prize speech, Faulkner makes a racist statement but is still willing to include Dilsey Gibson in his universal vision: "the will of man to prevail will even take the nether channel of the . . . black race" (5). But in the heated atmosphere of racial controversy in 1958—the governor of Virginia "had promulgated a doctrine of 'massive resistance' to federal pressure for integration"—the pressures of cultural mapping eventually generate in Faulkner the need to construct in the social and political realm a map as coherent and emotionally meaningful as his vision of master writers in the literary canon (Blotner 1685). This map is a talk called "A Word to Virginians," which introduces a session in February 1958. Faulkner begins by deploring a society with a permanent group of second-class citizens, but he also recoils from the idea of full integration, and he associates black people with a lack of "self-restraint, honesty, dependability, purity . . ." (211). In the context of a southern town, black people are no longer even a "nether channel" for the human spirit, but "five hundred unbridled horses loose in the streets . . ." (209). Elsewhere the staunch defender of individualism, Faulkner assumes that black people are an undifferentiated group. He prescribes for them a complete loss of their blackness because he sees their identity as negative at its core: "[The black man] must learn to cease forever more thinking like a Negro and acting like a Negro" (211).

Underlying this erasure is a vision of Virginia as an origin and moral center for the South. If southerners want to uplift black people, the place "to begin is Virginia, the mother of all the rest of us of the South. Compared to you, my country—Mississippi, Alabama, Arkansas—is still frontier, still wilderness. . . . Let this be the voice of that wilderness, speaking not just to Mother Virginia but to the best of her children—sons found and chosen worthy to be trained to the old pattern in the University established by Mr. Jefferson to be . . . the enduring fountain of his principles of order within the human condition and the relationship of man with man . . ." (212). Like Faulkner's canon of literary masters, this is a transcendent vision, invoking order, historical continuity, and a universal view of humankind. It also reproduces a familial pattern, with Mother Virginia joined by Mr. Jefferson, the namesake of Yoknapatawpha's chief town, as father. But in this discourse, when we read of the South looking toward Virginia "as the child looks toward the parent for a sign" (212), we find none of the irony and complexity of Faulkner's fictional portrayal of Charles Bon's anguished waiting for a sign of recognition from his father, Thomas Sutpen, in *Absalom, Absalom!*—an action that Morrison rewrites for her character Joe Trace in *Jazz*.

Eventually, as the Virginia audience starts to probe Faulkner's image of "unbridled horses"—which may, ironically, be linked in part to the memorable spotted horses episode in *The Hamlet*—he abandons the image as an "unfortunate simile" that he chose in order to achieve quick communication within a particular "environment": "I used something that we were all familiar with . . ." (218). This crisis in discourse, with its uncomfortable recognition of racism, leads to an absurdity: "We could reverse it and [talk about] a community of fifty thousand horses with five hundred loose men moving around in it . . ." (218). Participating in a public discourse on race with his audience, Faulkner loses access to the resources of form and language that have made his fiction endure, even for those who reject his public racial views. In the distance between Faulkner's fictional achievement and his statements at Virginia, we see a space where the work of cultural mediation, the probing and linking of discourses, urgently needs to be done. Until then, the relation between these two kinds of racial discourse will remain, in Morrison's words, an unspeakable thing unspoken.

Notes

1. See Philip M. Weinstein's discussion of gender and race in *Faulkner's Subject*, and Judith Bryant Wittenberg's essay "Race in *Light in August*."

2. See especially James A. Snead, *Figures of Division*, and Minrose C. Gwin, *The Feminine and Faulkner*.

3. For a full elaboration of the Circe/Clytie pairing, see Nancy E. Batty's essay in this volume. On Clytie and silence, see Keith E. Byerman's essay in this volume.

4. See Robert Dale Parker's *Faulkner and the Novelistic Imagination* for a stimulating examination of the problem of knowledge and of Faulkner's strategic withholding of secrets.

5. For a detailed discussion of this chapter, see my essay "Miss Rosa as '*Love's Androgynous Advocate.*'"

6. For a detailed discussion of Faulknerian elements in *Jazz*, see Roberta Rubenstein's essay in this volume.

7. See Patrick O'Donnell's essay in this volume for another discussion of *Playing in the Dark*.

8. For a discussion of Faulkner's individualism, including its relations to southern culture and to the Cold War, see Lawrence H. Schwartz, *Creating Faulkner's Reputation*.

9. See Joel Williamson's excellent summary of the changes in Faulkner's response to race relations in *William Faulkner and Southern History*, 336–37.

4. DAVID AND SOLOMON

Fathering in Faulkner and Morrison

Philip M. Weinstein

Slavery ended officially over 130 years ago, but what Faulkner would call its repercussion shows little sign of ceasing. This essay is about legacies—both the specific historical legacy of slavery itself and the more general (and patriarchal) legacy that we might understand as the "territory" passed by the father to his progeny: the entry into custom and law, the inheritance of property. Differences coded to race could hardly be starker in this domain, for the role of the postbellum black father is burdened by a unique set of pressures. Indeed, the Emancipation Proclamation of 1863 bequeathed a legacy of continued impotence. For later generations of blacks such a legacy may act, in a reversal of the very intention of legacies, as a menacing parental bequest, in the form of disabling cultural memories and material humiliations. Morrison attends from the beginning of her career to the repercussions of this patriarchally inflicted wound, and she seeks increasingly to imagine her way past the gender assumptions that underlie it. At the same time, Faulkner's texts show, more vividly perhaps (because he is a postbellum southern writer) than those of any other twentieth-century Western novelist, a white dysfunction wrought as well into the heart of the patriarchal model of property-descent: a dysfunction that registers in the damage done to and (even more) by the father.

Faulkner and Morrison explore the failure of the paternal function in significantly different ways. These differences attach, I wish to argue here, to racially different stances toward the Oedipal itself.[1] For the Oedipal model of maturation operates as the normative psychic model underlying white Western patriarchy's design for regulating the descent of gender identity and the cultural inheritances that gender subtends. This model was not designed, so to speak, with blacks in mind; and Morrison's black males aspire to it at their peril. Faulkner's fathers, by contrast, have no choice: the Oedipal/patriarchal paradigm for male maturation and the descent of gender identity is the only model his culture has valorized. In both writers the model fails. How the white southern male writer and the black nonsouthern female writer attend to such dysfunction is my subject.

David and Solomon: the names take us to *Absalom, Absalom!* and *Song of Solomon*, and they suggest, at the outset, that Faulknerian paternity will circulate about disinherited sons as recurrently as Morrisonian paternity will involve a search for Solomonic stability and wisdom. I will not attempt to reconstitute the father as he arises, component by component, from a totalizing vision of each writer's texts. Rather, I will proceed across the range of fathers that emerge in two careers full of paternal imagining. The father I pursue changes from novel to novel, showing a different face when juxtaposed against the other writer's paternal figures. Yet he retains a certain structural insistence (there is no avoiding either his presence or his absence) tinged with pathos. He would bequeath and enable. Insofar as he is invested in a patriarchal model of paternity turned incurably dysfunctional, he cannot succeed at either task. My questions are the following: What material and emotional legacies pass from fathers to their offspring? How does a white father differ from a black father? How does a black female writer engage these questions differently from a white male writer? In a word, what stories do Faulkner and Morrison tell when they tell the story of the father?[2] I begin with the most suggestively troubled fathers of Faulkner's and Morrison's early fiction: Mr. Compson in *The Sound and the Fury* and Cholly Breedlove in *The Bluest Eye*.

I. The Sound and the Fury *and* The Bluest Eye

Mr. Compson is the most engagingly impotent father in Faulkner's fiction. John Irwin (*Doubling*), André Bleikasten ("Fathers"), and Richard Moreland (*Faulkner*) have cogently analyzed his competitive relation to his son Quentin, his unshakable alcoholism, and his reactionary cast of mind; yet, his portrait in *The Sound and the Fury* is nevertheless infused with tenderness. His defining attribute is incapacity; he is the one who can make nothing happen. Faulkner's representational strategy ensures this impression by severing

Mr. Compson's behavior from his words. We hear him repeatedly in this novel—Benjy's notation of his telling the children to "mind Dilsey now" (24), Quentin's incessant "Father said"—but we do not see him act.

He comes into narrative focus as the father whose blueprints for behavior cannot affect the real. He cannot keep the Compson gate closed ("How did he get out?" [52] he asks his son Jason), leading to Benjy's castration. Here, in microcosm, we see his failure to shepherd his offspring through the Oedipal crisis, for the role of the father is to *suspend* the possibility of castration over the son's rebellious desires, leading to the latter's successful self-discipline and eventual gender maturation. He is not to permit the castration actually to happen; otherwise what are fathers for? He can't keep Caddy in tow any more than he could Benjy, and her exit from Compson mores is steadily driving him to suicidal drink, whatever he may say about the fictitious value of a daughter's virginity. Nor, despite a continuous pouring forth of advice (much of it acute, all of it intended as enabling), can he keep his dearest son Quentin from suicide. Finally, he fails to imbue his namesake Jason with any of his virtues. Perhaps the most revealing testimony to his failure lodges in the spectacle of his son Jason's reversal of the father's paternal functions. As "a different breed of cat from Father" (201), Jason systematically abuses his own siblings—the offspring Mr. Compson could not protect.

There is one moment in which, through Benjy's perspective, we see the father equal to his paternal role: "Caddy and Father and Jason were in Mother's chair. Jason's eyes were puffed shut and his mouth moved, like tasting. Caddy's head was on Father's shoulder. Her hair was like fire, and little points of fire were in her eyes, and I went and Father lifted me into the chair too, and Caddy held me" (72). The harmony is precarious; for an instant the father serves as a sort of bodily ground uniting these three offspring, letting them nest upon him as they brush up peacefully against each other. More often, though, his sons' perspectives show us a man in bodily isolation, furtively or defiantly drinking by himself, a man whose gnomic phrases about the meaning of life lack local grounding. His children can do nothing with his advice. It comes from a source removed from their experience, and it does not help them adapt to current conditions.

This is so because the only world view he would bequeath them is an antiquated one in which he no longer believes. Honor is the mainspring of his behavior—he takes in Caddy's child without asking questions, quietly defying his deal-making wife—yet honor has become for him like the family watch he bequeaths Quentin. Both are meant to signal the ceremonial ordering of time from generation to generation, but time can no longer be ordered. The watch should at least still tell time, but after Quentin smashes it it does nothing but tick. Its mainspring is indestructible—it keeps ticking—but it no longer orients, like Mr. Compson's irrelevant but still insistent mainspring of honor. It insists therefore in the form of its own negation: "reducto absurdum." The dimensions of the real register on him not as possibility or even challenge but as a slap in the face—a reduction to absurdity of his once pertinent system of values.

Mr. Compson's "reducto absurdum" (76) offers no subjective space for grounding him in the present. His lengthy speeches are about the nonbeing of what used to be. Ungrounded, he imagines himself as not there—like a shadow or like death itself, "only a state in which the others are left" (78). Others are left alive to move about on his periphery, but he is distant from them, suspended, enervated. "It's not despair until time it's not even time until it was" (178), Quentin remembers his father saying, and this formula conveys the inbetween temporality within which his father passes his life: a ticking watch/code which tells him that he no longer "is" but is not yet "was."

The mental set he can neither relinquish nor successfully bequeath is the ideology of southern honor.[3] Within that frame a father is a gentleman who passes on to his offspring both the proper sense of "gentle" and the resourceful, will-enabled sense of "man." Born after the War, Mr. Compson lives in a social scene that refuses both of these senses. A mercantile cash-nexus (which his namesake Jason will actively engage) has replaced the cavalier mythology he believes disappeared in 1865, and he has withdrawn from this vulgar situation into an impotent world of books. He utterly lacks a current project. His Latin tags orient no better than his other gnomic sayings, but they at least reveal that he knows of a way of life less mean than the one before him. Meanwhile he takes to drink, sells off the land parcel by parcel, and addresses his present moment in the relentlessly ironic mode of "reducto absurdum" (as though he were saying, "I who speak to you at this moment am not really here and now but there and then, suspended in an other scene whose values have of course become absurdly irrelevant today").

Faulkner's creative energy in this text is invested less in the failed father than in the loss inflicted upon his needy children. All four of them go radically awry—the daughter unable to use her father as a buffer against her mother's attacks upon her burgeoning sexuality, the eldest son unable to draw emotional sustenance or masculine resolve from his father's nihilist stance toward Caddy's fall from honor, the middle son repelled by his father's elegant incapacity to grapple with postWar material conditions, the most helpless third son abandoned first to the castrating knife and eventually to the impersonal asylum in Jackson. So great is Quentin's need of the father's guidance that he insistently constructs his crises as appeals to the father ("Father I have committed . . ."). Indeed, he half invents this necessary judge of his defective behavior: "*I am my fathers Progenitive I invented him . . .*" (122). It is as though, given the intensity of his children's need, his paternal blankness explodes in each of them as a social alienation beyond healing. The southern codes he would patriarchally bequeath collapse into a quietly corrosive irony as they pass through his discourse. Yet, and this is perhaps the source of his appeal, his more aggressive wife rages with a passionate intensity next to which his lack of all conviction appears virtually benign. The mother's defection outweighs his own, and on this note we may now turn to the different construction of parental figures in Morrison's fictional world.

Although the destruction of Pecola Breedlove in *The Bluest Eye* reveals a cultural dysfunction traceable equally to the father and the mother, Cholly Breedlove fails the more dramatically. The text announces his failure immediately, informing us as early as the third page of the doomed daughter impregnated by her father. Even before this opening there is the Dick and Jane prologue, typographically jumbled phrases that will reappear as incoherent chapter epigraphs (in that space where the reader usually finds nuggets of wisdom). These muddled Dick and Jane passages announce that this will be a story of propertylessness, of failed proprieties. "Knowing that there was such a thing as outdoors," Claudia the narrator says, "bred in us a hunger for property, for ownership" (18). "Outdoors" is economic territory, the unprotected territory (shaped by racial injustice) where blacks who cannot pay their bills to white merchants are exiled. Claudia's (unrepresented) father passes this test, but Cholly supremely fails it. Morrison paints this portrait through the misery of his ragged possessions—"the furniture that had aged without ever becoming familiar" (35). Economic defeat passes metonymically into emotional ravage. Cholly and Pauline have forged a marriage out of their mutual failures—"she needed Cholly's sins desperately" (42)—and we are urged to trace their dysfunction back to childhood wounds.

Cholly's wound, first mentioned just prior to the ugly fight that erupts between him and Pauline, takes on the resonance of trauma. As a young man he had been caught in his first act of intercourse by white men. Their flashlight on his behind and their sadistic sexual urging transformed desire into disgust and hatred—not for the whites who were watching but for the frightened girl beneath him. We shall return, as Morrison does, to this scene, but we can identify already a number of damaging elements that coalesce into a single syndrome. First, Cholly's dysfunction is sexually charged—intercourse will henceforth be revenge as much as release. Second, the dysfunction is white-inflected. It is as though the white flashlight reoriented his glandular and emotional systems; the act of sex is now subjectively accompanied by phantom onlookers. Third, the early sexual encounter and the present fight with Pauline circulate about the motif of a naked black body. "Black e mo. Yadaddysleepsnekkid" (65), Maureen taunts Pecola, and the taunt has its disturbing edge of truth. Cholly's impotence (literal in that early scene) registers in the form of a humiliated and exposed black body. He has been seen naked—first by abusive whites, next by his cringing daughter—without the dignity provided by clothes. This early sexual dislocation seems to lead inexorably to the final sexual outrage, his rape of his daughter Pecola.

In all of this the patriarchal/Oedipal model is failed utterly. Nakedness seems coded economically even more than sexually. Cholly has nothing—no parents, no lineage, no job, no possessions: no social coherence—he can call his own and can bequeath to his child. Futureless himself, he plays no role in shaping his daughter's maturation. "How dare she love him?" he thinks, just before abusing Pecola: "Hadn't she any sense at all? What was he supposed to do about that? Return it? How? . . . What of his knowledge of the world and of life could be useful to her? What could his heavy arms and befuddled brain accomplish that would earn him his own respect, that would in turn allow him to accept her love?" (161–2). His exposed black body suggests a black man arrested in infancy, in a state of dishonor, one whose will has no efficacy in the world. Cholly's own childhood was bereft of legacies that would enable his adult entry into the social realm, and he eventually leaves his daughter with a sexually humiliating wound similar to the one by which he reads himself. Propertyless, he respects no proprieties, he lacks the "proper" of achieved masculine identity. Within a white model of paternity as achieved self-possession permitting the passage of cultural goods to one's offspring, he emerges as a disastrous father, the first in Morrison's subsequent gallery of men who missed some turning in the ritual of maturation and who remain BoyBoys forever. Cholly is the most disturbing of these; yet, already, this novel is suggesting other, more provocative ways to view him. In a beautifully Faulknerian move Morrison goes on to revisit the child after delineating his adult collapse; the revisiting lens transforms the portrait.

Like Joe Christmas who changes before our eyes from pain-inflicting adult to pain-absorbing infant, Cholly now comes to the reader as an orphaned child, desperately in search of a father-figure. Aunt Jimmy, as the name suggests, played this role as best she could, but Cholly yearns for the missing male who would embody an adult grasp upon the social world that he could emulate and in time make his own. It is during this unsponsored state, aggravated by Aunt Jimmy's death, that the traumatic sexual event occurs: "The flashlight wormed its way into his guts and turned the sweet taste of muscadine into rotten fetid bile" (148). It would be hard to envisage a purer moment of self-alienation. The white gaze has penetrated to his guts and will henceforth (dis)orient his desires. Stung by these upheavals, he takes off for Macon, Georgia, in search of a man called Fuller—whom he believes to be his departed father. The scene of Cholly's discovery of Fuller in a card game (with other black men likewise discarded by the social system) is sublime. Cholly stares at the man whose mysterious potency begot him, amazed by Fuller's "hard, belligerent face" and vulnerable body smaller than his own:

> "What you want, boy?"
> "Uh. I mean . . . is you Samson Fuller?"
> "Who sent you?"
> "Huh?"
> "You Melba's boy?"
> "No, sir, I'm . . ." Cholly blinked. He could not remember his mother's name. Had he ever known it? What could he say? Whose boy was he? He couldn't say, "I'm your boy." That sounded disrespectful.
> The man was impatient. "Something wrong with your head? Who told you to come after me?"
> "Nobody." Cholly's hands were sweating. The man's eyes frightened him. "I just thought . . . I mean, I was just wandering around, and, uh, my name is Cholly. . . ."
> But Fuller had turned back to the game that was about to begin anew. . . . [Eventually] he stood up and in a vexed and whiny voice shouted at Cholly, "Tell that bitch she get her money. Now, get the fuck outta my face!" (155–6)

Recoiling in a daze, Cholly wanders into an alley, trying to hold himself together. Then "his bowels suddenly opened up, and before he could realize what he knew, liquid stools were running down his legs. At the mouth of the alley where his father was, on an orange crate in the sun, on a street full of grown men and women, he had soiled himself like a baby" (157). He runs to the river, sits "knotted there in fetal position" (157), enters the water to cleanse himself and his clothes, then thinks for the first time since her death of Aunt Jimmy: "With a longing that almost split him open, he thought of her handing him a bit of smoked hock out of her dish. . . . And then the tears rushed down his cheeks, to make a bouquet under his chin" (158).

I have quoted this scene fully because it embodies a male rite of passage that perfectly fails—as prelude to going beyond—the Oedipal model. Unfathered, sexually disoriented (confused as to racial and gender identity), Cholly seeks out the father, who once again disowns him. He regresses to a liquid and infantile economy, an unlearning of the constraints that had permitted his earlier precarious coherence. He soils himself, reenters the urine and feces that normally precede birthing, then—glimpsing in his mind the woman who gave him the only fathering he would ever receive—dissolves into tears. Like Paul D in *Beloved*, he is undone by a kind of absolute self-dispossession. Split open by longing, he loses the last shreds of individuation that allowed him to recognize himself as himself. The sequence is saturated in those infantile liquids that boys must learn to control if they would become men. Within a patriarchal/Oedipal economy grounded in the expectation of property, an economy whose legacies guide proper gender discipline, Cholly is an unmitigated disaster, and Morrison knows it.

She also knows that "the pieces of Cholly's life could become coherent only in the head of a musician. . . . Only a musician would sense, know, without even knowing that he knew, that Cholly was free. Dangerously free . . ." (159). His terrible way of failing a white gender model, his making of his life a series of contingent adventures rather than a cumulative sequence of projects—this is at the same time an unco-opted way of being black and male whose rhythm only a jazzman could intuit. Damaged to the core, all identity-sustaining boundaries overrun, Cholly ceases to be, on one model, and comes into being, on another. The second model is nonOedipal and nonpatriarchal. This Cholly has received no shaping legacy, will never own anything, is incapable of parenting. He is also, and dangerously, free. Indeed, he embodies the true threat promised in Morrison's later name of Stamp Paid, for he has paid his final dues ("there was nothing more to lose" [160]), opted out of all schemas of duty and the accumulation of goods, and is in the clear. No ideology of the will, of possession, can hold him. He rewrites, as a black man, the gender pact for humanizing time, going for unrelated moments of authenticity rather than a developmental sequence that would yield maturity and mastery.

If Cholly is for Morrison a breakthrough, he is no less an unresolvable problem. The man who breaks out of the cycle of male heartbreak is also the father who abuses his own daughter. Morrison narrates this climactic event strictly from within Cholly's perspective, for even her courage might fail if she were to invite us to feel (as Faulkner's Temple Drake feels) what being raped is like. The text then dances abruptly into Soaphead's crazed mind (a lens upon Cholly's?), before finishing in Pecola's crazed mind. Cholly exits from the representational schema altogether, allowing this tragedy to come to conclusion but leaving open the question that will engage Morrison for the next twenty years: how can a black man achieve masculinity outside a white model of manhood?[4] The figures through whom she pursues this inquiry are not always fathers, but they share increasingly the primary paternal resource: the capacity to enable others' growth. Stamp Paid and Paul D are stepping stones toward her latest musically-paced attempt at an answer—Joe Trace of *Jazz*.

II. Repercussions

In 1970 (the year of *The Bluest Eye*), Stamp Paid, Paul D, and Joe Trace are a long way off, hardly beckoning as eventual solutions. Instead, in a brilliant turn that focuses and releases a new source of power, Morrison transfers the dangerous masculine freedom of Cholly Breedlove to the female sphere. Cholly's first inheritor is Eva Peace, and this gender shift enables a social one. As Kathryn Stockton has suggestively argued, the "Bottom" in *Sula* is central to an organizational departure from white norms that is simultaneously economic and libidinal. ("The little nuclear family," Morrison argued in a *Time* interview, "is a paradigm that just doesn't work" [cited Stockton 98]; the savaged Dick and Jane snippets of *The Bluest Eye* were already pointing this way.) Eva's domestic sphere cuts loose from the organized libidinal repression of patriarchal models. Taking that model's masculine prerogative into herself, paying its male price (the castration/loss of her leg), she achieves separation on her own terms and becomes the architect of her black realm, sovereignly giving and taking life. Whites—and white ways—are kept out.

Black males enter her world freely, but always under the sign of economic incapacity (kept down by the patriarchal model), BoyBoys in the social sphere however Ajactive their sexual prowess. Chicken Little, the Deweys, Tar Baby, Plum, Shadrack—these are males shattered by or kept on the nearside of the social contract for males. Orphaned, disowned, picked up (if at all) only by Eva, they have inherited nothing and they bequeath nothing. They cannot, in Stockton's words, "convert the penis to the phallus" (104). Like Tar Baby, each enacts a version of "drinking himself to death" (*Sula* 40). They are as futureless as Hannah's husband Rekas, a "laughing man . . . who died when their daughter Sula was about three years old" (41): a male whose textual introduction serves equally as his epitaph, whose novelistic life lasts all of one vivid sentence. Failed fathers here are colorful, epitaphic ("a laughing man"), not the material of sustained analysis. It is as though nothing further is expected of them, as though, knowing they will turn emasculate—will deflate from Ajax to Albert Jacks— when forced to negotiate the patriarchal sphere, Morrison prefers to leave them their penis intact, not ask of them the social stability and norm-providing authority that only the paternal phallus brings.

Sula leads—even more than her mother and grandmother—a life outside of patriarchal constraints. Cut off like Cholly from all legacies, she becomes, like him, dangerously experimental: "As willing to feel pain as to give pain, to feel pleasure as to give pleasure, hers was an experimental life—ever since her mother's remarks sent her flying up those stairs, ever since her one major feeling of responsibility had been exorcised on the bank of a river with a closed place in the middle. The first experience taught her there was no other that you could count on; the second that there was no self to count on either. She had no center, no speck around which to grow" (118–19). In Cholly this experimental stance was foredoomed. A man without connection, yet with a family, is in trouble; his ultimate trouble will be to experiment with his own daughter. But Sula is intoxicatingly free of her family. The novel's most tonic passages are all enactments of familial disowning—of Chicken Little's unregretted disappearance into the water, of Plum's maternally engineered and incandescent departure, of Hannah's flaming dance that her daughter Sula watches with interest. Early in adolescence she had invaded masculine as well as occupied feminine territory, wielding the knife upon her finger as her grandmother had done on her leg, testifying to an unchecked will (capable of limitless damage to self and other) that makes antagonists shrink away from her. She is radiantly herself alone. To her grandmother's petulant plea—"When you gone to get married? You need some babies. It'll settle you"—she answers, "I don't want to make somebody else. I want to make myself" (92).

I want to make myself. The figure of Sula lets Morrison raise the fatal questions concealed beneath the articulate surface of *The Bluest Eye.* How does an unaided human life essentialize itself, purify itself of all excrescences, finding its way to the naked and inhuman loam (past flesh, past even bone)? What possibilities lie outside of all legacy (much of which has been white-deformed), such that the old stories are overthrown and a new one can come into being? What resources are available on the other side of orphanhood—the mother refused and the father all but unknown? How does a death sentence become—once it is embraced rather than resisted—life-enabling? Of all of Morrison's novels this is the most death-centered, the most lyrically committed to encountering with style, without fear, the annihilation of self that is death. If *The Bluest Eye* is a complaint launched from the shadow of a death always to be inflicted, *Sula* is an affirmation rising from within the substance of a death already imposed and accepted. In this book death is taken in, turned inside out, and reborn as a life-form. No more victimization at the hands of white convention; black life will issue (will issue only) from native black resource. There are no more laws, no more authorized values, no guiding legacies. Morrison will not rest here—a self that is no self, recognizing no family and no lawful values, offers little resting place—but she could never have found her way into the generosity of Pilate without passing through the crucible of Sula. As for the indistinguishable BoyBoys who accept their nonmanhood, they will reappear as the paired hunters—Milkman and Guitar—in search of the father.

If one of Morrison's abiding projects, from *Sula* forward, is to free the black experience of maturation from the shackles of a white value-system, we may return to Faulkner by saying that the collapse of this system generates the inexhaustible fallout of his fiction. He makes his tragedies out of an encountered outrage—a humiliation of inherited values and of the masculine will that sustains them—that Morrison seeks increasingly to read in other terms. Such outrage has been long recognized as Faulkner's keynote. There has been less scrutiny, however, of the emotional and intellectual syndrome subtending outrage: the syndrome of innocence. From Donald Mahon through Chick Mallison, Faulkner's commitment to male innocence is absolute, however complex his judgment of it. This innocence involves, always, a dream of the intact will, a fantasy scenario in which subject and world coincide as though meant for each other.

As a black woman who has virtually absorbed the defeat of the sovereign will with her mother's milk, Morrison differs fundamentally. She is as repelled by innocence as Christians are by corruption. In her work it casts an equivalent and indicting odor: "An innocent man is a sin before God. Inhuman and therefore unworthy. No man should live without absorbing the sins of his kind, the foul air of his innocence" (*Tar Baby* 243).[5] The contrast becomes clear. On the one hand, the Faulknerian project of the father, involving the indispensable twin features of innocence and outrage, unfolds as a drama of the disinherited son's humiliated will: a white male story of American failing. On the other hand, the Morrisonian project of the father, beginning with Cholly Breedlove, involves not the failed transmission of a once-intact legacy, but the suspended threat of an impotence descending from slavery itself.

John Irwin (*Doubling*) and André Bleikasten ("Fathers") have given us our most cogent readings of the damaging Faulknerian father, and Carolyn Porter has recently proposed a stunning revision of their claims. Irwin reads the Faulknerian father as a grown-up son, authoritative only in the eyes of his own rebellious offspring. Irwin's Mr. Compson embodies a generations-repeated imposture. Appearing powerful to his son, he in effect confesses to the son that he too was undone earlier by the apparent power of his own father, that no father is powerful inasmuch as every father is a son caught between his own father on whom he would seek revenge and his own son seeking similar revenge. Irwin draws on Nietzsche to propose a model of time as Chronos, the inhuman power that eventually undoes all sons grown first to fatherhood and then back into the impotence of old age. Bleikasten's Faulknerian father is equally beleaguered, mainly because he comes at a time—after the Civil War—in which he has no authority left to bequeath. Insofar as the father can pass on to the son only those legacies that the larger culture has kept intact, the postWar South guarantees Mr. Compson's impotence. Bleikasten reads Faulkner's antebellum fathers—the Hightowers, Sartorises, Sutpens, and McCaslins—as serenely unapproachable by their confused twentieth-century progeny: of no use whatsoever for current cultural adaptation. Porter's revision involves, by way of a politically slanted Lacanian lens, a reseeing of the entire paternal dynamic. The Faulknerian father emerges, by the time of Sutpen, as the figure of cultural authority itself. His power is based upon a successfully survived Oedipal ordeal—the eventual occupation of the position vacated by the original and hostile father that characterizes every Oedipal passage—which is itself the psychological motor of patriarchal politics, the logic of the descent of property and other perquisites from father to son. When *this* father comes apart, Porter argues, his self-destruction and destruction of others reveals nothing less than Faulkner's extraordinary diagnosis of patriarchy's intrinsically racial and gendered injustice.

Without further complicating this portrait of the father (for I do not know how to improve on Porter's analysis), I would point to the three sequences of Faulkner's fiction (all of them circulating in different ways around the son's outraged innocence) that it impels. First there is the sequence of the impotent father, he who fails to protect the son. Mr. Compson inaugurates this lineage, though we may say that the all-but-absent Judge Drake in *Sanctuary* and the present-but-useless Old Bayard in *Flags in the Dust* are preparatory figures. Their paternal ineptitude (Porter elaborates on Lacan's definition of the father as the father who does not know he is dead ["Symbolic" 99–106]) underwrites the assault—at once stylistic and substantive—that these novels deliver. (Indeed, what would better motivate such ferocious assault than the twin insults of a culture gone bankrupt in both the substance it would bequeath and its very style of bequeathing?) Malraux knew long ago that Faulkner's subject was "the irreparable," to which I would add that "the irreparable" becomes dramatic only when the drama of outraged innocence in its presence is supplied. Rape and rupture—a humiliation of will, a failure of legacy—are the obsessive events, and Faulkner's art is lavished upon showing that there is no getting used to these abuses. Benjy Compson embodies most purely a nonadaptation equally visible in Quentin and Jason, in Darl and Jewel, in Joe Christmas and Temple Drake.

When Faulkner returns to Temple, some twenty years after *Sanctuary* in *Requiem for a Nun*, the failed legacy and humiliating wound remain beyond

adaptation. Indeed, the wound has festered, poisoning the lives it touches—
Temple's, Gavin's, Nancy's, the baby's. As Temple says to the doomed Nancy
late in the novel, "Why do you and my little baby both have to suffer just
because I decided to go to a baseball game eight years ago?" (*Requiem* 277).
Despite its endless circulation around this question and its cognates, the text
can come up with no answer beyond Nancy's mysterious "Believe." There may
be some ultimate sanction justifying this suffering, but it is beyond knowing,
even perhaps, the text may suggest, beyond white believing. What strikes me is
Faulkner's unresisted urge to keep the wound mortal, to collapse the intervening
days and years into so much inauthentic time passed under the shadow of a
concealed self-betrayal. We are in the presence of an authorial insistence upon
disaster, one focused not on the event's further possible meanings (for the event
reduces here to pure evil), but rather on its irreparable consequences. The
pretenses of a sutured self (Temple's, Gowan's) are tirelessly torn apart. The text
all but revels in its protagonists' pain and in the futility of any parental figure's
attempt to address that pain.

The pattern I have been tracing—the humiliation of the will, the discovery of
impotence consequent upon a failed legacy—begins arguably with the paralyzed
Donald Mahon and nourishes many of Faulkner's characteristic portraits.
Bayard (of *Flags*), Benjy, Quentin, Horace, Joe Christmas, Henry Sutpen,
Charles Bon, Ike McCaslin: these are above all disappointed sons, young men
orphaned and humiliated by the parent or the parental culture. They lack
resource, they are overwhelmed by the trouble they find themselves in, they
tend toward the denouement of the corporal in *A Fable*: crucifixion. Out of
this overwhelming Faulkner makes very great art, perhaps his greatest. There
may be no better way of indicating the magnitude of cultural bankruptcy that
he witnessed (the South's incapacity to diagnose its dilemmas and reroute its
legacies) than by creating a gallery of unavailing male protagonists. Yet, without
derogating the significance of their failure, we might note its insistent racial and
gendered assumptions. For we are dealing with a white male topic, an infatuation
with immortal wounds suffered by those who had such other expectations. And
we are asked, in the reading, to register the priceless value of male hearts and
minds going down to defeat. Charles Etienne St. Valery Bon—he of the long
name and short life—epitomizes the beauty and hopelessness of this Faulknerian
agon, and something of this figure lies concealed within the entire gallery
of failed young men I have been examining. They find themselves radically
unparented, with no resources for encountering the collapse of their dreams,
the defeat of their innocence. "His trouble was innocence," it is famously said
of Faulkner's Sutpen. The diagnosis bespeaks a trouble common to the larger

white male illusion of an intact will. When, by contrast, Morrison speaks of "the foul air of innocence," she gestures toward a territory on the other side of that illusion, a space in which the broken will—an absorption of "the sins of one's kind"—is inaugurative rather than conclusive. For reasons that have nothing to do with biology and everything to do with cultural placement, this latter territory is black.

Faulkner produces other paternal configurations as well, one of which (to which I shall return) might be called "the ameliorative." Figures in this group include the later Ike McCaslin, the amiable Ratliff, and the indefatigable Gavin Stevens. But the most famous Faulknerian fathers, the "giants before the flood," remain Sartoris, Sutpen, and McCaslin. These figures suffer not from an incapacitation of the will but from its excess. Taking what they want, brooking no quarter, self-possessed to a fault, they not only exercise their own freedom at others' expense, but they can come into their own, it seems, only through others' expense. Sartoris's heroic statue makes no reference to the murdered Burdens, but we may mentally supply those two corpses, just as we eventually see that the statue of Sutpen omits reference to the murdered Charles and abused Eulalia and Rosa (figures who make him what he is), and just as Old Carothers's ferocious self-sufficiency (so sought after by Lucas Beauchamp) requires, as its complementary features, an immolated Eunice and an impregnated but disowned Tomasina. It takes a passel of abused people to account for three solitary heroes, and Faulkner's texts work carefully to produce the pathos of the missing corpses. The main point to make is that such epic fathers leave a violence-filled legacy that their twentieth-century offspring (forced to confront the racial and gendered consequences of an unchecked male will) can neither accept nor escape. As Faulkner puts it with unforgettable force:

> *Yes. Maybe we are both Father. Maybe nothing ever happens once and is finished. Maybe happens is never once but like ripples maybe on water after the pebble sinks, the ripples moving on, spreading, the pool attached by a narrow umbilical water-cord to the next pool which the first pool feeds, has fed, did feed, let this second pool contain a different temperature of water, a different molecularity of having seen, felt, remembered, reflect in a different tone the infinite unchanging sky, it doesn't matter: that pebble's watery echo whose fall it did not even see moves across its surface too at the original ripple-space, to the old ineradicable rhythm thinking Yes, we are both Father. Or maybe Father and I are both Shreve, maybe it took Father and me both to make Shreve or Shreve and me both to make Father or maybe Thomas Sutpen to make all of us. (Absalom 210)*

Perhaps the entire Faulknerian dilemma is here. We have the insistence upon disaster, upon an unhealing wound and an unavailing legacy, in its purest form.

The vignette is eloquently, maybe even unknowingly, gender-biased, revealing a structure in which agency is male, reception female. The key event is the pebble's fatal entry into the water; the repercussions of that phallic penetration are immortal. The ripples on the water are mere effect to pebble-cause, and the various pools' differences over time, however considerable, can be no more than superficial. The drama is rigorously commanded by a single (sovereign) male action forgotten yet generative of a foredoomed genealogy: "*maybe Thomas Sutpen to make all of us.*" Omitted at every level but the figurative is female agency, for the passage's essential hubris is to imagine a procreative descent— a virtual orgy of begettings—enacted exclusively through male couplings. This incapacity to give name to the women who make generation possible (an incapacity at the heart of *Absalom*'s plot) is quietly upbraided by the figurative logic of the passage, in which, insist as they will, male pebbles remain indebted to a liquid structure that permits echo to occur. For this is simultaneously an umbilical scene, deep in the territory of the female. But if only the white male players are named, if action is coded white and male and reaction coded black and female, then what would the result be but the repeated outrages that constitute *Absalom, Absalom!*? Morrison, for her part, narrates this drama of the sought-after father's bequests and omissions but once—with differences as marked as the similarities. For this narration we turn from David to Solomon.

"The fathers may soar/ And the children may know their names"—so reads the epigraph of *Song of Solomon*. The epigraph cues us to the transcendent father sought after in this text, Solomon, a figure so epic that even his immediate offspring, Macon Dead Sr., appears (in memory) as larger than life:

> He had come out of nowhere, as ignorant as a hammer and broke as a convict, with nothing but free papers, a Bible, and a pretty black-haired wife, and in one year he'd leased ten acres, the next ten more. Sixteen years later he had one of the best farms in Montour County. A farm that colored their lives like a paintbrush and spoke to them like a sermon. "You see?" the farm said to them. . . . "Here, this here, is what a man can do if he puts his mind to it and his back into it. . . . Grab it. Grab this land! Take it, hold it, my brothers, make it, my brothers, shake it, squeeze it, turn it, twist it, beat it, kick it, kiss it, whip it, stomp it, dig it, plow it, seed it, reap it, rent it, buy it, sell it, own it, build it, multiply it, and pass it on—can you hear me? Pass it on!" (235)

The passage is resonant, and if it sounds familiar that is because the first sentence uncannily echoes the advent of Sutpen, equally from nowhere, equally boundless in his ambition. Macon Dead appears here in poignant contrast both to the fleeing youth first sketched to us in the naming scene, and to the desiccated sequel embodied a generation later in his son Macon Jr. In between, after the War and before the rise of segregation, the tendering to blacks of the American dream (during the period of Reconstruction) has been accepted and exploited. We witness a self-making focused on the will and on the Lockean dream of identity-as-property.[6] A black dynasty is being envisaged, its rhapsodic phrases not to be sounded by Morrison again until Baby Suggs's sermon in *Beloved*. Macon's farm focuses and enables a virtual explosion of the will, that penultimate sentence lavishing twenty-three different verbs in the imperative mode—each a call to action, a celebration of black identity as a capacity enacted through the possession, improvement, and bequeathing of property.

As Morrison well knows, this was a short-lived (barely one-generational) dream for blacks, and Macon Sr.'s property-project is also his undoing. His last soaring is five feet into the air, rent apart by a white man's shotgun while trying to protect his property. His soaring and his falling are inseparable. He leaves, like his transcendent father, orphans behind. Macon Dead Jr., in fact, never recovers from the murderous theft of his father's land. Taking from his father only his passion for material possession, dedicating his life to the pursuit of property, he urges his son: "Let me tell you right now the one important thing you'll ever need to know: Own things. And let the things you own own other things. Then you'll own yourself and other people too" (55). Envisaging human value as a possessible thing, Macon Jr. subtly deforms all the lives that come into his domain. His urge to own is simultaneously competitive and paranoid—what he cannot bound frightens him—and he remains locked in a contest with his father-in-law, Dr. Foster, that lasts well beyond the old man's death. Dr. Foster and Macon Jr., however inimical, resemble each other finally, sharing the next black generation's early-twentieth-century yearning for success at any cost and on white terms. Both men achieve such success, and in so doing complete an alienation from cultural roots that orphans those nearest them. Morrison brilliantly explores a black class system coded to the lightness of skin color, a system on whose tenets Corinthians and Magdalene are splayed/displayed as crucified exemplars. Macon Jr. may be incapable of forgiving his light-skinned father-in-law's white airs—he dilates obsessively on the repellent whiteness of the Doctor's corpse—yet, like Sutpen, he emulates what he detests, driving the Packard to prove his class superiority, withholding his daughters from darker-skinned or uncultivated suitors. In some repressed part of himself, moreover, Macon Jr. knows that his financial success masks a human failure. Covertly watching from outside, as though hypnotized, he sees his disowned sister Pilate move through dinner with her family with a rhythmic grace—alternately singing, eating, braiding, sewing, none of this programmed, all of it pleasure-productive—long since banned from his white-routinized life.

If Dr. Foster and Macon Jr. both fail as parental guides (their model for success simultaneously an erasure of their racial heritage), there remains one further paternal claim in the midst of this novel's mid-century racial turbulence: the Seven Days. A paramilitary group intent on revenge against the whites, the Days propose simultaneously a reading of black history, a recovery of black dignity, a model of black masculinity, and a task for black males that (as the name suggests) gives order to time.[7] In the name of community they band together, a sassing and amiable group of black men congregating around the pool bar and the barber shop when not on a mission. Milkman's only friend, Guitar, is their youngest convert, and this would be a different novel if Morrison could see in such parentage a successful nourishing. To measure the depth of the need to which the Days respond, even if finally without success, we must turn to the third generation of black males in search of racial grounding, Milkman and Guitar.

"Everything in the world loves" a black man, Sula told a disgruntled Jude (*Sula* 103). Men white and black, women white and black—all dilate, with whatever different motives, upon the black man's charged body ("Somewhere beneath all that daintiness, chambered in all that neatness, lay the thing that clotted their dreams" [*Sula* 51]). I use the verb "charged" to convey a body never neutral in the imaginary of both races and genders, and to convey as well, and in consequence, the body on which so many claims are charged, so much violence is discharged. It is a body riddled with imaginary over-investments, and Morrison's phrasing intensifies when, three years later, she has Guitar echo Sula: "Everybody wants the life of a black man" (*Song* 222). The grim insight in this phrasing accommodates both Faulkner's understanding of the white insanity (male and female) that black male bodies provoke and the wry self-awareness of the black male subject himself. A player in everyone else's fantasies, what is left over for himself? What unsought legacy could possibly serve as a mirror for his own self-unfolding? This problem becomes a crisis when his model of manhood would equate identity with unfettered potency, and when everywhere he finds himself economically cut off, racially and sexually stereotyped, a participant only in others' schemas. Is it any wonder that the radical solution proposed by the Days—eye for eye, act for act—has its appeal?

Morrison shares with Faulkner the courage to follow her insights absolutely, to refuse compromising resolutions, and she ends this novel (as Faulkner ends *Absalom, Absalom!*) in a moment of perfect tension—Milkman leaping into an apotheosis we simply cannot predicate. Whether, and on what terms, he lives or dies is unsayable. But we can note that her attempt to imagine fathering in the Faulknerian key of supreme authority imposes considerable costs. Not only are Corinthians and Magdalene virtually undeveloped in this text of the son, but Milkman's triumphant recovery of Solomon is ringed round with female suffering and exclusion. How, for example, are we to respond to Hagar's sudden death, to Pilate's smiling subordination to Milkman at the end (accompanying him to her death), and to Ruth Dead's continued exile from the text? How, further, should we read the text's sexual offer of Sweet as Milkman's earned male reward? And, finally, what are we to make of the closing fraternal embrace— "My main man" (337), Guitar murmurs as he moves toward Milkman—an embrace paid for by a certain number of dead and disowned black women? "We don't off Negroes" (161), Guitar had assured Milkman. Yet something in the internal binary logic of this text understands the saved life of a black man in terms of the yielded life of a black woman. Henceforth Morrison will approach the male search in different terms. From Son through Paul D and Stamp Paid to Joe Trace—this drama proposes, increasingly, the black male's recovery of his manhood less through pursuit of the father outside than through reconciliation with the woman within.

III. Later Developments, Tentative Conclusions

I would conclude this study of fathering tentatively because Morrison's career— while amply before us—is still in the making. Yet she seems to have reached her own version of an autumnal stance that permeates Faulkner's later work as well. What appears in *Jazz* as a nostalgia funded by the middle years reveals the paternal principle in a different—softer, less urgent—light. Commenting briefly on three texts, *Intruder in the Dust, Beloved,* and *Jazz,* I want to explore the bearing of these later developments.

Lucas in *Go Down, Moses* runs the gamut from child to old man. He stands as figurative counterpart to Ike McCaslin, as literal father to black offspring, and as symbolic father (or is it competitor?) to Roth Edmonds. When Faulkner takes Lucas up again in *Intruder in the Dust,* he is older yet, and this time carefully lifted clear from his black culture. "Solitary, kinless, and intractable" (*Intruder* 301), the text delights in calling him. Later we read: " 'I aint got friends,' Lucas said with stern and inflexible pride" (331–2). Removed from a black web of identity-shaping associations, Lucas can thus be inserted in a white web of values.[8] In *Intruder,* that web is insistently parental and filial: parental insofar as he emerges as Chick Mallison's fantasy-father (Chick falling into Lucas's creek, being covered with Lucas's cloak), yet filial insofar as Gavin Stevens (the other symbolic father in this text) will insist on seeing and renaming him as the entire South's offspring: Sambo.

As fantasy-father, his portrait is suffused in the same admiring terms earlier bestowed upon Faulknerian male icons. Regardless of the scene we find him in, Lucas is inscrutable, impenetrable—at his own fire and hearth or imprisoned in the Jefferson jail. Rising out of the water as though into a second birth, Chick first discovers Lucas's eyes upon him, "watching him without pity commiseration or anything else" (287). Lucas's face has no pigment, his bearing is "not arrogant, not even scornful" (288); and these "not" formulae do their work of producing him textually without penetrating within. "Within" is a sanctuary of maintained self-sameness that no stress can violate, and the text cooperates in preserving this male bastion of virginity. He remains immaculately self-possessed, assuring Gavin that "never nobody knocked me down" (331), aligning himself insistently with his trusty Colt 41 (an heirloom from Old Carothers). Three times he presses to have this pistol back, as though that phallic accompaniment would take care of all problems, whereas it is in fact his vanity over the pistol that allows Crawford Gowrie to entrap him in the first place. Finally, this is a virtually silent father whose authority is constructed outside the field of speech.

The inevitable segue here is to Gavin Stevens, the other father figure in *Intruder in the Dust*. Gavin tells Chick; Lucas shows him. Lucas's enactment of dignity counters Gavin's interminable talk of dignity, and this split is suggestive. It is as though the social realm itself—the space of law, education, culture, politics—were becoming for Faulkner increasingly garrulous and unreal at the same time; its name is Gavin. Perhaps the sadness that saturates the later novels locates itself most precisely in this figure whose unflagging energy never quite conceals a deeper hopelessness. But if Gavin is sad, he is not (like Mr. Compson) nihilistic, and his advice seems followable. John Irwin ("Horace Benbow") has recently commented on Gavin as an older and mellower Mr. Compson, and Jay Martin has urged us to recognize, especially in Faulkner's later work, a reliance upon the male mentor. Avuncular rather than more closely blood-related, liberated from the complicities of marital involvement, freed as well of the need to do, Gavin tirelessly advises. The caretaker of the realm of culture, he will yet never complete his translation of the Old Testament back into its original Greek. He too is virgin.

The father in the social realm of endless talk is white; the father in the fantasy realm of focused silence is black. Both are free of the female, both are innocent. The political implications of this split in the figuring of authority are considerable. The "homogeneous" white South that Gavin would preserve from northern interference is itself anachronistic, a retreat (as the rabidly Latinate-insistent vocabulary and ceaseless syntax of Gavin's speech are a retreat) from New South vulgarities that nevertheless will have to figure in the region's future. Intact himself, Gavin projects a similar intactness upon his culture. In both cases the intactness screens a deeper impotence—indeed the absence of any intrinsic Southern culture left to be bequeathed. Lucas, for his part, is accessed by Faulkner in such a way as to be alienated from his own black culture; he despises "field niggers" as wholeheartedly as whites do. More, he is ushered into white protection on a single, all-encompassing condition: that he cease to be a "nigger." The mob, of course, would leave him be if he would only act like a nigger, but Gavin and the privileged few who know better see his eventual emancipation in reverse terms, as a transcendence of his racial legacy. The Negro must "learn to cease forever more thinking like a Negro and acting like a Negro," Faulkner wrote later in the 1950s (Peavy 81); this stance recurs in *Intruder in the Dust.* Black smell, black food, black irresponsibility: all these "habits" can be unlearned, surpassed, and Lucas's masculine courage testifies to such a surpassing (which is in reality an erasing).[9]

If Gavin's white model of authority is latently impotent, so then is Lucas's black model. His power is revealed as illusory by his other textual name, Sambo. Faulkner incoherently envisages his region's racial future as a sort of improved return to the past. He sees the white South (no northerners needed, thank you) eventually freeing its silent and dignified blacks. Lucas, the plot of this novel elaborately guarantees, is incapable of freeing himself. Indeed, what kind of authority could he possess if his virtues are imagined as essentially outside the realm of speech?

Within the Oedipal framework that I have developed, we see two fathers who, in equal and opposite measures, succeed on the surface but fail at a deeper level. Lucas is the archaic imaginary-father, the figure of unblinking courage ready to face death with his manhood intact. Gavin is the impotent symbolic-father, the weaver of words and speaker of the social drama, yet inept, a well-intentioned mentor at best. Chick apparently learns from both of them, though Faulkner cannot show us anything bearing on race that Chick (or any other character) might learn, for he never writes a fiction seriously attentive to racial turmoil on the other side (post-1948) of Lucas Beauchamp's crisis. The Oedipal legacy ends by being bypassed rather than secured. Faulkner is simply unable, in the South of the late 1940s, to imagine a successful transmission of cultural values for which the Oedipal paradigm is the blueprint. Bypassed, not dismantled, not even attacked: Lucas and Gavin both retain a masculine integrity perhaps all the more poignant for its inability to affect the real. Protected from a more damaging immersion in the racial currents of their time, they survive intact, and in so doing leave behind the Faulknerian tragedy of humiliated will, the outrage to male identity that has virtually served as this writer's novelistic signature. Faulkner finishes, thus, upon the sweetness of *The Reivers*, where the legacy of male innocence returns unchecked (that is, checked only in ways that can be overcome). For a take upon manhood outside this protected register, we turn to Morrison's *Beloved* and *Jazz*, texts saturated in a racial experience that ensures that "no man should live without absorbing the sins of his kind, the foul air of his innocence."

Paul D is a man in profound touch with women and a man who has lost his innocence. These go together inasmuch as innocence is a notion lodged within a white male paradigm of values. (It was men, Mr. Compson tells his son, who invented virginity, not women.) Morrison introduces Paul D as "the kind of man who could walk into the house and make the women cry" (*Beloved* 17). Women find themselves confessing to him, Sethe soon realizes that his hands are wise enough to take on "the responsibility for her breasts" (18). His gift is an empathic quickness that registers the shifting feelings of the other: "as though all you had to do was get his attention and right away he produced the feeling you were feeling" (7–8). More, this capacity to enter others' emotional range is not limited to females; he is a lover but he is not just a lover. His name (however slavery-imposed) intimates as well that, unlike a Faulknerian isolate, he lives in a fraternal world, sharing his identity with other males. He touches men's bodies casually, engages in a kind of intimate horseplay with the other Pauls that seems outside the range of Faulknerian white male behavior. This somatic/fraternal ease allows him to step into the space vacated by Halle (almost another brother) without competitiveness or stress, and it allows him as well to survive the ordeal of slavery. Shackled men must come to terms with their own bodies and those of others as free men never need to. He may vomit at the threat of a white penis in his mouth, and he may go half-mad at the imposition of the bit upon his tongue; but he has bonded with his black confederates and he has come to terms with that chain.[10] Moving together, their bodies synchronized, the slaves work with the chain, not against it, to secure their freedom. Their singing together, their sign language for checking on each other's bodily endurance—these betoken a body regime, an achieved and shared somatic intimacy, beyond the experience (outside the training) of Faulkner's white males.

His is also an experience of self-annihilating abuse. Owned and manhandled by slaveowners, forced to realize his radical impotence, he sees he cannot be a man on the terms proposed by Garner. If he would become a man on other terms, he must yield up his white model and its judgmental code—cease viewing Sethe as a creature with four legs, not two—and begin to reconceive manhood on the other side of an intact body and an intact law. This involves the relinquishment of identity as a maintained possession, an intrinsic property, and its replacement by a model of identity shaped to the pressures of psychic and bodily interpenetration. In this second model the would-be creator—the male whose identity is synonymous with the reach of his will—cedes some space to the actual creature: the male who must learn to live his identity as a variable resource dependent upon an identificatory and reciprocal commerce with others. On this schema, identity operates relationally or not at all. Stamp Paid has had to learn, precisely, to resee himself in such communal terms. Joshua was extinguished by a wound to the male ego too deep to be borne, but this wound need not extinguish life as well. Reemerging as Stamp Paid, he managed to accede, as only the pain of nonintactness could teach him, to another way of being male: one beyond the luxuries of innocence and outrage. The institution of slavery, I wish to argue, taught black people to acknowledge a kind of radical interdependency of identity without which they would have perished: an interdependency at the core of survival itself (for none of us makes it all alone) but one which Western white males are still fleeing from in numbers too vast for counting.

In my reading of Morrison's career, *Beloved* is the novel in which she finds her way into this new vision of black manhood, with its potential for a different kind of paternity. She finally turns off that white flashlight coiling in Cholly Breedlove's guts (telling him he must be male on the white master's terms or not male at all). She starts to envisage a recovery of paternal dignity that moves, not through the heroic mastery of Macon Dead Sr. and his mythic father Solomon, but rather through Paul D and Stamp Paid, toward the damaged but indestructible Joe Trace. All these males are orphaned, but they are at the same time, increasingly, immersed in the resources of a shared community. Morrison's novelistic trajectory makes its way past the innocence and outrage of *Song of Solomon*, issuing into the shamelessly fallen world of *Jazz*.

As insistently as the surname of Paul D, Joe Trace's surname reveals his status of nonmastery. His orphaned identity is founded upon a void itself—a mother who disappeared "without a trace" (*Jazz* 124). Joe lives in the contingent: "Before I met her [Dorcas], I'd changed into new seven times" (123), each identity change dependent upon a change in time and place. Contingent, yes, but not to be confused with Camus's Meursault or any other figure suffused in white Western alienation. Joe is cut off but not alone, unsponsored but not unrelated. The mother Joe would "trace" is herself Wild, and her unapproachable blackness whispers of Africa further back. A hunter's hunter, Joe has picked up the

Shalimar virtues as well—his orphaning does not read as an abandoning—and this figure, when we follow him in the city, is no victim of urban anomie. Rather, he is all but limitlessly open to a shaping context, and his emotional quickness echoes Paul D's: "A sample-case man. A nice, neighborly, everybody-knows-him man. The kind you let in your house because he was not dangerous, because you had seen him with children, bought his products and never heard a scrap of gossip about him doing wrong. . . . He was the man who took you to your door if you missed the trolley. . . . Who warned young girls away from hooch joints and the men who lingered there. Women teased him because they trusted him" (73). Like Paul D, but a generation older, living domestically in the city, Joe Trace is yet capable of betraying utterly the aura of reliability radiated by this passage. In a different kind of novel—a mystery story, or even Conrad—that betrayal would reveal the true figure beneath the conventional facade. But *Jazz*'s commitment to the mobile surface of things, to the pressures of contingency, is absolute. There is no master-model for sorting Joe's surfaces from his depths. He is trustworthy, yet he could do anything—a twentieth-century black man both hemmed in and seething with life. A current runs through him, and that current is the African-American genius that Alain Locke saw in the 1920s as shaping the "New Negro" of the Harlem Renaissance.[11] The deepest achievement of *Jazz* registers not in the plot or the characters but in the music of the black language itself. "[W]hat was meant," the narrator says of a black parade charged with pride and anger, comes not from the hoisted banners: it comes "from the drums" (53). Joe Trace's emotional life and characteristic moves are nourished by these same drums. As he himself acknowledges, "You could say I've been a new Negro all my life" (129).

If we seek to understand why Joe killed Dorcas, we find ourselves far from any interior psychoanalytic paradigm of isolated and repressed motivations. No (white) model of individual depth operates here; no Faulknerian exploration of the psyche's secrets. Rather, the explanations (insofar as they exist) are cultural and temporal: outside pressures affecting them all. The cultural context is the intoxicating black culture of the "City" itself, resulting from a migration from the South that reached its headiest moments in the 1920s and that seems to turn America's largest urban space of that time into a village. Joe (like Violet and Dorcas and Alice and the others) lives immersed within a ceaselessly humming communal world made up of migratory strolls for business and pleasure, vibrating chords of street and bar music, the casual interlocking of male and female lives, the rhythmic circulation of alternately fanned and repressed desires, and the thickened medium of black urban folkways of the 1920s. Morrison works to get us to take in this story of romance, heartbreak, and murder as a black folktale of the city, if not a piece of jazz itself.

The pressures upon Joe Trace are temporal as well as cultural, though; his story is saturated in the passage of time through his sensibility. Seeking his unknown mother's hand, wanting just the touch of acknowledgment but not receiving it, he enters (chronologically decades later, but textually on the next page) into the relation with Dorcas as a renewal, in a different key, of the search for the mother. Though he is on the far side of fifty and she is on the near side of twenty, Joe and Dorcas are both orphaned, and they pass their evenings released through mutual memories as well as passionate lovemaking. It is their own gathered incompleteness they pour into each other, and Joe needs this since his wife Violet—fiercely battling her own menopausal changes and now hopelessly childless—has withdrawn from him. Dorcas is represented fleetingly (tentatively) as the withheld mother, the fantasy daughter, the momentary lover; they each play multiple roles. It all makes for an indecipherable explosion of violence, next to which the assessing of Sethe's murder of her child seems relatively clear:

> "Why did he do such a thing?" [Alice to Violet]
> "Why did she?"
> "Why did you?"
> "I don't know." (81)

Such not-knowing denotes not ignorance but the opening into mystery. It is radically not clear why people do what they do, though we see the age-old pressures (both cultural and universal) at work upon their incurable incompleteness. Orphans all, exiled from Oedipally descended norms of right and wrong, of achieved identity, these characters move musically, so to speak, in an almost tangible atmosphere of physical and emotional interpenetration. This is Morrison's supreme novel of touch, and touch—the root of contingency— seems not only to replace knowledge, it brings a sort of experience unamenable to knowledge. Unlike Faulknerian dramas built upon the collapse of innocence, the outrageous refusal of the real to meet one's dreams of mastery, *Jazz* circulates about a cast of characters who have long ago lost their innocence and who have ceased to judge the real by the criteria of innocence. Their negotiations with the real are instead steeped in an accommodation of the irreparable in which wound and dance—injury and performance—are inseparable constituents.

If we call this condition tragic, we miss its most stunning dimension: that it turns the collapse of mastery into the enabling framework of the music. The narrative begins rather than ends there. Not the dream-innocence of a single male's intact will, then, but the shared life-intensification that follows the breaking of the law. Here is Joe to Dorcas: "I told you again that you were the reason Adam ate the apple and its core. That when he left Eden, he left a rich man. Not only did he have Eve, but he had the taste of the first apple in his mouth for the rest of his life. The very first to know what it was like. To bite it down, bite it down. Hear the crunch and let the red peeling break his heart" (133). Solomon does not speak in *Song of Solomon*; only in *Jazz* do we get the words he might have uttered. Heartbreak as wealth, love as necessarily including betrayal, any life worth living as one transgressing the law that prohibits the apple, any identity worth enacting as one born of an accommodated self-shattering. By the time of *Jazz*, the commerce of parent and child involves not the legacy of lawful property and propriety, not the dream of an individual's intact descent, but instead a larger community's taking hold and savoring of its lived adulteration, transforming those who are often seen as last into the first, "the very first." Beyond innocence and outrage, this Solomon would speak—if he spoke—the survival of a people who have taken into themselves everything that white America could impose upon them: and made of it an unsentimental, unspeakable music.

Faulkner's David withholds his legacy, or he suffocates his offspring in bequeathing it, or his legacy (like Hubert Beauchamp's cup of silver) has lost its value by the time it is drawn upon. Whatever the case, when Faulkner thinks of David, his mind turns to Absalom. He sees several sons, some legitimate and some not, all clamoring for the father's blessing. The tragedy of these needy sons balked of their inheritance gives Faulkner the substance of his fiction, and that substance registers as the outraging of innocence. The inheritance is Oedipal/patriarchal, and its model for the descent of property and the proper excludes women (politely) and blacks (brutally) from positions of acknowledgment. The deepest thing Faulkner knows is that the women and blacks will suffer from these exclusions in such a way as to dispossess the men as well. His greatest fictions present and re-present a racial and gendered nightmare—a design gone irreparably wrong and yet uselessly repercussing rather than replaced by something better. This is his tragic story of America. He is incapable of revising it, for nothing in his culture's norms or in his relation to those norms positions him to see his way past this disaster. His last fathers are less disabling, and his last sons are better instructed, but these are scenes of descent in which the blacks have been removed and the women kept on the margins. The fiction of his final decade becomes pastoral; it plays for lesser stakes. Morrison's Solomon rarely speaks. The black father first enters her work in the desperate form of Cholly Breedlove, and Morrison somehow manages to see this damaged and damaging figure with remarkable generosity. It would take a musician to find the coherence in Cholly's contingencies, she writes, and rather than take up that task in *Sula*, Morrison transfers the vital principle from male to female. But *Song of Solomon* pursues the father again—it is a song in search of Solomon—this time a figure of achieved power mythically removed from Cholly's errancies. Finally, *Beloved* and *Jazz* begin the work of reconceiving the black male outside the Oedipal/patriarchal frame in which he is doomed to fail. A male broken into and dispossessed of the dream of innocence in which his identity might be coextensive with his intact will, a male who has learned to be in touch with others' bodies and their minds (male and female), a male whose creatural experience has taught him to recognize the woman within, a male for whom identity begins on the other side of adulteration and the broken law—such a figure starts to beckon in her work. He is not yet a father, but he has something to bequeath. He does not yet speak, but his life seems to cohere as an African-inspired music.[12]

Notes

1. I argue later in this essay, and more extensively in the larger study from which this essay is adapted (Weinstein, *What Else But Love*), that the patriarchal and Oedipal models are versions of each other: paradigms for securing traditional gender development and for stabilizing the descent of goods from father to son. For further analysis of this connection, see Carolyn Porter's provocative essays ("Symbolic Fathers" and "(Un)making").

2. For a useful collection of essays on the possibilities of a postpatriarchal father, see Patricia Yaeger and Beth Kowaleski-Wallace's *Refiguring the Father*.

3. Wyatt-Brown's is the best discussion of the Old South as a culture centered on an honor-shame set of values. Wadlington's *Reading Faulknerian Tragedy* draws acutely on Wyatt-Brown for his understanding of Faulkner's tragic universe.

4. It is becoming increasingly recognized that the organization of family roles in African-American culture, in Marianne Hirsch's words, "radically challenges the very bases on which the mythos of the patriarchal Oedipal family rests" (70). See also Hortense Spillers ("Mama's Baby").

5. See Terry Otten for a book-length study of Morrison's treatment of innocence. Essentially, Otten places Morrison in the Romantic tradition, but I think Morrison goes further, rejecting the entire (white male) orientation guiding Western thinking about innocence (including Faulkner's thinking), in order to imagine the conditions of a permanently postlapsarian world.

6. For further commentary on the Lockean premise of property as the keynote of normative (read: white male) American identity, see my "Mister: The Drama of Black Manhood in Faulkner and Morrison."

7. For a more negative reading of the Days as black exploiters of women hardly different from their white counterparts, see John Duvall ("Doe").

8. I have developed this argument more fully in *Faulkner's Subject*, 64–81.

9. Peavy quotes (with apparent approval) Faulkner's sinister criterion for black equality. At the University of Virginia in 1958, Faulkner spoke of the "Negro" as

prepared, as yet, for only "second-class citizenship. His tragedy may be that so far he is competent only in ratio of his white blood" (cited 81). The implication seems clear: American assimilation may well require racial erasure.

10. A suggestive visual contrast between Faulknerian and Morrisonian manhood emerges if we compare two males under duress: Mink Snopes bound to the sheriff's surrey in *The Hamlet* and Paul D bound to the slaveholder's chain in *Beloved*. Mink seeks his freedom through brute and self-damaging resistance to the instrument that thwarts his will, nearly breaking his neck in the process. Paul D eventually gets free by studying the regime of the chain and cooperating with its rhythms in order finally to outsmart it.

11. Alain Locke's introduction to the anthology of creative and critical writings he published in 1925 proudly announced the advent of a New Negro: a figure finally emerging from the "protective social mimicry forced upon him by the adverse circumstances of dependence" (3).

12. This essay is a revised version of a portion of *What Else But Love* by Philip Weinstein. Copyright © 1996 by Columbia University Press. Reprinted with permission of the publisher.

II   Pairings

5. RIFF, REFRAIN, REFRAME

Toni Morrison's Song of Absalom

Nancy Ellen Batty

I.

> *In the field of the unconscious the ears are the only orifice that cannot be closed. Whereas* making oneself seen *is indicated by an arrow that really comes back towards the subject,* making oneself heard *goes toward the other.*
> —*Jacques Lacan*

Toni Morrison insisted that she is "not like [William] Faulkner," but rather that her "effort is to be *like* something that has probably only been fully expressed in music" (Interview with Nellie McKay; rpt. Gates and Appiah 408). This insistence invites us to speculate on an intertextuality that operates somewhat like the "riffing" of a jazz piece. Morrison herself repeatedly describes her own work in terms of music, particularly jazz:

> Classical music satisfies and closes. Black music does not do that. Jazz always keeps you on the edge. There is no final chord. There may be a long chord, but no final chord. And it agitates you. Spirituals agitate you, no matter what they are saying about how it is all going to be. There is something underneath them that is incomplete. There is always something else that you want from the music. I want my books to be like that—because I want the feeling of something held in reserve and the sense that there is more—that you can't have it all right now. . . . That is a part

of what I want to put into my books. They will never fully satisfy—never fully. (Interview with Nellie McKay; rpt. Gates and Appiah 411)

Just as Morrison has concluded about Faulkner's work that, in it, "there is always something to surface" ("Faulkner and Women" 297), she senses in jazz music an analogy to her own novels as indeterminate, or as having submerged potential: "There is something underneath them that is incomplete."

But jazz is also an inter-subjective musical form. Alternately listening and playing, repeating and improvising, jazz performers essentially create an intertextual space that crosses both individual and racial boundaries. Not only do musicians "jam" together, both repeating and improvising on each other's phrases, but even jazz soloists "quote" frequently from the canon of both European and African-American musical compositions.[1] Moreover, the jazz session suspends and violates conventional notions of marked time and the impulse toward symmetry, creating an economy that can best be described as circulatory and infinite, tentative rather than teleological: "there is always something to surface."

Such a "jazz" economy can be usefully compared to the intersubjectivity of a Lacanian psychoanalytic session in which desire circulates around an unobtainable object. No sooner is desire expressed than its echo, hollow and unsatisfactory, is heard: what is important is both the expression itself and the attentive ears and improvising voice of the listener.

Madan Sarup inadvertently describes how we might arrive at a view of intertextuality that mediates between jazz and Lacanian theory by considering the origins of Lacan's notion of "full speech" in Heideggerian thought: "Heidegger makes an important distinction between authentic and inauthentic forms of existential discourse. The authentic form he calls 'Saying.' This he identifies with our ability to *listen* and thus genuinely respond to the voice of Being. The inauthentic form he calls idle talk, which he goes on to define as opinionated chatter unmindful of human Being" (54).[2] What occurs between the texts of Morrison and Faulkner, I will argue in this paper, is a form of "Saying" the "Other" in full speech, as Lacan defines full speech as "ceas[ing] to speak of oneself as an object" (Sarup 55). But what this process involves is not what might be called a deliberate recovery or recycling of Faulkner's speech in Morrison's work; rather, when we overhear Faulkner while reading Morrison, or vice versa, we become aware of the ceaseless desire of language itself to circulate within a wider cultural field and to establish new relations to subjectivity.

Both Faulkner and Morrison use the lyrics of the "blues" and African-American spirituals in their work, and the relationship between certain texts is characterized by a "jazz" economy, which is, of course, also a Lacanian economy in which the metonymy of desire fuels circulation.[3] Morrison is absolutely correct when she says she is not *like* Faulkner in the sense of sharing with him an aesthetic identity; rather, her works speak to and with those of Faulkner in something like the language of one musician *listening to* and *speaking with* another, the style of each "distinguishable" and "recognizable," but in conversation nonetheless. Moreover, Morrison's insistence on appropriating musical models when forced to confront questions of influence and intertextuality, particularly as these questions pertain to connections with Faulkner, points to something beyond conscious articulation—"something rogue" (*Jazz* [228])—in much the same way that Lacanian psychoanalysis is oriented toward the impossibility of apprehending the Real.

While my elaboration of the jazz analogy initially suggested by Morrison and confirmed by many of her commentators provides a potentially useful heuristic model for writing and intertextuality, however, I must clarify here as well the limitations for its use and qualify the status of music itself in some psychoanalytic theory. Kaja Silverman notes that music—or more precisely non-vocative, rhythmic sound—is more closely associated with the pre-Oedipal stage of human development and with "infantile pleasure" (96) than with the Symbolic. As such, music may be seen to have a "lulling" or pacifying effect on the subject that would seem to nullify its potential for meaningful communication. But if music is associated with the maternal voice, then by analogy, as Silverman implies in her critique of the Kristevan chora as a "regressive fantasy" (124)— that is, an Imaginary site that is retroactively constructed from the place of the Symbolic—it may also play a similar role to that of the maternal voice in "inaugurating desire" (137). Lacan theorizes that it is the mother's speech, or more precisely the expression of her desire for the father—"the link of love and respect, by which the mother does or does not put the father in his ideal place" (*Écrits* 218)—that produces the paternal metaphor which governs entry into the Symbolic and therefore establishes the child's relationship to desire.

From a psychoanalytic point of view, then, music already has an ambivalent signifying potential which can only be magnified and complicated by its incorporation into the discursive form of the novel. However, I am less interested in elaborating the more technical or stylistic contributions of music or rhythm *per se* to the works of Morrison and Faulkner (neither of whom has claimed a technical interest or expertise in music) than in locating moments of orality/aurality that serve to rupture the closed economy of the gaze. These moments in both Faulkner and Morrison are often connected to the lyrics of song, particularly gospel or blues, as both writers employ music and song strategically in their work.

Thadious M. Davis has pointed to Faulkner's use of music and particularly African-American spiritual music as "a mode of development" ("From" 84) of black characters, a technique characteristic of even some of Faulkner's earliest work. Davis points to one of the New Orleans sketches, "The Longshoreman," in which Faulkner portrays a day laborer singing "Swing Low, Sweet Chariot" and "All God's Chillen Got Wings" as he works, obviously dreaming of freedom from his earthly burdens: "I got wings, you got wings; all God's chillen got w-i-i-n-g-s-s!" (9). Seeming almost to anticipate the theme of flying in Morrison's *Song of Solomon*, Faulkner also suggests in this brief sketch the transcendent, compensatory qualities of gospel music that allow the laborer to tolerate the inhuman conditions under which he works.

In another early work, *Soldier's Pay*, Gilligan and the (white) rector stand outside the circle of warmth in a black church, listening to the music from within: "Feed Thy Sheep, O Jesus. All the longing of mankind for a Oneness with Something, somewhere. Feed Thy Sheep, O Jesus. . . . The rector and Gilligan stood side by side in the dusty road. The road went on under the moon, vaguely dissolving without perspective" (221). But while Faulkner's portrayals of the laborer and of the black congregation seem at first glance to be positive, as Davis suggests, these scenes are also heavily invested with racist overtones: the historical subjugation of the black race can be justified or excused in direct proportion not only to what is seen in these passages as the ability of the African-American to benefit spiritually from oppression, but in direct proportion also to the everlasting damnation endured by the white oppressors who are denied access, by virtue of their crimes against African-Americans, to spiritual redemption. Witness Gilligan and even the rector standing *outside* the spiritual circle, looking bleakly onto a road "without perspective." A similar example of white exclusion from the compensatory qualities of African-American spirituality can be found at the end of the story "Go Down, Moses" itself, when the well-meaning but essentially patronizing Gavin Stevens is literally driven out of the Worsham home by Molly and Hamp's mournful, dual-voiced rendition of the title spiritual, a scene which is uncannily reenacted by the impromptu choir outside Nancy Mannigoe's jail cell in the later *Requiem for a Nun*.

The connection between rhythmic voice and an African-American spirituality that is both superior and inaccessible to the defeated and morally bankrupt white gentry of the American South is made even more explicit in the often-cited Dilsey section in *The Sound and the Fury*. Not only are all the white characters, except for the childlike and innocent Benjy, excluded from witnessing Reverend Shegog's sermon, but also, as Alexander Marshall III has argued, Faulkner's attempted approximation of African-American voice in this section may have the additional effect of excluding, or at least distancing, the white reader from full understanding of Shegog's message. At any rate, during the church service itself, song and call-and-response preaching meld into a kind of transcendent and transfixing ineffability: "And the congregation seemed to watch with its own eyes while the voice consumed him, until he was nothing and they were nothing and there was not even a voice but instead their hearts were speaking to one another in chanting measures beyond the need for words . . ." (294). In a novel full of the "sound and fury" of the futile white voices of the Compsons, hope finally rests in an incorporeal, voiceless surrender to spirit, a condition to which, however, only the African-American and the child-like Benjy can aspire.

In situating Faulkner's use of African-American spiritual music, we discover Faulkner's repeated attempts to use gospel forms to disrupt a specular, colonizing white gaze and to offer an alternative, if somewhat transcendent and exclusive (of whites), version of the recursive, doomed trajectory of white history in the South. In other words, as each of these examples adduces, the very central problem of verbal repetition itself in Faulkner seeks a solution not only in some apocalyptic aural moment *outside* of language, but, more importantly, in some apocalyptic moment *outside of* and *unavailable to* white experience. The idea that the subjugated African-American is morally superior to his or her white oppressors can then be used (as it is, for example, by Ike McCaslin in "The Bear" and "Delta Autumn") paradoxically and specularly to support the idea that freedom can only corrupt and demean the black man or woman as it has the white.

While gospel music in Faulkner's work often signals the transcendence of voice over the materiality of the body and the gaze to which it is subjected, secular music such as blues and jazz tends to signify a return to the material and, particularly, to Faulkner's less palatable idea of the "dark," mysterious, and potentially violent sexual materiality of the black race, especially black women. A case in point is "That Evening Sun," in which the allegedly promiscuous and pregnant Nancy holds the entire Compson family hostage to fear of her jealous lover Jesus. Nancy's fear is repeatedly expressed in a "sound that was not singing and not unsinging" (309): the title of the story suggests that this refrain represents a variation of the blues, specifically W. C. Handy's "St. Louis Blues," the title riffing ironically on the lines "I hate to see that evening sun go down" because "my man done left this town." Once again, however, the inarticulate expression of Nancy's suffering sets her entirely apart from the white characters in the story: she becomes a spectacle, a dark mirror of all of the children's fears about the bogeyman, suffering, and death, the evil kept at bay by Jason's desperate chant, "I aint a nigger" (297, 298, 309).

II.

Not so long ago, a little girl said to me sweetly that it was about time somebody began to look after her so that she might seem lovable to herself.
—*Jacques Lacan*

If Morrison riffs on Faulkner, she does so in a way that addresses Faulkner's "good Negro/bad Negro" dichotomy (the gospel-singing Dilsey vs. the bluesy Nancy), a dichotomy that not only prevents Faulkner from fully portraying African-American subjectivity, but also prevents his white characters from exploring their common humanity, and therefore their common history and destiny, with the African-Americans with whom they share their lives. Much of the repetition in Faulkner, I believe, stems from his vision of the history of the South in terms of the culpability and doom of whites, the oppression and potentially redemptive force of African-Americans, and the perforce mutual exclusivity of these destinies. While Morrison locates most of her work solely in the African-American community, she nonetheless riffs on Faulkner's themes to suggest an alternative to this view: when her narrator in *Jazz* says "I was so sure . . . [t]hat the past was an abused record with no choice but to repeat itself at the crack and no power on earth could lift the arm that held the needle" (220), she might be echoing Quentin Compson: *"I am going to have to hear it all over again I am already hearing it all over again I am listening to it all over again I shall have to never listen to anything else but this again forever"* (*Absalom* 222). But listen to how Morrison improvises on this theme: "I was so sure, and they danced and walked all over me. Busy, they were, busy being original, complicated, changeable—human, I guess you'd say, while I was the predictable one, confused in my solitude" (*Jazz* 220). In her unpredictable, funky novel *Jazz*, Morrison appears to offer improvisation as a form of secular redemption.

Morrison's riffs on Faulkner's ambivalent concepts of African-Americans and their music begin as early as her first novel, *The Bluest Eye*, whose very title potentially puns on the idea of a reconciliation of the voice and the gaze as a means of perception: The Blues[t] Eye. Certainly, Morrison puns on the word "blue" in *The Bluest Eye* to register a protest against the harmful internalization of white standards of beauty and social adequacy in the African-American subject. But by using the idiom of the blues to portray central characters in her novel, Morrison literally re-embodies African-American subjectivity as she redefines for readers steeped in Faulkner's doomed cosmology the complex, signifying relationship among white and African-Americans and their expressive forms.

In a scene remarkably similar in some ways to the portrayal of Reverend Shegog's service, eyes and voice also merge in the "blues" eyes of a mother comforting her daughter Claudia by initiating her not into the ineffable promise of heavenly reward, but into the bitter-sweet mysteries of earthly, adult desire: "If my mother was in a singing mood, it wasn't so bad. She would sing about hard times, bad times, and somebody-done-gone-and-left-me times. But her voice was so sweet and her singing-eyes so melty I found myself longing for those hard times, yearning to be grown without 'a thin di-i-ime to my name.' I looked forward to the delicious time when 'my man' would leave me, when I would 'hate to see that evening sun go down . . .' 'cause then I would know 'my man has left this town' " (17–18). Incorporating the lyrics of "St. Louis Blues," Morrison riffs on Faulknerian cadences and rhythms at the same time as she grounds her idea of transcendence in the language of a secular music that dares to aspire to earthly pleasures, rather than heavenly reward. By alluding to "St. Louis Blues" in her description of a deeply loving mother-daughter relationship, Morrison reinvests African-American secular music with a redemptive spirituality. At the same time, however, she contextualizes the potential for intra-racial violence to which Faulkner alludes in "That Evening Sun" precisely in the colonizing effects of the gaze in a white hegemonic society, a gaze which ultimately fuels the violation of young Pecola Breedlove's body and destroys her mind, a gaze that can only be neutralized by "blues eyes" and a loving dialogue between decolonized subjects.

By increasingly focusing on music in her novels, Morrison unsettles the Imaginary economy of the gaze with an emphasis on voice and a revaluation of the aural senses over the visual ones. She explores both the implications and limitations of Faulkner's own experiments with lyrical voice by inserting the voice of her narrator or her characters into those moments in Faulkner's texts when the gaze threatens to short-circuit the verbal exchange between white- and African-Americans. Not surprisingly, *Song of Solomon*, with its evocation both of lyrical voice and of the Biblical source of Faulkner's title *Absalom, Absalom!*, is a novel which invites us to discover such textual/intertextual structures.

III.

You cant know yet. You cannot know yet whether what you see is what you are looking at or what you are believing.
    —Absalom, Absalom!

> *What one looks at is what cannot be seen.*
> —*Jacques Lacan*

While critics such as Susan Willis have noted the similarities between *Song of Solomon* and *Absalom, Absalom!*, they have focused primarily on the way that the three-woman household of Pilate, Reba, and Hagar in Morrison's novel parodies the Clytie-Judith-Rosa triumvirate in *Absalom, Absalom!* Instead, I will focus on the remarkable intertextual resonance between Quentin's encounter with the Sutpen's house servant, Clytie, and Milkman's encounter with the Butlers' servant, Circe. I am inspired first by the numerous similarities between Clytie and Circe: their classically inspired names, their wizened appearances, their apparently extreme ages. Each guards, if for very different reasons, a former master's house. And if we think back to Clytie's avatar, Raby, in Faulkner's early story "Evangeline," they both also carefully tend their masters' German-bred dogs. But I will also suggest that Circe is more than just an ironic inversion of either Raby or Clytemnestra: her presence in *Song of Solomon* provides Morrison with an opportunity not only to riff on Faulkner's version of master-slave relationships in *Absalom, Absalom!*, but also to challenge, through a highly acoustic improvisation, the scopic impulses that dominate inter-racial relationships in Faulkner's work.

Indeed, Faulkner presents Quentin's encounter with Clytie almost entirely as a visual experience. It is "seeing" Clytie that provides Quentin with the final clue or clues as to the identity of Charles Bon, as Shreve suggests: "you wouldn't have known what anybody was talking about if you hadn't been out there and seen Clytie" (220). Clytie has consequently always served as something of a hermeneutic knot in Faulkner's novel, her face and skin color a symbol, both for the narrators in the novel and some of its critics, of the "debacle" of the Sutpen family: her significance to Quentin and these same critics is apparently entirely visual. Quentin's verbal engagement with Clytie, however, is brief and hesitant, even fearful, almost as though what he fears most is Clytie's knowledge about the events of the past, a knowledge that Quentin appears to seek, yet paradoxically resists discovering. Although Clytie speaks to Quentin, implying even that she *does* possess some of the first hand information about the Bon-Henry-Judith affair that Quentin seeks—"Whatever he done, me and Judith and him have paid it out" (296)—Quentin passes her on the stairs without so much as acknowledging her words.

In *Absalom*, Quentin does not *listen* to Clytie, although he does obey her command to follow Rosa up the stairs of the Sutpen mansion (something he probably would have done anyway, out of sheer curiosity). If he had listened to Clytie, or shown an interest in listening to her, Quentin might have learned something. Instead, Quentin appears to be driven by an infantile, specular impulse, the overwhelming desire to "see" and be seen by what is hiding upstairs. Since Faulkner allows us so little information about Clytie's motivations, whether to emphasize her taciturn nature or Quentin's failure to address her, her defense and torching of the Sutpen mansion are implicitly viewed as an extension of her loyal service to the Sutpen family: she is, after all, Thomas Sutpen's daughter. At any rate, we never discover what it is that Clytie knows, or what motivates her to guard the Sutpen mansion so fervently that she will commit suicide and murder to prevent outside interference.

The earlier version of *Absalom*, the short story "Evangeline," features, instead of Quentin and Shreve, an unnamed narrator and his friend, Don. Here the "Clytie" character is much less taciturn. Like Clytie (and, as we shall see, Circe), Raby is "incredibly old: a small woman with a myriad wrinkled face in color like pale coffee and as still and cold as granite" (594–5). What is particularly striking, from an intertextual viewpoint, is that Raby employs dogs to guard the white man's mansion and, like Circe's Weimaraners in Morrison's *Song of Solomon*, Raby's dogs are German (shepherds), descended from a line imported by the white master.[4] But while the use of dogs in both narratives is perhaps inherently interesting, it serves my purpose rather to point to other aspects of "Evangeline" which, by suggesting the possibility of a dialogic relationship between a white male character and a black female, can serve as a commentary on both Quentin's encounter with Clytie and Milkman's encounter with Circe in *Song of Solomon*.

Once the narrator of "Evangeline" has "passed" the dog guarding the Sutpen mansion, Raby readily complies with his demands for information. She appears to tell him everything she knows about Charles Bon and Judith and Henry Sutpen: essentially that Henry murdered Bon because Bon was already married and therefore had committed bigamy when he married Judith. Raby also surprises the narrator by telling him that Henry Sutpen is her brother. But she comes to a point in her story when she refuses to go on, when she coyly tells the narrator, "You'll hear what I going to tell you. What I aint going to tell you aint going to hear" (602). What the narrator discovers after speaking to Raby, and it is not clear whether he learns this by actually interviewing Henry or by imagining that he does, is that Bon, too, was Henry Sutpen's brother, a fact which would have made the marriage to Judith not only bigamous, but incestuous. The final "surprise" in the story, which ends after Raby's torching of the Sutpen mansion, is the narrator's discovery of a picture which suggests that Bon's first wife had negroid features. Like the novel which Faulkner developed from it, the story ends with both a spectacular display and a specular reaction, as the narrator is left to ponder the mystery (and at least for Quentin, the horror) of racial indeterminacy.

The relevance to my intertextual study of both the narrative details and the way they are disclosed in "Evangeline" is made clear by Raby's response to the narrator's question, a question that Quentin, apparently, could never bring himself to ask of Clytie: "Why did you do all this [hide him for forty years] for Henry Sutpen? Didn't you have your own life to live, your own family to raise?" (604). It is this question that elicits the information regarding Raby's biological status: "She spoke, her voice not waisthigh, level, quiet. 'Henry Sutpen is my brother'" (604). Confessing to the ties of blood with the white man whom she hides, Raby clarifies the issue of her sacrifice with a simple statement of fact. While Clytie never makes such a confession in *Absalom, Absalom!*, either some vestigial residue of Raby's character in her or some intricate web of Western, Eurocentric logic within the minds of the novel's critics seems to compel us to draw the same conclusion about her: a powerful filial bond, not merely servile loyalty, motivates her. As we shall see, it is precisely this arrogant assumption on the part of both Quentin and Faulkner's readers that Morrison will explode in *Song of Solomon*.

When Milkman Dead, on his quest for gold, approaches the ironically named Butler house he has been told was once occupied by their servant Circe, a woman who had helped his father and his aunt escape the white men who had killed their father, he does so, like Quentin in *Absalom, Absalom!*, with a great sense of dread. What he least expects to find there, however, is Circe herself, who the elderly Reverend Cooper tells him "Was a hundred when I was a boy" (233). His discovery of Circe in the house is narrated in terms of a fairy tale, or a dream: "He had had dreams as a child . . . of the witch who chased him down dark alleys, between lawn trees, and finally into rooms from which he could not escape. . . . So when he saw the woman at the top of the stairs there was no way for him to resist climbing up toward her outstretched hands, her fingers spread wide for him, her mouth gaping open for him, her eyes devouring him. In a dream you climb the stairs" (239). The scene partakes of the logic of a dream, and Milkman surrenders himself to that logic as if under a spell. But what breaks the spell and forces him to "surface" from the dream is "a humming sound around his knees" (240) coming from the Weimaraners. "Daytime" logic is then further tested when Milkman confronts the discrepancy between Circe's appearance and her voice: "She was old. So old she was colorless. So old only her mouth and eyes were distinguishable features in her face. Nose, chin, cheekbones, forehead, neck all had surrendered their identity to the pleats and crochet-work of skin committed to constant change" (240). But "out of the toothless mouth came the strong, mellifluent voice of a twenty-year-old-girl" (240).

Milkman's encounter with Circe is a trial of both his senses and his intellect: he must overcome the nausea that the smell of rotting flesh and dog feces induces in him; he must acknowledge the "reality" of the living presence of a woman who should, by rights, be dead; and he must somehow reconcile the fact that Circe's "dainty habits . . . matched her torn and filthy clothes in precisely the way her strong young cultivated voice matched her wizened face" (242). In short, he must unravel the threads of "common sense" that have previously comprised for him the very tapestry of Western bipolar logic. Central to this process, as Circe repeatedly tells him, is the ability to *listen*, not just to Circe's words, but to what she is *saying*.

Raby tells the narrator of "Evangeline," " 'You'll hear what I going to tell you. What I aint going to tell you aint going to hear.' " Circe will tell Milkman, " 'You don't listen to people. Your ear is on your head, but it's not connected to your brain' " (249). Milkman, like the narrator of "Evangeline," skeptically listens to, without hearing, the story of an old woman living alone, caring for her master's property—in this case, the dogs—and, seeing how she remains at the mansion tending to their needs even above her own, asks: "You loved those white folks that much?" (246). Circe responds with a story:

> "Do you know why [the mistress] killed herself? She couldn't stand to see the place go to ruin. She couldn't live without servants and money and what it could buy. Every cent was gone and the taxes took whatever came in. She had to let the upstairs maids go, then the cook, then the dog trainer, then the yardman, then the chauffeur, then the car, then the woman who washed once a week. Then she started selling bits and pieces—land, jewels, furniture. The last few years we ate out of the garden. Finally she couldn't take it anymore. The thought of having no help, no money—well, she couldn't take that. She had to let everything go."
>
> "But she didn't let you go." Milkman had no trouble letting his words snarl.
>
> "No, she didn't let me go. She killed herself."
>
> "And you still loyal." (246–7)

Circe's indignant outburst—" 'You don't listen to people' "—is a blues song accompanied by the music of the dogs' steady humming. Still governed not only by a bipolar visual logic—Circe is there; therefore she must be emotionally attached to the mansion—but also by Eurocentric notions of economy, implanted by his father, in which proprietorship is always only associated with the desire for gainful acquisition, Milkman fails at first to hear in Circe's words the hatred of her former masters that compels her to oversee the total destruction of the Butlers' mansion. Circe is not "just singing the blues": her lyrics feed and sustain her very existence. Circe's life, in fact, appears by some obscure agency to be prolonged just so that she may survive long enough to accomplish this feat. Unlike Clytie or Raby, Circe will never torch the Butler mansion: such an act, we might speculate, would be too humane, would amount almost to an act of forgiveness or mercy.

The lesson that Circe teaches Milkman is not a lesson in hate, however; it is a lesson in how to listen. Milkman must *ignore* what he sees (and ignore all his other senses as well: Circe thanks him for pretending her house "didn't stink" [248]), not just Circe's appearance but the appearance of servitude that her continued presence in the Butlers' house implies. Only by suspending everything he has been taught by his parents and his community, and by fully entering the logic of the waking dream, can he learn that lesson. In other words, Circe asks Milkman to forget "knowledge" and listen to "truth," the truth of the unconscious that the dream state sometimes allows one to overhear. Milkman's meeting with Circe is ideal preparation for listening to the rhyme of the children in Shalimar (the spelling of which is, significantly, discordant with its pronunciation, Shalamone): "Milkman took out his wallet and pulled from it his airplane ticket stub, but he had no pencil to write with, and his pen was in his suit. He would just have to listen and memorize it. *He closed his eyes* and concentrated while the children, inexhaustible in their willingness to repeat a rhythmic, rhyming action game, performed the round over and over again. And Milkman memorized all of what they sang" (303, emphasis added). John Leonard notes, "If not for a Pilate and a Guitar, Macon (Milkman) Dead would not have learned to fly" (39). It is Circe, however, who opens Milkman's ears to the sound of the beat.

In *Absalom, Absalom!*, Quentin "sees" Clytie, but we cannot be so sure that he "hears" her. Certainly, he does not interrogate Clytie the way the first-person narrator of "Evangeline" interrogates Raby, nor does he listen to her the way that Milkman learns to listen to Circe. Of course, most of the information provided by Raby in "Evangeline" is already known to Quentin before he meets Clytie. He does not have to ask her why she has remained at the mansion, why she continues to remain with Henry: by the same logic that not only appears to underwrite but actually *produces* the knowledge that Charles Bon would willingly die for the acceptance and love of his white father, the reader is asked to assume that Clytie would die protecting, not her sister Judith, who narrators in the novel lead us to believe shared Clytie's hardships, but her murdering white brother.[5] Her silence, as opposed to either Raby's or Circe's willing disclosure, perhaps dignifies Clytie, but this same silence does not necessarily dignify critics of the novel. Perhaps we need to take a lesson in listening from Circe: "Your ear is on your head, but it's not connected to your brain."

By suggesting that Morrison perhaps "hears" Clytie in a different register than most other critics of the novel, and that Clytie's voice can somehow be heard coming out of the mouth of Circe in *Song of Solomon,* I may appear to be overlooking one fundamental difference: Circe is not her master's daughter. To that objection I can only reply that we do not know whose daughter Circe is. We can hear only what Circe "going to tell" and what she tells us, I think, is that it does not matter whose daughter she is: nothing will change the fact that she was once a slave and that her mistress killed herself rather than face similar deprivation. To say that Faulkner idealizes and perhaps even romanticizes the relationships produced by miscegenation in *Absalom, Absalom!* in much the same way as he idealizes incest, is merely to argue that his novel demonstrates the inevitable failure of *vision* in a society which is utterly obsessed with color but can neither curb its own lusts nor control the product of its desires. Shreve tells us as much when he informs Quentin: "I think that in time the Jim Bonds are going to conquer the western hemisphere. Of course it wont quite be in our time and of course as they spread toward the poles they will bleach out again like the rabbits and the birds do, so they wont show up so sharp against the snow" (302). Clytie is both implicated in and escapes the logic of such a vision: what she ain't going to tell we ain't going to hear.

Near the end of *Song of Solomon,* Milkman once again closes his eyes, but this time to recite the names of black men and women as a way of reclaiming his connection to the past: "He closed his eyes and thought of the black men in Shalimar, Roanoke, Petersburg, Newport News, Danville, in the Blood Bank, on Darling Street, in the pool halls, the barbershops. Their names. Names they got from yearnings, gestures, flaws, events, mistakes, weaknesses. Names that bore witness. Macon Dead, Sing Byrd, Crowell Byrd, Pilate, Reba, Hagar, Magdalene, First Corinthians, Milkman, Guitar . . ." (330). As the names of such legendary musicians as Muddy Waters, Fats, and Bo Didley come "angling out from these thoughts," we are reminded that Morrison's art is both profoundly aural and profoundly intertextual. In *Song of Solomon,* Morrison uses voice and music to disrupt the relentlessly specular impulses of white male characters such as Quentin Compson in *Absalom, Absalom!* and to resituate in the latter text the unvoiced but not unlocatable site of black desire. It is precisely through the musicality of her language and the language of music that Morrison's repetition of Faulknerian refrains has the effect of exposing and unsettling our hegemonic readings of Faulkner's texts. Like those of a jazz musician, Morrison's riffs offer repetition with a difference to establish a truly intertextual economy.

But rather than replying directly to and therefore potentially silencing Faulkner, Morrison's voice and the voices of her characters—her style—signify "the place where a new passage through otherness can be opened up, and only if one is attempting to follow an imperative *not to stop there*" (Johnson, *World* 31; emphasis added). There is yet always "something to surface," not only in jazz, but in Morrison and Faulkner, as well: whether or not we are eavesdropping, their voices will be heard "Answering each other from yard to yard with a verse or its variation" (*Jazz* 226).[6]

Notes

1. Miles Davis's improvisation on "Favorite Things" comes to mind.

2. To this, we might add Daniel Gunn's emphasis on the act of "listening": "If there is a 'truth' of psychoanalysis, I have suggested, it is ultimately an unconscious truth. This means, of course, that such truth, while it can be sought, cannot rightly be 'discovered,' in the way that treasure chests or gold nuggets are discovered. It cannot be known, retained, and then recycled. It can only be uttered, only encountered. It is less heard than overheard" (217).

3. The link I am proposing between African-American literary and musical forms has been previously theorized in the work of Houston A. Baker, Jr., in *Blues, Ideology, and Afro-American Literature: A Vernacular Theory*. But rather than elaborating on Baker's idea that the blues define an exclusively African-American aesthetic, I want to suggest that African-American gospel, blues, and jazz form part of a wider signifying culture and their "vernacular" can be employed strategically and to different effect in the works of both white- and African-American writers. In other words, I do not wish to propose a displacement of essentialism "from sight to sound" (Fuss 90), that is, from the signification of skin color to the signification of vernacular as an intrinsic racial characteristic, but rather a way of exploring the "junction where . . . texts, norms, and values meet and work upon each other" (Iser, "Towards" 216–17). In particular, jazz, with its emphasis on both repetition and innovation, translates the idiom of the Lacanian psychoanalytic encounter into a cultural space shared, but inhabited differently by, Morrison and Faulkner.

4. I do not know if Morrison was familiar with "Evangeline" when she wrote *Song of Solomon*: the story was collected for the first time in 1972, five years before *Song of Solomon*'s publication, but long after Morrison's research for her Master's thesis on Faulkner and Woolf was completed. Nonetheless, it is striking that both writers, perhaps attuned to a Ulysses intertext, depicted Cerberus-like dogs guarding the white man's mansion.

5. In "The Riddle of *Absalom, Absalom!*: Looking at the Wrong Blackbird?", I make the rather unorthodox claim that there is evidence in the text that points to the possibility that Clytie dies to protect her *black* half-brother Charles Bon.

6. Sources for epigraphs: I: *Four* 195. II.: *Four* 257. III.: *Absalom* 251 and *Four* 182.

6. NARRATIVE TIME/ SPIRITUAL TEXT

Beloved and *As I Lay Dying*[1]

Karla F. C. Holloway

Ev'ry time I feel the spirit, moving in my heart I will pray.
  —African-American spiritual

The trees drooped wisteria still, my third summer south—enduring, despite what often seemed unendurable times, returning, dependable and resilient to a springtime perch where a grip that only seemed precarious attached soon-to-be fragrant blooms to branches or telephone poles without bias or distinction. They held firm there, as if waiting for me to discover that this was indeed the wisteria that I once could only imagine in Faulkner, that this was the scent and the blossom of those southern stories.

Is telling a time like telling a story? No. Not if a spirit imposes itself between the story's time and the story's text.

Several years ago, after my first reading of Toni Morrison's *Beloved,* I wrote the first line of an essay about that novel. Talking back to no one in particular and everyone in general I began that review this way: "No, this is not a ghost story, it is a spiritual" (*"Beloved"* 179). Knowing that it is not a necessarily consistent habit of mine to still believe what I have said when I return and reconsider (a situation that makes reflective moments particularly bold and courageous occasions for me), I returned to that pronouncement with not a little trepidation. I am relieved to report that I not only still believe this to be true—that *Beloved* is not a ghost story but a spiritual—but that I believe it now with even more assurance than I did in 1989.

This return and reflection bring me to my wondering of how one tells a spiritual. Where is the place for inscription when that space is spiritual? And how do you tell them so that their persistence is felt like the return of wisteria that relentlessly pursues its chosen heights each summer in the South?

Certainly one can tell a ghost story. In *As I Lay Dying*, William Faulkner tells Addie's story despite the displacement her own pronouncement places onto the narrative. "As I lay dying" what, Addie? Where's the focus of this adverbial modifier? Did something happen? Did something "pass on" like Beloved's story could not?[2] Did someone speak? As I lay dying . . . what?

Morrison and Faulkner both have explored a territory of certain spatial configuration and uncertain dimension. It is a hybrid territory for each of them, and this is the intertext I want to explore with this essay. These novels share a notion of what I call "spiritual hybridity" wherein an uninhabited territory gains the dimension of terrain. Here, the character of space is critical to its identity. Spiritual hybridity depends upon a diaphanous quality that is unrestricted in its reach. The contours of what was a "common ground," in the sense of an "ordinary place"—northern or southern—are vulnerable to the impurity or, if you will, the chaos of hybridity.

Rivers, trees, and even fish shift their shapes when they meet the uncertain terrain of a spiritual space. In turn, these narrative discourses insist upon intimacy for their character—a closeness to home, sweet, or otherwise.[3]

What are these homeplaces that re-envision spiritual identity and that make a disparate community—familial, ancestral, and even geographic—cohere when sense and wisdom and especially when history argue against viability? These narratives share like disturbances in language, family, childhood, as well as in composition. Both Faulkner's *As I Lay Dying* and Morrison's *Beloved* explore these likenesses as they privilege dissonance and violence in the telling of their stories.

My text for this particular contemplation honors my own community's tradition of selecting a text to undergird and support a telling. I select Ralph Ellison's classic novel *Invisible Man* because of my deep respect for the immutable character whose forty-year-old resilience resists any closure of time or literary era. This novel and its author (whose recent departure from our territory leaves me with profound sadness) certainly inhabit a spiritual space. So the text that underlies my reflection on Morrison and Faulkner is from *Invisible Man*.

My citation comes from the novel's final chapters—a time when the Invisible Man wanders the streets of Harlem, and watches as they dissolve into disarray. A riotous time looms as night falls. The Invisible Man notes the oncoming darkness, and the disarray. It seems to him a "merging fluidity" and he wonders, "could this be the way the world appeared . . . ? 'For now we see as through a glass darkly but then—but then—' I couldn't remember the rest" (491).

Ellison positions the loss of memory as essential to sighting the darkened text—stories I would argue are like *As I Lay Dying* and *Beloved*. Each of these is a memoir. Faulkner's depends on the memories and voices of an ensemble of narrators. There is not one voice to mediate the text for the reader and to offer the assurance of a singular and stable presence. Instead, multiple narrators whom we know, through their revealed frailties of spirit and body, are nothing if not unreliable are pressed into usefulness because they are the only storytellers we have.

I recall Toni Morrison's powerfully assuring presence as she read from what was the then recently published *Beloved* in an auditorium in the Blue Ridge Mountains in Virginia.[4] Before her reading, she spoke to this packed lecture hall of her concern about the telling of *Beloved*'s difficult story. Morrison understood the way in which the novel held a certain danger, especially in its slippage into historic and spiritual spaces that we'd rather remain buried and silent. So she constructed, she said, a narrative voice that would be reassuring and calming in its presence, inviting readers into its difficult dominions and accompanying us through the troubling story. This narrative voice, calm and stable, would emerge along with us at the story's end, whole and intact, because *Beloved*'s would not be a story to "pass on."[5]

Both *As I Lay Dying* and *Beloved* are narratives of mourning—a state of mind and being that exists to ontologize, to give body to the dead. Whether the spirit poses or decomposes itself, we are aware of the violence in each of these stories that interrupts narrative time—dislodging and decomposing its spectral moments. So when, in Faulkner's novella, Vardaman declares his mother to be a fish, we understand his vulnerability to psychic violence to be akin to the little boy who, looking for bait back of 124 Bluestone Road after Beloved's body had been disposed by the singing women who gathered at Sethe's house, saw a naked woman with fish for hair: "Later, a little boy put it out how he had been looking for bait back of 124, down by the stream, and saw, cutting through the woods, a naked woman with fish for hair" (267).

Both narratives explore the processes of dislocation. It seems to me that this is a process like decomposition. Consider the challenge of a narrative that is undermined by its own interior. These narratives decompose as they impose a spirit to occupy the disembodied space. Whether it is the spirit of Addie

Bundren's death-bed promise exacted from her family, or Beloved's insistent acting out within her family—spirits occupy the essential decomposed spaces of each narrative. In *Beloved* it seems to have the felt-life quality of a poltergeist and appears as

> . . . a pool of pulsing red light. . . . It was sad. Walking through it, a wave of grief soaked him so thoroughly he wanted to cry. . . . Paul D looked at the spot where grief had soaked him. The red was gone but a kind of weeping clung to the air where it had been. . . .
> "We have a ghost in here . . ."
> "[N]ot evil. But not sad either"
> "What then?"
> "Rebuked. Lonely and rebuked." (9, 10, 13)

The weeping that clings to the air in Morrison's novel shares its persistence with the pungent scent of Addie Bundren's decomposing body that follows her family on their journey.

If the dominating discourse of these novels often seems manic and chaotic, it is because these are narratives that exist, as Shakespeare's Hamlet discovers, when "the time is out of joint. O cursed spite,/That ever I was born to set it right!" (*Hamlet*, I.v.).

The experience of the Danish prince is not unlike the disjointed time when the presence of those who are no longer present controls the behavior of the survivors. Addie Bundren and Beloved both instantiate a responsibility that unhinges the present. Each enacts the lesson of Toni Morrison's earlier novel, *Song of Solomon*, a story where members of the "Dead" family (Macon, Pilate, and Milkman) learn that "you just can't go off and leave a body" (333).[6] The omissions and lapses between narrators in Faulkner's novella and the lapses in Beloved's present and past declare by themselves that the time is disjointed.

Whether we inherit these spirits like Beloved's because of our violence and the violence of the narrative/story-telling times, or whether we inherit a responsibility to their last requests like Addie's exacted promise to be buried in Jefferson with her people, that Anse take "me back to Jefferson when I die . . ." (173) to "lie among [my] own people" (23), we come to learn that inheritance belies its seeming benevolence. It is, instead, an exacting task. All inheritors collaborate to construct a composition of mourning. These are the stories that are composed after Addie's and Beloved's death. Both stories resurrect—that is, reconstitute—their spirits.

So what happens, one might ask, when the untimely appears? When death composes as it decomposes? Faulkner's story suggests that this moment of untimeliness provokes the kind of stillness that riveted Darl to his mother's deathbed where he "just stood and looked at [her], his heart too full for words" (25). Faulkner warns, early in the narrative, that the time—"out of joint"— would be too full for the words that flood the pages of this brief story. Morrison links Beloved's reappearance to her signifying use of "rememory"—a phrase that marks both a re-appearance and a re-membrance. The latter implicates a menacing bodily reconstruction: "Remembering seemed unwise" (*Beloved* 275).

It seems that what we may learn from these stories and the craft of their authors lies within the coalescence of strategies that collectively inhabit a particularly provocative terrain. Here, the character of the land—that is, the space *and* composition of ground, is critical not only to the author's vision, but to the spirit's successful migration across these spaces. Nothing but spirit is able to inhabit a heart-felt terrain. Darl's, after all, was too full for words. Baby Suggs's heart-weary center was full as well: " . . . no *matter*, for the sadness was at her center, the desolated center where the self that was no self made its home" (140, emphasis added).

Darl, addled as he might have been, fractured as he surely was, was no better a narrator for Faulkner's story than was Baby Suggs for Morrison's. Baby Suggs's mourning over a loss of color and texture—the "*matter*" of life—indicated the open and vulnerable spiritual terrain left once there was no matter, no substantive self to center her: "[s]uspended between the nastiness of life and the meanness of the dead, she couldn't get interested in leaving life or living it. . . . Her past had been like her present—intolerable—and since she knew death was anything but forgetfulness, she used the little energy left her for pondering color" (3–4).

As Morrison gives fabric and texture to the idea of rememory, she reconstitutes the spirit as the ephemeral, shining, and deeply disturbing presence of Beloved. Morrison's composing is different only in degree from Faulkner's giving texture to the life of Addie Bundren. He reconstitutes Addie out of the shards of her children's pitiful living. Morrison constructs Beloved out of the mournful spaces of motherlove lost.

The common denominator, because it does indeed divide these narratives and because it is ordinary, is violence. Violence is the intimately shared feature of these two spiritual texts. It successfully negotiates the chasm between the physical and the spiritual worlds. It insists itself into a mediatory presence that Faulkner's narrative eschews and Morrison's narrative requires if we are, as she has assured, to survive this story's telling. Violence is the narrative's objective correlative. It is a sure and reliable touchstone that allows the readers to recognize—albeit darkly—the "rest of the text" that would be forgotten, or buried, or left, were it not for its ubiquitous presence.

Consider the range of physical violence in *As I Lay Dying*: that done to Dewey Dell's body and that she would do; the cement cast that allows gangrene to advance up Cash's leg; the raging river current that tosses Addie's body and her children's against submerged logs; the drill that pierces her and the traumatizing sorrow that pierces and fractures her smallest child's heart. These are violent incidents all and they, along with the flames of the burned barn and Darl's scalded psyche, pursue this narrative. They cling to Addie's dead body as relentlessly as her family clings to her rotting corpse. Ironically, its progressive stench is the most certain and reliable indicator of time's passage in the story.

As I Lay Dying gathers up an ensemble of psychic violence, spiritual pain, physical abuse, and loss. The tenacity of its violent undercurrent makes certain that the character of the terrain we learn to rely upon (because a singular narrator's voice is absent and the collective narrative voices are unreliable) is harsh and brutal. This is what we recognize as the rest of the text. Face to face, the narrative's timely disposition of event reveals a striking similarity—a visual mirror as the darkened text is unambiguously revealed (even restored) as the violent coupling of terrain and character. The southern land is like the southerners who inhabit it.

Their migration across the land does nothing more dramatic than to cause the land to claim their characters as its own. The melodrama of buzzards, the unforgiving ground, the floodwaters and fire all find their simulacrum in the addled Bundren family. Their diminished capacity for any kind of existence other than a troubled one is enacted upon a land that understands, intimately, how to characterize, that is, how to give character to trouble.

Here, then, is the craft that Morrison recognizes in Faulkner and carries to her own work. I do not mean to suggest there is an intentional link of thematic or stylistic device between the two, but certainly and significantly, there is a shared understanding of the reach of violence and the vulnerability of terrain to its effect. No thing and no one is immune to this particular thesis. Spiritual hybridity is occasioned exactly when the interior character of the land and its people is interdependent—a symbiosis formed by violent, needful exchange of a trauma that defines the narrative, gives it its character, and even brings to it some measure of stability. In narrative and violent times, "time" is out of joint and spirits inhabit a story's telling.

There are parallels in the two novels with violent elements—the rain that makes the river's current swell and rage in *As I Lay Dying* and the rain in *Beloved* that invades the trenches where Paul D is imprisoned in a box. The rain changes the ground to a muddy slime that threatens Paul D with suffocation.

The precarious situation also creates a flush of water that eventually becomes a mudslide. Its force breaks apart the box that imprisons him. His destiny—suffocation or liberation—is finally a *matter* of time.

Both novels express an urge towards redemption. Within *As I Lay Dying*

> . . . the women begin to sing. We hear the first line commence, beginning to swell as they take hold, and we rise and move toward the door.
>
> The song ends; the voices quaver away with a rich and dying fall.
>
> In the thick air it's like their voices come out of the air, flowing together and on in the sad, comforting tunes. When they cease it's like they hadn't gone away. It's like they had just disappeared into the air and when we moved we would loose them again out of the air around us, sad and comforting. (91)

Because this is a story of migration, the Bundrens will move again, and the air around will ready itself for another moment in the cycle of their redemption and their pain.

That fragile moment of stillness that heralds an eventual migration is not unlike the moment in Morrison's novel where thirty women gather in the front of the house at 124 Bluestone road as if " . . . the clearing had come to her with all its heat and simmering leaves, where the voices of women searched for the right combination, the key, the code, the sound that broke the back of words. Building voice upon voice until they found it and when they did it was a wave of sound wide enough to sound deep water and knock the pods off chestnut trees. It broke over Sethe and she trembled like the baptized in its wash" (261). Redemption is the spirit's salvation. Its persistence composes despite the decomposing violence of narrative times. It does not matter what is the character of that spirit—these are not stories to pass on.

So what does this have to do with trees, rivers, and fish? Here is where the enduring scent of wisteria, the trails of chokecherries, the sketch of scars on Sethe's back, and the scarred living of Addie's children collide and collapse—articulating themselves through a shared, intimate text of violence, but enduring because the *sense* of the living had joined itself to the *scents* of the dying—or nearly dead, or almost dead, or may-as-well-be-dead dead. Recall Baby Suggs who spent her last days in an *extra*territorial space "suspended between the nastiness of life and the meanness of the dead" (5).

A hybrid spirit inhabits exactly this nether world, collecting the living, newly dead, old dead, and the not yet born-to-die dead. Addie Bundren's father constantly reminded any who would listen that "the reason for living was to get ready to stay dead a long time" (169). A hybrid spirit collects all these into its disjointed time where we learn to tell a spiritual rather than a story or time, and where the operative text for the spirit is, as is Ellison's Invisible Man (the quintessential spiritual hybrid), membrance.

> *"For now we see as through a glass darkly but then—*
> *but then—" I couldn't remember the rest.*

Toni Morrison and William Faulkner both re-member the text, and, in giving body to the spirits of Beloved and Addie, remind us that, regardless of our capacity to "feel the spirit," "you just can't go off and leave a body."

Notes

1. This essay was originally given as a talk in 1994 at the American Literature Association conference in San Diego, California.

2. The final pages of *Beloved* repeat: "It was not a story to pass on. They forgot her like a bad dream. After they made up their tales, shaped and decorated them . . . in the end, they forgot her. . . . Remembering seemed unwise. . . . It was not a story to pass on. . . . This is not a story to pass on (274, 275).

3. In *Beloved*, Sethe, Paul D, and Baby Suggs have all escaped from a plantation ironically named "Sweet Home."

4. The lecture was delivered at Virginia Polytechnic Institute in Blacksburg, Virginia, shortly after the publication of *Beloved*.

5. I read the repetition of "It was/this is not a story to pass on" (see note 2 above), as a signifying gesture, encouraging the reader to view the lines with the syntactic complexity that "pass on" allows if we consider "pass on" both as a verb with a bound particle and a verb followed by a free adverbial modifier. The latter syntactic construction (especially) encourages its interpretation to mean that this was not a story to die out or terminate. Instead it is a story, like the phrase itself, to be repeated. I discuss this possibility in greater detail in *Moorings and Metaphors*. See especially chapter eight, "Spirituals and Praisesongs: Telling Testimonies."

6. Pilate and Milkman return to Shalimar, Virginia, to bury her father's (his grandfather's) bones. The line, however, has more resonance than its accompaniment to their burial rites. The novel reveals as well the legend of Solomon, the great-grandfather of the Dead clan, who was of the tribe of flying Africans, and who left (the bodies of) his children and his wife, as he escaped slavery by flying back to Africa.

7. THE GRANDFATHER CLAUSE

Reading the Legacy from "The Bear" to *Song of Solomon*

Lucinda H. MacKethan

In William Faulkner's "The Bear" (part of *Go Down, Moses*), when sixteen-year-old Isaac McCaslin takes down the ledger books in the plantation commissary, he learns fully for the first time the story of his grandfather's defining actions, the incest and miscegenation that have shaped the lives of his progeny down to this "direct male descendant of him who saw the opportunity and took it" (245). In *Song of Solomon*, Toni Morrison's grandson character, Milkman Dead, sits in front of Solomon's store and listens for the first time to the full text of a song he has heard in fragments all his life. It is this song that gives him the story of his grandfather and of his great-grandfather's defining action, the slave Solomon's flight back to Africa. The shared theme of "The Bear" and *Song of Solomon* is the making and reading of texts centered on the past, in which grandfathers represent how the past is passed on.[1] Both novels operate through a series of "reading scenes" in which information, often in the form of a sign, name, gesture, or whole story, is placed before characters who are charged with making sense of it.

In "The Bear" the written word defines Ike's past and thus is his legacy—his inheritance of identity, purpose, and prospects. The commissary ledgers, his Uncle Hubert's I.O.U.'s, the Keats poem that his cousin Cass reads to him—all of these written documents take precedence as sources of knowledge

99

and frames of reference. The ritual of the hunt, seemingly the source of such a different kind of knowledge, actually provides no meaningful alternative. Faulkner's wilderness operates through rigid codes embedded in stories that make sacrosanct and thereby maintain white male power and privilege. Morrison, in *Song of Solomon*, reconfigures written, printed signs of "The Bear" as well as its ritually repeated stories. Through song, through stories which must constantly be revised, through parodies of inscribed white male rituals like the hunt, Morrison redefines reading as active listening, building on an African-American legacy of oral tradition.[2] Lessons in attention to the spoken word, demanding engagement as well as memory, give Milkman a legacy denied to Ike, the legacy of access to creative change in his own life, his own story.

Ike and Milkman are defined in their stories primarily as readers who face the task of finding roles for themselves from "scripts" shaped in the past, specifically in the past of their grandfathers. Significantly, Ike's grandfather Carothers McCaslin comes to him out of his signature in written, bound books, his will, and the ledgers that his twin sons, Buck and Buddy, and then his grandson Cass Edmonds keep as a record of family as well as business transactions. Milkman's grandfather comes to him in stories told orally to him by his father, Macon Dead II, by his aunt Pilate, and then by the Danville, Pennsylvania, community that knew and respected Macon Dead I. Both texts target literacy, through either the faith in book knowledge or the naive attachment to written words that many characters exhibit. Buck and Buddy write almost illiterately in the ledgers; their handwriting looks as though it "had been written by the same perfectly normal ten-year-old boy," and one of the ledger's many ironies is that their first entry concerns a slave, a "*Bookepper*," about whom one of them writes: "*No bookepper any way Cant read. Can write his Name but I already put that down My self . . .*" (255). In *Song of Solomon* the freed slave Macon Dead I is totally illiterate. His son tells Milkman that "He never read nothing. I tried to teach him, but he said he couldn't remember those little marks from one day to the next" (53). Pilate reads only from a fourth grade geography book but also demonstrates extensive knowledge of the Bible. Milkman becomes his father's bookkeeper, and Macon Dead II sums up his own faith in literacy by saying of his father, "Everything bad that ever happened to him happened because he couldn't read" (53).

I.

Faulkner and Morrison work with several figures which exist exclusively to be read. We can begin by looking at one such figure in both texts, a figure that offers a paradigm for the way that signs shape identity and fate according to how they are "read." In "The Bear" Faulkner sets up the print of the great bear himself as an emblem for the written word and its relation to the reader. In *Song of Solomon*, Morrison gives us Pilate's smooth stomach, her missing navel, to offer an alternative way to read, and by extension, to live.

In Section One of "The Bear," Ike's own first experience, at age ten, of "reading" his bear—the great, seemingly imperishable gigantic bear named "Old Ben"—comes when Sam Fathers leads him to a place deep in the woods and uncovers for him the bear's footprint in "wet earth" by a rotted log. Almost as though thus set on parchment, Ike sees "the print of the enormous warped two-toed foot" (192). Through the bear's print, his unmistakable two-toed foot whose mark has been left in wet earth, Ike can "see"—sense, form knowledge of—the nature of the bear itself as a "real" creature, which he now calls specifically a "mortal animal" (192). Later, in tracking the bear one summer, he again sees "the crooked print, the warped indentation in the wet ground which while he looked at it continued to fill with water" (200), and he can again read what this print must mean—its exclusive, single referent. This time, because the print is fresh and repeats itself in the earth, he can follow it, certain that it will lead to the ancient two-toed bear. By the time Ike is thirteen, in section two, he "[knows] the old bear's footprint better than he [does] his own," he can distinguish not only the crooked print, the bear's most particularized signature, but the prints of his three sound paws as well, from those of any other bear (201). Faulkner's use of the word "print" for the bear connects the animal's sign with the print of books that Ike later reads, and specifically with the handwriting of his grandfather, father, and uncle in the ledgers. Faulkner's characters make reading print a matter of relating signs to their referents, in which there is a fixed and therefore logocentric relationship. "Print" is associated with patrimony then, to what is given, fixed, and, like death, finally cannot be repudiated, relinquished, or escaped.

For young Ike, the bear's print speaks always to a notion of the bear's absolute existence, yet Faulkner has given the great animal missing toes, perhaps his own warning that there are absences that his character needs to use to qualify his fixed readings. Morrison in *Song of Solomon* is clearly aware of the power of absence. Pilate's smooth stomach is for her text a dominating sign of absence, something missing, a lack. In her essay "Unspeakable Things Unspoken: The Afro-American Presence in American Literature," Morrison talks of "invisible things" in a way that is instructive for the sign involved in Pilate's lack. She says: "We can agree, I think, that invisible things are not necessarily 'not-there'; that a void may be empty, but is not a vacuum. In addition, certain absences are so stressed, so ornate, so planned, they call attention to themselves; arrest us with intentionality and purpose, like neighborhoods that are defined by the populations held away from them" (11). Pilate's lack of a navel is just this kind of "stressed absence," calling attention to itself and causing marked reactions. Pilate has a stomach which indicates, as her brother knows, that "she had come struggling out of the womb without help" (27). In a parallel manner, everyone, including Pilate, must creatively read the text of her smooth stomach without help. Pilate associates it first with another lack, her lack of a penis, and so assumes that this appendage "not there" is, like the other, a mark of gender. For the series of communities who reject her, the "lack" means that Pilate is unnatural; the absence makes a presence—a defect, which in turn makes Pilate a freak.

Beyond the mystery of its presence-in-absence, Pilate's smooth stomach indicates a gap in all texts that is filled as it is read and misread, interpreted like any other mark, out of its readers' experiences and understanding. In this capacity, the smooth navel acts as a "gap" or "blank" of the kind described in Wolfgang Iser's theory of reading: "Even in the simplest story there is bound to be some kind of blockage, if only because no tale can ever be told in its entirety. Indeed, it is only through inevitable omissions that a story gains its dynamism. Thus whenever the flow is interrupted . . . the opportunity is given to us to bring into play our own faculty for establishing connections—for filling in the gaps left by the text itself" (*Implied* 55).

Morrison echoes Iser, but adds the agency of the writer in the process, as she explains specifically her method of writing *Song of Solomon*: "These spaces, which I am filling in, and can fill in because they were planned, can conceivably be filled in with other significances. That is planned as well. The point is that into these spaces should fall the ruminations of the reader and his or her invented or recollected or misunderstood knowingness" ("Unspeakable" 29). Thus although Pilate's smooth stomach seems to be a "theatrical failure" because there is "nothing there to see" (149), in reality, for each perceiver, this sign engages narrative filling-in of all kinds. Faulkner's bearprint fixes meaning in an absolute mark that can only be followed until it dissolves, and so far as Ike is concerned, refers only to one object. Morrison's smooth stomach layers and disperses meaning in an omission or emptiness betokening not a "vacuum" but the necessity of creating meaning in engagement with what can never be fully "there." The many misreadings of her smooth stomach serve to point not only to the mysteriousness of this sign, present in its absence, but to the way that readers participate in the making of meaning in signs. Reading itself is creating.

II.

In *Song of Solomon* Morrison reads "The Bear" in several of her book's maneuvers involving objects, gestures, and even whole narrative patterns. As we look at several significant instances of her reading of Faulkner, what becomes clear is that each reading is a filling-in of gaps that also constitutes what we can call a creative misreading. Morrison parodies, shifts, or reverses the direction that Faulkner takes. In her signifying, Morrison is unravelling the stress that Faulkner's characters give to writing and the written word. Like Faulkner, but without his fatalism, she seeks a way to challenge the tasks that words are assigned and the parameters that are designated to them in the dominant culture. One example of her revising of Faulkner's tragic sense of the limitations of language involves an emblematic object, the silver cup filled with gold coins that Ike's godfather Uncle Hubert ceremoniously presents him as his legacy (Faulkner begins this section with the portentous words: "there had been a legacy" [287]). Sealed with Uncle Hubert's own seal and wrapped in "inscrutable burlap," the cup is brought out each year without being unwrapped, "passing . . . from hand to hand" to be examined by each member of the family for weight and sound (290). The cup in its burlap remains *covered* (like an unread book?) until Ike is twenty-one; then he and his cousin Cass register no surprise at finding in the burlap only a tin coffee pot filled with a few coppers and I.O.U.'s "all dated and signed" (293). The written signature, like the bear's two-toed print, announces to Ike a fixed identity while it also infers something lacking. The bag which should contain gold in actuality contains scraps of paper; Hubert signs his name to, and thus identifies with, empty "notes" that commodify relationships, as does the language of the ledger books.

Faulkner uses the story of Uncle Hubert's failed "legacy" to repeat the imprint of Ike's legacy from his grandfather, the legacy that also entailed upon Ike the duty of carrying out the decree of old Carothers McCaslin's will. There, in yet another written document, Grandfather McCaslin in his "bold cramped hand" (257) arranged the inheritance of his estate, most of which must eventually come to Isaac, "not only the male descendant but the only and last descendant in the male line" (245), as his cousin Cass reminds him. Yet Carothers also bequeathed one thousand dollars to the son born of his incestuous relationship with his slave daughter, herself born of his union with his mulatta New Orleans concubine. "*Fathers will,*" as Buck and Buddy write, and Hubert's I.O.U.'s share the fixity of legality, of language attempting both to substitute for and to control human interactions. Ike understands that Carothers wrote his legacy to his black son in his will because "*that was cheaper than saying My son to a nigger*" (258). Carothers chose a "cheap" escape into written language, which could substitute in his absence, over the communion of relationship that *saying* the word "son" in the present, and in his presence, would signify. Uncle Hubert takes the same way out, using written language to substitute for spoken, living contact.

Morrison takes Faulkner's theme of the incapacity yet also the tyranny of written language and shifts its weight in her story of Pilate's bag of bones. In *Song of Solomon*, Pilate carries a large green sack everywhere she goes, finally hanging it from the ceiling of her home in Southside. Her brother Macon believes that the sack contains bags of gold nuggets that they had discovered as children while hiding in a cave from their father's murderers. Pilate had refused to let Macon carry off the gold then, but he believes that she betrayed him and took it for herself. The fact that Pilate calls the sack her "inheritance" (164) confirms his suspicion, so he pressures Milkman into stealing the sack for him. Like Faulkner's burlap wrap, Pilate's "grass green" sack turns out to contain no gold at all. Yet unlike Ike's legacy of scraps of paper and signatures giving testimony to his Uncle's written "borrowings," Pilate's "inheritance" contains bones, which for her testify to her duty to a human being whom she believes she helped her brother to murder back in the cave where the gold was found.

Morrison makes several plays on Uncle Hubert's cup from "The Bear," in one instance through her reference to weight. As Ike participates in the yearly rituals of holding and shaking the cup in its wrappings, he recognizes that Hubert's "legacy" has changed in both weight and shape. Likewise Milkman and his friend Guitar, as they cut down Pilate's sack, find the bag "much lighter than they had anticipated" (187); Macon, when he had lifted one of the bags of gold as a boy, had been "amazed at its weight" (171). In Ike's cup, there has been a substitution; Milkman and Guitar find to their chagrin what seems a similar kind of substitution, not worthless paper and writing, but within Pilate's green sack, human bones. To them the bones constitute a worthless exchange and a cruel trick. Pilate, however, "reads" the bones as organic remains, for which she bears responsibility; as she explains, "You can't take a life and walk off and leave it. Life is life. Precious" (210). How precious these bones are even Pilate does not know until Milkman discovers the whole story of his grandfather, the first Macon Dead.

Pilate's stunned response to Milkman's story of their family heritage—"I've been carryin Papa?" (337)—is Morrison's extra twist to Faulkner's story of Uncle Hubert's substitutions. The various changes/exchanges in the bag's contents enable Morrison to stress what is fluid about the past and about race, as well as what language can and cannot fix. Most significantly, in Morrison's text there has never been any actual substitution of one thing for another in Pilate's sack: in a continual progression of reading what is under the "cover" of the sack, what people know determines what they think is there. Morrison insists that as knowledge is the product of a fluid, ever-changing process, so are the realities it transposes.

When Pilate and Milkman take the first Macon Dead's (finally known as Jake Solomon's) bones back to Virginia for burial, Pilate buries with them the piece of paper on which her father had written her name: "Then she made a little hole with her fingers and placed in it Sing's snuffbox and the single word Jake ever wrote" (339). The original writing of the name, described in a story told much earlier, is evoked at this concluding moment: how Jake chose the name Pilate out of the Bible solely because of its shape, the capital "P" looking "like a tree hanging in some princely but protective way over a row of smaller trees" (18), and how he laboriously copied out the name on a scrap of paper. Jake's printing of Pilate's name, like his choosing of it, shows language working in a different kind of system than the one that directs Hubert's scrawling of his name with the symbolic letters "I.O.U." For Jake, it is the meaning of the shape of the word (princely and protective), not the semantic level of the word itself (Pilate means "Christkiller," his horrified neighbors tell him) that signifies. Since Jake's death, Pilate has carried the paper with its writing in an earring fashioned from her mother's snuffbox, the snuffbox like a book containing a whole text in one word. Yet where Pilate has carried this "box" is testament to yet another way the word means—carried close to her ear, the name as she can hear her father's voice saying it is what matters. She listens to his voice instead of reading "the one word" he ever wrote (53). The burial of the bones and snuffbox and written word together marks another of Morrison's many mergers of signs that stress the constructed, infinitely variable, everchanging nature of knowledge within language. The fact that a bird carries away the name and "box" at the end reinforces this revitalizing capacity of words.

Pilate's gesture of burying her written name with her father's bones stresses what Milkman has just begun to understand, that recorded words do not have to, indeed cannot, themselves finally bear the full weight of their referents. There is always more happening than simply words being shaped to control or fix reality when human identities and relationships are recorded in language: "[u]nder the recorded names were other names, just as 'Macon Dead,' recorded for all time in some dusty file, hid from view the real names of people, places, and things" (333). In the world Faulkner constructs for Ike McCaslin, the family names are fixed in the dusty files of the ledger books; Hubert tries to fix his debt as he scrawls his name with legal finality on his I.O.U.'s; Ike's cousin Cass, trying to fix the concept of living truth, resorts to a poem printed in a book, a poem whose subject is two lovers frozen in passion without hope of consummating their love. In marked contrast, Pilate's gesture, releasing her recorded name with her grandfather's bones, frees and reconstitutes her identity and her father's along with both the name and the memory of the man whose bones are buried. Ike's tragedy, as Faulkner understands all too well, is his entrapment in a world of recorded names that cannot be released or reconfigured. It is a tragedy that Faulkner names but does not move his character beyond. Ike, attempting to achieve his own stable space, cannot endorse the principle of change which might truly revive him.[3]

Just as she does with the bag of bones, Morrison subjects "Pilate" as name to numerous revisions. Indeed, for Morrison, all names of necessity come to be "misread" and therefore meaningful in this way.[4] Pilate is not Christkiller, but her brother does believe she has betrayed him. Her name is not spelled "Pilot" as some think, although she is certainly a pilot for Milkman (one who will not fly in an airplane, however). Guitar can't play a guitar, First Corinthians and Magdalene have no love in their lives, Ruth Dead cleaves to her father, not her husband's family. The Dead family is alive, but soon begin their quests for "owning things" which Morrison associates closely with death, so that the soldier who renamed Jake Solomon as Macon Dead heard wrong, but in some ways named (predicted) right. The name of the town, "Shalimar," and the slave "Solomon," are pronounced similarly—neither name is exact, and which came first? The word "Sing," which Pilate's ghost-father repeats, seems to command her to sing, and so she does, crooning songs which bring comfort and sustenance to herself and others. Finally Milkman can point out to her that she has completely misread the meaning of the word for her father—he was simply repeating the name of the wife he lost when Pilate was born. So too, in assuming that her father has told her to go get the murdered white man's bones, Pilate misunderstands, for it is his own bones that the father is sending her to find, while he also indicts the white murderers who left him unburied. Misreading—skewing meanings out of lack of knowledge, need, limited experience—makes all knowledge-gaining creative guesswork among shifting possibilities of meaning, none of which are stable. Far from being a curse, however, this fluidity of language is consistent with the nature of the world. It is what gives life its creativity, and for Morrison, it is a literally lifesaving attribute of words.

Possibilities for creative misreading are denied to Ike, in the commissary and indeed in the forest. He is charged consistently with finding the one place, the one print, the one meaning, that then directs his actions. The meanings, through all the dialogues and debates—between himself and Cass or between his father and uncle in their ledger commentaries—do not change. In the ledger his uncle had written of the slave Eunice, "*June 21th 1833 Drownd herself,*" and his father's hand in reply wrote "*23 Jun 1833 Who in hell ever heard of a niger drownding him self.*" The uncle in turn scrawled, "with a complete finality,"

"*Aug 13th 1833 Drownd herself*" (256). The meaning of that drowning Ike finds in reading the entries that surround it, but the meaning never changes, and there has been no dialogue—Uncle Buck's and Buddy's handwriting and behind it their thinking are indistinguishable, a "rubber stamp" (256) of each other's. Once Ike had thought that "what the old books contained would be after all these years fixed immutably, finished, unalterable, harmless" (256); the truth becomes that the writings are for Ike and all Carothers McCaslin's progeny never finished, or harmless, precisely because they are accepted as "fixed immutably" and "unalterable." The words, a part of McCaslin's legally binding patrimony, never change their meaning or their significance for Ike's life. In "The Bear," words substitute for and fix reality.

Carothers McCaslin's will (both senses), written and thereby seemingly ratified, presides over all.

III.

Morrison, in her creative misreading of Faulkner, insists upon the need to misread the function of signs themselves, and words as signs most of all. Objects, words, and names as signs change with their collisions against and mergers with other signs in *Song of Solomon*. They are read, misread, and then must be continually re-read to make sense, to be usable. Gestures and patterns of action work in the same way. As Morrison reads "The Bear" as a hunt story, she copies several gestures that carry special significance in that context; her novel's hunting sequence is in its entirety a parody, a deliberate misreading, as well as a parable, an expansion and interpretation, of Faulkner's elaborate, elegiac witness to white male bonding and coming of age. Morrison has indicated that her novel provides "Sotto (but not completely) my own giggle (in African-American terms) of the proto-myth of the journey to manhood" ("Unspeakable" 29). This comment provides a key to Morrison's development of Milkman's quest; both to set him into and to free him from the tyranny of the Word, she simultaneously plays from and distorts several literary, mythological sources—including Hansel and Gretel, *The Odyssey*, as well as "The Bear," with its highly stylized, linguistically ornate patterning of the Adamic "proto-myth of the journey to manhood."

As Morrison's all African-American hunting party gets ready to go after raccoons in the dark of the night, almost as a tip of a hunting cap Morrison has one of them say, "Don't shoot no bears, now" (*Song* 276). Among many of her carefully calibrated reloadings of Faulkner's hunting script is Milkman's gesture of taking the change from his pocket when he is told it will make too much noise and thus interfere with the hunt. Ike, hoping to see the bear, is told by Sam Fathers that he will have to leave behind his gun, and later he also sets aside his compass and watch, after which the bear comes into view. Likewise, as Milkman enters into the hunt's world of men, wild prey, dogs, and guns, he gains new insight and some power over experience—or at least how he understands experience—by shedding the objects of status that belong to the civilized world. As Milkman sits under a sweet gum tree (Ike found Boon Hoggenback frantically trying to load his gun under a gum tree at the end of "The Bear"), he thinks, "There was nothing here to help him—not his money, his car, his father's reputation, his suit, or his shoes. In fact they hampered him" (280). Freed for the first time from his dependence on values defined outside of him, Milkman discovers a different kind of language that he hears in the interacting sounds of men and dogs—signs of pure communication, "what there was before language. Before things were written down" (281). He understands that the Shalimar man he has followed into the woods was adept at "pulling meaning through his fingers," and he imitates that way of knowing himself, "trying to listen with his fingertips, to hear what, if anything, the earth had to say" (282). The knowledge he gets is literally lifesaving, for at the moment he uses ears and fingers to ask the earth for knowledge, he is able to sense a threatening presence behind him in time to prevent Guitar from choking him.[5]

Milkman's relinquishing of his materialistic dependencies allows him insights similar to the wisdom Ike learns in the woods, but this parallel holds only up to a point. Milkman's ultimate bonding is with a group very different from the hunter class who are Ike's designated equals in "The Bear." Here, as with the gestures of forest relinquishing, Morrison reads, then skews, Faulkner's hunt. Ike hunts in exclusive company: Jefferson, Mississippi's most respected white citizens, the largest landowners, men of both means and honor. Accompanying them are their servants, some former slaves, who perform the menial duties and only in the case of Sam have earned the stature of the upper-class white hunters. In constituting her hunt scene, Morrison rewrites roles for Milkman's hunters to show that if this were Jefferson, Milkman and his cohorts would be serving in the capacity that the "Negroes" served for Ike's hunting parties—exclusively as cooks and mule wagon drivers, not real hunters. In their free time, Faulkner tells us, the "Negroes" who went with the white hunters to the summer camp in the forest ran the "coons and cats" "scorned" by the "proven hunters," Major DeSpain, General Compson, Walter Ewell, and Cass McCaslin (196). The black hunters from Shalimar specifically look for coons and are delighted when the hounds track a bobcat. Faulkner's "Negroes" cannot be heroic bear hunters, and what Morrison thus reads in Faulkner's bear hunt is a ritual that works by exclusion as much as by endurance, a script prohibited to people whose lives are defined by prejudice instead of by privileges which make the hunt, as

Faulkner calls it, "the ancient and unremitting contest according to the ancient and immitigable rules" (184). "Unremitting" and "immitigable" are words that name the kind of fixity and rigidity that Faulkner's white hunters revere but which Morrison's very differently cast black hunters must learn to challenge.

Faulkner's concluding section of "The Bear" reiterates Ike's reverential and fatalistic attachment to the hunt as a validation of a closed white male mythology. There Ike visits the closed and shrunken wilderness to see for the last time the graves of Sam Fathers and the dog Lion before the land is given over completely to the logging interests. As he imagines Sam's and Lion's "immutable progression . . . being myriad, one," their immunity to time, he thinks of a conversation he had held years earlier with his cousin Cass back in the town. He had been fourteen, and was trying to explain to Cass why he had not shot the bear when he had the chance. To help him, Cass had gone "*to the bookcase beneath the mounted head of his first buck, and returned with the book and sat down again and opened it*" (283). What Cass read then was Keats's "Ode on a Grecian Urn." The lines that Faulkner has Cass repeat with special emphasis are: "*She cannot fade, though thou hast not thy bliss. . . . Forever wilt thou love, and she be fair*" (283). In the woods standing over the graves, much as Cass had stood under the mounted buck head, Ike thinks, "the long challenge and the long chase, no heart to be driven and outraged, no flesh to be mauled and bled" (313). He looks to "the book," as had Cass, to resolve the agonies of experience, and looks to a poem which expresses the paradox of art, that it can endure out of time only with the sacrifice of movement, change, life. Faulkner's rendering of Ike's thoughts up to this deliberate paraphrase of Keats's "Ode" has been an elegiac tribute to a Keatsian ideal of a deathless world of nature; Faulkner himself never clearly embraces this ideal. In fact, the turn into the poem that Ike takes represents a retreat into written language.[6] Faulkner seems to be stressing the Urn only as a medium of a mixed message. The reference represents an acknowledgement of Ike's dependence on the word which is also an acknowledgement of the poem's ambiguity about both art and nature. Whatever its answer, Ike ultimately has nowhere to go in his wilderness meditation except back into the books and records that define his future, what he inherits from the past.

IV.

In both town and wilderness, in Cass's library and at the burial site in the shrinking forest, reality is frozen in repetitions of the past. In "The Bear," not just words but stories themselves, and storytelling, are limited in this way. Early in Section One, Ike thinks at age sixteen that "For six years now he had heard the best of all talking," and then he conjures the scenes of storytelling *about* hunts which have taken place in town and in camps: "the best of all listening, the voices quiet and weighty and deliberate for retrospection and recollection and exactitude among the concrete trophies—the racked guns and the heads and skins" (184). The best of all talking and listening for Ike involves "retrospection and recollection and exactitude," significantly among dead, stuffed "trophies." Stories become tightly constructed versions of the past marked by the frozen, preserved but also lifeless "game" that provides the source of the story. In "The Bear" stories are bound by the weight of the past and ritual, by "retrospection" and "exactitude" and death.

Against Faulkner's fatalistic prescription of the function of words and story, Morrison shapes stories that insist on expanding the possibilities of language, through an affirmation of traditions which Ike—with his grandfather's will and ledgers as his legacy—cannot inherit. Morrison clarified the particular tradition that she inherits as a black writer when she commented in an interview: "So I do a lot of revision when I write in order to clean away the parts of the book that can *only* work as print. . . . [O]ne of the major characteristics of black literature as far as I'm concerned . . . is the participation of the *other*, that is, the audience, the reader, and that you can do with a spoken story" (Interview with Christina Davis 147). In "The Bear," language works for the characters as print, as fixed, recorded story, and the "other" as audience does not interact with the materials that make the record. While Faulkner makes Ike's story a mystery, for the reader a complex detective story of how Ike comes to understand his past, he makes it clear that the tradition of print which Ike accepts does not provide him with viable knowledge or ways to know because it is a tradition which exalts the closing of meaning in fixity, which is death.

In *Song of Solomon,* storytelling and stories are moving parts of other experiences, generated out of actions as well as recording them, changing the shape of reality as well as changing themselves. In "The Bear" stories mark returns to the past but they provide no way into the future. Part of the reason that they are static and only backward-looking is that they are locked into both ritual and records that exclude new kinds of readers and readings. Ike, remembering the drinking that was part of the hunt's storytelling rituals, thinks that it seemed as if the stories themselves had been "distilled into that brown liquor which not women, not boys and children, but only hunters drank" (184). Only white men both make and "drink" the stories. For Morrison, storytelling and stories must be both open and inclusive, involving men, women, and children of different races and classes and regions as tellers and subjects of tales. It is a woman, Pilate, who first sings the song that tells the novel's story (she also provides the liquor, her bootleg wine); it is the children of Shalimar who play their "game" with the story/song that becomes Milkman's text. Furthermore, never are the stories occasions, as Ike sees them, that are separate from living contexts: Macon tells Milkman a story to explain his treatment of his wife; Pilate tells Ruth a story to keep her away from Hagar; several people tell Milkman stories in response to specific questions that he has about his family, the "living Deads." The stories and their contexts mix and merge factors of gender, race, time, and purpose.

In *Song of Solomon*, everyone has stories to tell, yet all of the stories are also partial, inaccurate, sometimes deliberately distorting, other times accidentally but also creatively misreading facts, objects, and gestures. Macon Dead tells his son Milkman one version of his wife's relationship with her father, based on what he thought he saw or wanted to see; Ruth tells Milkman a different version, based on her own needs. Pilate tells Ruth the story of her early life, misconstruing some of the things that happened; Macon Dead, covering some of the same material with Milkman, also mistakes many signs. When Milkman arrives in Pennsylvania, Reverend Cooper and Circe, the aged woman named out of fable herself, provide missing details, but they, too, know only parts of the whole. Milkman, for his part, finds that he can tell a story, the story of his father that the old men back in Pennsylvania want to hear. Yet this story, too, is purposefully inaccurate, shaped to the needs of its hearers; Milkman sees that they need a hero to replace the first Macon Dead, shot down because he was a strong and successful black man, so he substitutes his father for his grandfather, and transforms his father's greed into the kind of heroics his listeners want to hear. For Morrison, such is the revitalizing nature of storymaking.

Morrison begins Part II of *Song of Solomon* with a reference to Hansel and Gretel. She is setting up Milkman's quest, which begins as his hunger for gold and ends with his search for the full story of his family. As he stands in front of Circe's house, which "looked as if it had been eaten by a galloping disease" (221), Morrison refers to the fairy tale of the children who were driven to the gingerbread house out of their deep hunger. She is playing again with story, how myths work and are unworked. Milkman is hungry for gold but needs most to discover, not just stories themselves but the capacity to hear them. This is Circe's wisdom and gift; she can indeed give him pieces of the puzzle of his family's past, but she gives Milkman the greatest gift when she tells him, in patently unheroic terms, "You don't listen to people. Your ear is on your head, but it's not connected to your brain" (249). Stories must be heard and understood in order to mean. Part of Milkman's development, the final, crucial element of his growth, involves his becoming an active audience for the stories that have been prepared for him to hear. His greatest early weaknesses involve his inability to relate actively to stories. He himself thinks, "Above all he wanted to escape what he knew, escape the implications of what he had been told. . . . He felt like a garbage pail for the actions and hatreds of other people. He himself did nothing" (120). In some ways these words describe Ike McCaslin at the end of Section Four of "The Bear." He is a receptacle, but not a creator, so stories can only control him, and he can only long to escape their implications.

Morrison's readings of "The Bear," through recognizable shifts of reference, reveal her to us as a reader as well as a writer of a text who does what all attentive reader/listeners do with stories: they pay attention, they carefully record the details and signs, but they at the same time fill in what is missing and add from their own sources to make the story new. This process of reading, promoting a theory of the active "listener" as co-creator of the text, is defined in an interview in which Nellie McKay comments on the effect of reading Morrison's novels: "When the reading is done, one is not through with the book"; Morrison replies that "People who are listening comment on it and make it up too, as it goes along. In the same way when a preacher delivers a sermon he really expects his congregation to listen, participate, approve, disapprove, and interject as much as he does" (420). Morrison adds that her textmaking is "a corollary, or a parallel, or an outgrowth of what the oral tradition was"; she does not reject written language but insists upon opening the written text to participation, to creative reader response.[7] Likewise when Milkman becomes an active listener, no longer a "garbage pail" for the words of others, he too can shape a meaning, and more importantly, a "synthesis." This is the drama of the closing pages of *Song of Solomon,* as Milkman listens carefully to the children's song, records it mentally without printing it, and returns to Susan Byrd for verification, elaboration, and revision of what he has heard.

Milkman sits outside in front of Solomon's store, after the exciting hunt and his evening with Sweet, listening to children singing a song that accompanies a game that they play. The scene revises Ike's reading of the ledgers, in which there is no transaction but only absorption, "as page followed page and year," until "the yellowed pages in their fading and implacable succession were as much a part of his consciousness and would remain so forever" ("The Bear" 259). In Shalimar the song is sung, with children taking different roles, and Milkman, the listener, fills in the meanings with his new knowledge, in conjunction with the children who oblige him by singing the song until he has committed it to memory, since he has no pencil to write down the words. Then he returns to Susan Byrd, the woman who the day before had given him little help with the story he was trying to collect. Her reason for withholding was the earlier audience—not just Milkman but a nosy neighbor who would *talk* too much. As Milkman listens to Susan, he for his part "sat back and listened to gossip, stories, legends, speculations. His mind was ahead of hers, behind hers, with hers, and bit by bit, with what she said, what he knew, and what he guessed, he put it all together" (327). This moment marks in some ways the fulfillment of Milkman's quest—the moment when a whole story is created, Milkman "making it up too," a story built by participation, listening, and acting, or "transacting."

On the way back north Milkman shows what he has learned about reading and signs: "He read the road signs with interest now, wondering what lay beneath the names" (333). When Ike asks the same question of the names in the ledger, he has no way of participating in any answer that can free him from what the words have been made to mean in their recording. Milkman, on the other hand, has learned to make adjustments; he has been taught that there is always more to know. Now he can revise the story, the song, as well as listen to it. His new power is evident when Pilate, dying, asks him to sing. He changes the words of Solomon's song for his listener, singing "Sugargirl don't leave me," as a creative substitution for the "Sugarman" of the song's earlier versions (340). Commenting on this ending, Morrison has written that Pilate's "longing to hear the song, finally, is a longing for balm to die by, not a submissive obedience to history" ("Unspeakable" 29). Ike submits to the history that is recorded in the ledgers, in the imprint of his grandfather's and the South's rigid imperatives. His response to his knowledge of the past, variously called "repudiation," "relinquishment," or "just plain quitting," allows him no future, no way to interact creatively with the world. Milkman "bit by bit . . . put[s] it all together," and then makes a song into the balm that his listener needs. Together Pilate and Milkman have found a way to fly, through a surrender to language in its best form, an open, spoken, shared story that cushions and directs their great leap into the unknown.

Notes

1. David Cowart notes that Milkman resembles Ike "interpreting the ledger entries when he analyzes the rhyme" in the children's song (88). Cowart argues that Morrison's themes are an "intertextual engagement" with Faulkner, among others. John Duvall's sense of Faulkner/Morrison relations in these two works is much closer to mine. He argues that Morrison's novel "reclaims Faulkner's in ways that question the male-centered world of the hunt" ("Doe" 95–96).

2. Many critics, and Morrison herself, stress her roots in an African-American oral tradition. See Middleton.

3. Werner's analysis of Ike is helpful. He relates Ike's narrative to the "narrative of endurance" that Faulkner designed for his African-American characters: "it is

static, not kinetic. Second, its temporal focus is on the past or present rather than the future" (713–14).

4. For discussion of naming in Morrison, see MacKethan and Hirsch.

5. Guitar's hunt for Milkman also parallels Faulkner's bear hunt. With the six men who form the race- and gender-defined revenge organization, the Seven Days, Guitar has pledged himself to the ritual that most closely and ironically parallels the hunt ritual in "The Bear." As different as Guitar might seem to be from Faulkner's hunters, especially Ike, he is bound to them in one significant respect: he lives by a ritual of justified killing that forces him to deny any other code. Duvall ("Doe") discusses this destructive masculine code, pointing to similarities between doe-killing in "Delta Autumn" and Guitar's story of killing a doe.

6. See Korenman and Gelfant. Both read Ike negatively as one who, in Korenman's words, "is seeking in the Keatsian unfulfilled state a way to define time and change" (19).

7. Louise Rosenblatt's theory of transactional reading relates closely to Morrison's imperative of opening the written text: "Instead of functioning as a rigid mould, the text is seen to serve as a pattern which the reader must to some extent create even as he is guided by it" (136).

8. BLACK MATTERS ON THE DIXIE LIMITED

As I Lay Dying and The Bluest Eye

Theresa M. Towner

> *The presence alone of Faulkner in our midst makes a great difference in what the writer can and cannot permit himself to do. Nobody wants his mule and wagon stalled on the same track the Dixie Limited is roaring down.*
> —*Flannery O'Connor*

The literary relationship between William Faulkner and Toni Morrison has been, in life, completely one-sided, as he was to live for only seven years after she finished her master's thesis on Faulkner and Woolf, and she would not publish her first novel until eight years after his death. As other essays in this volume indicate, Morrison has confronted the magnitude of Faulkner's achievement—the fact of O'Connor's "Dixie Limited" (45), as it were—throughout her career and in a variety of ways. A careful examination of the relationship between Morrison's and Faulkner's fictions can balance the portrait of their relationship by tracing its mutual intertextuality, or what Henry Louis Gates, Jr., has called "the nonthematic manner by which texts—poems and novels—respond to other texts" ("Preface" 68). In this essay, I will use two concepts born of African-American literary theory in order to address the question of how Morrison's early fiction responds to several significant techniques and themes of Faulkner's. Ultimately, I will propose that a reading of Faulkner's work in light of Morrison's reveals new insights into the construction of the well-worn tracks of the Dixie Limited.

The first of these two concepts is what Michael Awkward has termed "inspiriting influence." In his study of narrative patterns in African-American women's fiction, Awkward argues that these writers do not suffer their male counterparts' "anxiety of influence," the state in which they must somehow confront and then top the achievement of their (male) predecessors, but instead enjoy and feel gratitude toward the female writers who came before ("Inspiriting" 1–14). These writing women, Awkward says, respond to one another's "inspiriting influence." He argues further that the task of the black writer is to add "black expressive cultural features" to Western cultural forms in order to "reflect, in black 'mouths' and 'contexts,' what we might call (in Bakhtinian terms) Afro-American 'intention' and 'accent'" (9). Awkward's formulations have sparked a good deal of my substantive readings of *The Bluest Eye* in this essay. The second concept I wish to explore in my comparison of Faulkner and Morrison is that of signifying, the black rhetorical tradition that Gates has so deftly connected to contemporary literary theory's investigation of textual meaning and instability. Signifying, he explains, is "the trope of revision, of repetition and difference" (*Figures* xxxi; see also *Signifying* 8–32). Already the student of Faulkner can think of many places in his fiction where Faulkner signifies upon himself, and I will argue in the following pages that, in a state of inspirited influence, Morrison's first novel signifies consistently and deliberately upon Faulkner's *As I Lay Dying*. No detail escapes her revisionist attention. Even the titles of the two works arise from sad puns at the thematic hearts of the novels. How a dead woman can narrate part of a novel, the initial mystery of the title *As I Lay Dying*, turns into a metaphysical speculation when we learn that she believed "the reason for living was to get ready to stay dead a long time" (169). The title mystery of *The Bluest Eye*—only one eye, and bluer than what?—turns into Pecola's crazed search for "the bluest eyes in the whole world" (203) and finally describes Pecola's pathetically isolated and lonely self. She is the Bluest I.

Morrison does not merely appropriate the details of Faulkner's book. She repeats and modifies nearly every major thematic and structural component of the Bundrens' trek to Jefferson in order to create a portrait of individual insanity within the larger frame of the institutionalized madness of American racism. Morrison recasts the Faulknerian mold in two important areas: the theme of disjointed language and the metaphors of the violated human body which support that theme. In the process of tracing and recoloring its model, Morrison's novel emerges as a brilliant original.

Central to *As I Lay Dying* is the axis of words and deeds that Addie describes: "words go straight up in a thin line, quick and harmless" while "how terribly doing goes along the earth, clinging to it, so that after a while the two lines are too far apart for the same person to straddle from one to the other" (173). When she has her affair with Whitfield, language and action unite for the first time in Addie's experience; language has meaning because love has given it life. Faulkner expresses that language in paradox as Addie reflects on her affair: "hearing the dark land talking of God's love and His beauty and His sin; hearing the dark voicelessness in which the words are the deeds" (174). She would not describe her feelings for Whitfield with the word *love*; that is Anse's word, and Addie struggles to make her words match the exquisite torment that for her transcends her husband's and Cora Tull's "high dead words" and "dead sound." In this synesthetic "dark voicelessness" Addie hears and sees "the duty to the alive," "the reason" for living that stands in contradiction to her father's cynicism (174). As Stephen Ross puts it, "In taking Rev. Whitfield, a master of the hypocritical word, as her lover, Addie gives in to language" (129). The end of her affair leaves her bitter not about "love" but about the possibility that language could reflect her injuries (Bleikasten, *Faulkner's* 136). Wounded psychically, she blames language, not Whitfield. The rest of her life is mere housecleaning.

Addie's axis of words and deeds reflects a good deal of Faulkner's own ambivalence about language spoken and written. As André Bleikasten argues, Faulkner's fiction (those who knew him would say that his life, too) contains diatribes against "talk" and "words"; but what made the man a novelist was "the recognition that immersion into experience, although indispensable, is not enough and that truth becomes a man's possession only after what he has lived, felt, and suffered has been transmuted into awareness, recorded by memory, and reordered by imagination." The "task of the novelist" is "to lend his voice to 'the old verities and truths of the heart,' to embody them in a language that respects their rootedness in experience and never yields to the glibness of abstraction" (*Faulkner's* 137). The act of reading *As I Lay Dying*, of negotiating Addie's axis for ourselves, produces what Warwick Wadlington calls "moments of reading vertigo related to one of the novel's key questions: where does the 'I' begin and end?" (*As I Lay* 75). Ultimately, "to be an 'I' is to be the shape and echo of words, the words of others as well as our own, in the sense that we radically depend on others' stories and the conventions that make them possible" (Wadlington, *As I Lay* 82). In a novel that investigates issues of identity and community and situates these issues inside a shifting axis of experience and language, Faulkner remains ambivalent.

In her examinations of generational conflicts, gender constraints, repressed sexuality, cathartic violence, and insanity, Morrison signifies on Faulkner's Bundrens as pre–World War II African-Americans struggling to find a way to live in a culture that shuns them, or at the very best tolerates their passage through it in order to take some kind of advantage of them. As Faulkner does, she develops these themes in *The Bluest Eye* alongside a rigorous investigation of the function of language and of its place in a world of often harsh action. Morrison, however, evinces none of Faulkner's ambivalence regarding how to interpret the relationships between language and experience. In the book's prologue, she highlights the "magic" created by the union of words and deeds that will appear on virtually every subsequent page: "so deeply concerned were we with the health and safe delivery of Pecola's baby we could think of nothing but our own magic: if we planted the seeds, and said the right words over them, they would blossom, and everything would be all right" (5). Exactly how everything is not all right is the subject of the novel, and to show this Morrison's language virtually equates words with deeds and often points to their absence—or silence—as a source of evil. Pauline and Cholly Breedlove fight, for instance, "with a darkly brutal formalism. . . . They did not talk, groan, or curse during these beatings. There was only the muted sound of falling things, and flesh on unsurprised flesh" (43). Pecola's parents breed but do not love. She must ask the MacTeer girls "how you get somebody to love you" (32), and she surmises from her parents' copulations, "Maybe that was love. Choking sounds and silence" (57). When Cholly rapes Pecola, her silence only excites him further: "the silence of her stunned throat, was better than Pauline's easy laughter had been" (162). Underscoring the connection between silence and evil, young Claudia says that adult speech is "a code to be broken by us" that nonetheless should extend to expressions of concern for Pecola and her unborn child: "we listened for the one who would say, 'Poor little girl,' or, 'Poor baby,' but there was only head-wagging where those words should have been" (190).

Yet words in this world, when clear and not encoded, are often weapons, the most dangerous of which foster and sustain black self-contempt. When Pauline simultaneously scolds Pecola and comforts a white child, for instance, her words for her daughter are "hotter and darker than the smoking berries" in a cobbler; "she spit out words at us [black children] like rotten pieces of apple," but for the white girl "the honey in her words complemented the sundown spilling on the lake" (109). Pecola is the novel's most self-contemptuous character—so much so that Claudia once wants "to open her up, crisp her edges, ram a stick down that hunched and curving spine, force her to stand erect and spit the misery out on the streets" (73–74). She is consequently made the town's scapegoat, but even Claudia knows the difference between a scapegoat and a savior. "All of us—all who knew her—felt so wholesome after we cleaned ourselves on her," Claudia reflects. "Her inarticulateness made us believe we were eloquent. . . . Even her waking dreams we used—to silence our own nightmares. And she let us, and thereby deserved our contempt." The scapegoating saves no one from self-contempt, and the final metaphor for that truth is (not incidentally) linguistic: "we rearranged lies and called it truth, seeing in the new pattern of an old idea the Revelation and the Word" (205–6). Morrison relies upon the power, the actionableness, of language to unpack the sources of black self-contempt and to illustrate what sacrifice that self-contempt demands. It is no less than a human sacrifice—first the body and then the mind of Pecola Breedlove.

In *As I Lay Dying,* images of physical disability and death represent the burdens the Bundrens endure as well as those they inflict upon others as they journey towards Jefferson, through life. Such images saturate the novel, and the list includes Addie's stinking corpse; Cash's twice-broken leg, set in concrete, the skin finally ripped away before gangrene sets in; Anse's teeth, old and rotted away or new and false; and Dewey Dell's swelling belly. In *The Bluest Eye,* the theme of black self-contempt accounts for the pervasiveness of Morrison's images of physical decay, mutilation, and deformity. These metaphors at first describe characters, like the relentlessly middle-class women who guard against "the funkiness of nature."[1] These women, who guard "the line between colored and nigger," even raise plants whose names evoke mutilation of the body— bleeding hearts and mother-in-law tongues (81–85). The major characters' individual disappointments and mutual antagonisms are revealed in these details of deformity. Pauline, with her stunted foot and missing tooth, revises Anse Bundren's toothlessness. His desire to "get them teeth" (52) in town finds its most poignant parallel in the moment Pauline loses her tooth in the local movie house, where she goes for refuge from real life and quickly assimilates the white film standards of romantic love and physical beauty. "*I was sitting back in my seat,*" she says of one visit, "*and I taken a big bite of that candy, and it pulled a tooth right out of my mouth. I could of cried. I had good teeth, not a rotten one in my head. I don't believe I ever did get over that. There I was, five months pregnant, trying to look like Jean Harlow, and a front tooth gone. Everything went then. Look like I just didn't care no more after that. I . . . settled down to just being ugly*" (123). In Morrison's all-encompassing vision of a rotting world, even Cholly elicits some sympathy. His character as a victimizer is formed when his first act of sexual intercourse is witnessed and brutally forced to consummation by shotgun-toting white men, after which he feels humiliation and its absence "like the space left by a newly pulled tooth still conscious of the rottenness that had once filled it" (150). The rottenness of the social world erupts in images of corrupted and dead bodies; finally, a dead dog and a crazed child result from Soaphead Church's decision, made as he licks a well-worn gold filling, to grant Pecola's request for blue eyes (174). As Stephanie Demetrakopoulos argues, "Morrison's images of the human body are radically scatological," and "unpleasant truths about being embodied are forced on us repeatedly" because Morrison wishes to "expose the romanticism of faith in [such] abstractions" as natural rhythms and human society (Holloway and Demetrakopoulos 32).

The metaphors of corrupted bodies also support and express Morrison's investigation of language. The scene in which a group of boys taunts Pecola exemplifies most clearly the dynamic relationship between black self-contempt, language, and the body: "It was their contempt for their own blackness that gave the first insult its teeth. They seemed to have taken all of their smoothly cultivated ignorance, their exquisitely learned self-hatred, their elaborately designed hopelessness and sucked it all up into a fiery cone of scorn . . . and spilled over lips of outrage, consuming whatever was in its path. They danced a macabre ballet around their victim, whom, for their own sake, they were prepared to sacrifice to the flaming pit" (65). In this passage, insults and the self-contempt that fuels them actually take human form, become literally and scathingly embodied, complete with teeth. At movies like *Imitation of Life* and *The Littlest Soldier*, Pauline slips on the straitjacket of self-hatred that the teasing boys have likewise collected from the streets.[2] "In equating physical beauty with virtue," Morrison says of Pauline, "she stripped her mind, bound it, and collected self-contempt by the heap" (122). Because she hates herself, Pauline will ultimately seal her own daughter's fate by refusing her word that Cholly has raped her. That she denies the reality of Pecola's ruined body is the saddest effect of embodied self-contempt; the rape itself, triggered by Pecola's unconscious repetition of a physical gesture that initially attracted Cholly to Pauline, is its most terrifying. Morrison uses a subtle yet shocking parallelism to describe Cholly's desire for his daughter, which thus contains its own refutation. Angry, "he wanted to break her neck—but tenderly"; then not angry, "he wanted to fuck her—tenderly" (161–63). The horrifying jolt of difference between the physical violence and the tenderness that violence must destroy reveals Morrison's condemnation of Cholly's actions. Vanessa Dickerson has pointed out that this novel reveals the extent to which "Western society has warped black fatherhood" (123). But several other commentators, completely misunderstanding Morrison's representation of Cholly as "a free man," blame Pecola for the rape (see Otten 21; Samuels and Hudson-Weems 15). On the contrary, Morrison, like Faulkner and Janis Joplin, knows that Cholly's kind of freedom is just another word for nothin' left to lose (see *The Bluest Eye* 160). In the "tenderly" passage above, we not only see the beginning of Pecola's destruction but also the novel's most brutal manifestation of Morrison's portrait of the relationships between language and black self-contempt (see Byerman, "Intense" 1982).

Just as Darl Bundren splits into interrogative and nonsensically responsive halves as a result of the trauma of his imprisonment—"Darl has gone to Jackson. They put him on the train, laughing, down the long car laughing, the heads turning like the heads of owls when he passed. 'What are you laughing at?' I said.

"'Yes yes yes yes yes.'" (253)—so Pecola splits into two personalities who speak only to one another as a result of the multiple traumas she has endured. Raped twice by her father and carrying his child, she goes to the pedophile Soaphead Church with a request for blue eyes. He "grants" her request by engineering the poisoning of the dog Bob, upon whose death her personality fractures:

> . . . You're looking drop-eyed like Mrs. Breedlove.
> *Mrs. Breedlove look drop-eyed at you?*
> Yes. Now she does. Ever since I got my blue eyes, she look away from me all of the time. Do you suppose she's jealous too?
> *Could be. They are pretty, you know.*
> I know. He really did a good job. Everybody's jealous. Every time I look at somebody, they look off. (195)

Pecola's internal dialogue reveals an even greater injury to the child than those previously inflicted. Mrs. Breedlove has refused her daughter's word that she was raped, and the turmoil in the household is reflected in the confused way in which Pecola tries to figure out the connections between love, sex, pleasure, and violence. Her splinter self, the sly voice that seems to understand that some pleasure might accrue from adult sexual intercourse, baits the child self repeatedly:

> *Well, she probably loved him anyway.*
> HIM?
> *Sure. Why not? Anyway, if she didn't love him, she sure let him do it to her a lot. . . .*
> *How could somebody make you do something like that?*
> Easy.
> *Oh, yeah? How easy?*
> They just make you, that's all.
> *I guess you're right. And Cholly could make anybody do anything.*
> He could not.

> *He made you, didn't he?*
> Shut up! (198–99)

This dialogue reflects Pecola's secret fear that she might have caused her own rape and, more significantly, that any notion of her own sexual pleasure would further discredit her word about the rape.[3] The splinter self goads:

> *I wonder what it would be like.*
> Horrible.
> *Really?*
> Yes. Horrible.
> *Then why didn't you tell Mrs. Breedlove?*
> I did tell her!
> *I don't mean about the first time. I mean about the second time, when you were sleeping on the couch.*
> I wasn't sleeping! I was reading!
> *You don't have to shout.*
> You don't understand anything, do you? She didn't even believe me when I told her.
> *So that's why you didn't tell her about the second time?* (200)

The tension between these two selves increases, and the splinter self finally abandons the child self, whose desire for blue eyes escalates into a wish for "the bluest eyes in the whole world" (203). Morrison's language reflects the ongoing self-contempt at Pecola's ruined inner core, which suffers abandonment and ridicule even in madness.

Describing the shell-shocked Shadrack of *Sula* as "very organized," Morrison once gave a definition of madness as "orderly . . . isolation, total isolation and order" ("Intimate" 223). The definition speaks as well to Pecola's state and has a prototype, I think, in Faulkner's Benjy Compson, who wants everything "in its ordered place" (*Sound* 321). Pecola has another obvious Faulknerian predecessor in Temple Drake of *Sanctuary*, but the most fruitful comparisons between them arise when we seek to understand them not solely as victims of rape but as figures around which a community organizes in order to define itself and to plot the means for its own survival. More simply put, Pecola's role in Lorain as a scapegoat whose word is refused inverts Temple's role in Jefferson as a scapegoat whose word is required (Rigney 21).

In the gap that exists between any of the stories that Temple tells Horace Benbow and the court and the version that Faulkner supplies us of the crimes against her, we see just how terribly her world misunderstands this violated woman. Perhaps most moving of all the things she tells him at Miss Reba's is her claim that she tried to protect herself from Popeye by imagining herself as first a boy, then a corpse, a forty-five-year-old schoolteacher, and an old man. She tried to cope with Popeye's hand on her belly by becoming first something Popeye would not expect—a boy—then something that reflects her own grief—a corpse with shucks in the coffin. The last two projections, however, are tellingly racialized: she thinks of Popeye as "a little black thing like a nigger boy" and of herself as "an old [white] man" who can make Popeye get "littler and littler" (219–20). The only way Temple can control any part of her situation the night before the rape is to make Popeye into a small black male presence who becomes steadily less threatening to Temple's white femaleness. At her very core stands the belief that violating presences are black and male, "inviolation" limited likewise to the white and male.

Even Horace, who feels so sorry for her, does not understand that she has been raped. He cares only for her story—for her—only insofar as it can clear Lee Goodwin's name. Yet this violated young woman reminds him powerfully of his own stepdaughter of about the same age. As he holds Little Belle's photograph in his hands and sees there "a soft and fading aftermath of invitation and voluptuous promise and secret affirmation" (223), the unsteady truce between physical desire and stepfatherly restraint disappears. So too does Horace's sense of himself as male. He becomes both violator and violated as he vomits, hearing in his imagination the shucks in Temple's mattress and seeing too "something black and furious go roaring out of her pale body" (223). In this curious passage, the line between rapist and victim, between male and female dissolves for Horace just as surely as it does for Temple during the night at the Old Frenchman place. Faulkner also complicates the imagery of whiteness and blackness that falls so neatly into place in Temple's consciousness. The "black and furious" something of vomit and blood turns into a "black tunnel" through which the pale victim, "like a figure lifted down from a crucifix," shoots into a "darkness" that contains the victim's only liberation from grief and terror: "an interval in which she would swing faintly and lazily in nothingness filled with pale, myriad points of light" (223). Horace's nausea, exhausted, mirrors Temple's detachment after her rape (136–38) and presages his response to Lee Goodwin's lynching (296). By linking the episode of Horace's nausea so closely with Temple's story of the night before Tommy's murder, Faulkner systematically dismantles race- and gender-based explanations of human behavior. This dissolution implies that, to Faulkner, human identity is shifting, nebulous, malleable, and hence infinitely corruptible.

To both Faulkner and Morrison, identity is also infinitely constructible, perhaps most fluidly so in language, where community is as possible as isolation. Jay Watson maintains that in *Sanctuary*, "[e]ven when a human life rests on the power of forensic narrative, Horace fails as a storyteller, so his arguments bow before a malevolent rhetoric, an amoral but persuasive theatricality" (75), which accounts nicely for Horace's disappearance from Faulkner's fiction. Bleikasten, Ross, and Wadlington all note the communal quality of the combined voices and reflected consciousnesses of the narrators of *As I Lay Dying*; Ross speaks most closely to my argument here when he writes, "[v]oice in *As I Lay Dying* also interrogates the metaphysics of *individual* consciousness, revealing characters' secret selves by immersing them in a *communal* discourse, making their private thoughts a function of how they hear, respond to, and render each other's speech" (125). Morrison manages a similarly provocative contest between storytellers as well as an interrogation of the metaphysics of individual consciousness in *The Bluest Eye*, where language can work like an ax to the head, words can both rot and be rotten, and self-contempt leads the attack and guarantees the wilt from within.[4]

She does so with the deceptively simple juxtaposed contending narratives that frame the novel, competing for our attention and approval. Her initial description of the Breedlove family (where love does not even exist, never mind breed) could also describe the Bundrens, whose name also puns (see Byerman, *Fingering* 206): "Each member of the family in his own cell of consciousness, each making his own patchwork quilt of reality—collecting fragments of experience here, pieces of information there" (*Bluest* 34). That line also fairly describes the form of *As I Lay Dying*—juxtaposed "cells of consciousness" that surface in modified form in the structure of *The Bluest Eye*. Four large sections entitled "Autumn," "Winter," "Spring," and "Summer" consist of Claudia's first-person narration and the omniscient voice of a narrator with more information about the world and the Breedloves than the nine-year-old Claudia can have. The novel begins with a Dick and Jane story, a primer tale of family—white—that contrasts starkly with the textured narrative produced by Claudia and the omniscient narrator. Morrison repeats the story three times, with decreasing levels of punctuation and concern for spacing, until the third version speaks in monotone, run-on: "Hereisthehouse . . ." (4). Sections of that run-on version introduce those sections of the novel that Claudia does not narrate. The sections are capitalized when pressed into this introductory service, from which perch they scream their simplistic morality, and their normalcy, at the text that follows. The effect is immediate irony, and often terror in hindsight. Cholly's introduction sends shivers down our spines:

SEEFATHERHEISBIGANDSTRONGFATH
ERWILLYOUPLAYWITHJANEFATHER
ISSMILINGSMILEFATHERSMILESMILE (132)

Trying to appropriate the text, this alternative narrative bludgeons the reader of *The Bluest Eye*. It is as real a fact of our reading as its white moral "normalcy" is to the black citizenry. It reflects, in Keith Byerman's phrase, "the exploitative nature of logocentric orders" (*Fingering* 185); and it exists to reproduce in the structure of the novel the essence of the perversions of the institutionalized racism that breeds and nurtures black self-contempt.

Yet as Claudia gently insists on Pecola's value as self and as story,[5] we recognize, as Michael Awkward says, "the inappropriateness of the white voice's attempt to authorize or authenticate the black text" ("Roadblocks" 59). We come to see an evil in silence and to hear the madness in the primer's scream, and that alternative narrative is finally subsumed into an astonishing parable of ugliness and beauty. Morrison thus signifies not only upon Faulkner's text but also upon various ways of reading all texts. She sets the issue of influence in the foreground of her first novel.

Faulkner would have recognized some of his Bundrens' features in Morrison's characters and would have heard some startling riffs on his themes in *The Bluest Eye*, and I think too that the man who once praised Ralph Ellison for not "being first a Negro" but "first a writer" would have discerned in Morrison's novel the eloquent rebuttal of his own facile distinction between racial identity and artistic achievement. He criticized Richard Wright on these grounds in the same interview at the Tokyo American Cultural Center in 1955 (*Lion* 185–186). In laying out the terms of evaluation thus, he was trying to say, I think, that Wright's work took a turn toward the explicitly political and away from the "artistic"; he did not believe that art had an agenda. Morrison would not accept this distinction. Moreover, she would take issue with its assumption that literature by white Americans is any less racially implicated than that by persons of color. She argues that an avowedly "apolitical" stance is "the most obviously political stance imaginable since one of the functions of political ideology is to pass itself off as immutable, natural, and 'innocent' " ("Unspeakable" 8).[6]

"The world does not become raceless or will not become unracialized by assertion," Morrison writes; "The act of enforcing racelessness in literary discourse is itself a racial act" (*Playing* 46). I think that observation is one that Faulkner would have applauded, especially given his moving portraits of black characters forced to confront both well-meaning white people who avoid articulating the American color line and the not-so-well-meaning members of both races who profit from racial exploitation. To see how we might understand Morrison and Faulkner's literary relationship—the influence question—from a purely intertextual perspective, unbounded by birth and death and publication dates, it is informative to take a look at the one place in *As I Lay Dying* that Faulkner racializes the Bundrens' journey. They have reached Jefferson's outskirts. Darl narrates:

> Three negroes walk beside the road ahead of us; ten feet ahead of them a white man walks. When we pass the negroes their heads turn suddenly with that expression of shock and instinctive outrage. "Great God," one says; "what they got in that wagon?"
> Jewel whirls. "Son of a bitches," he says. As he does so he is abreast of the white man, who has paused. It is as though Jewel had gone blind for the moment, for it is the white man toward whom he whirls. (229)

The white man, who has a knife, takes offense. Jewel immediately transfers his anger to the white man from the blacks who originally prompted his name-calling because he assumes that the white man, as a "town fellow," looks down on him. Darl restrains Jewel, but when the town fellow will not drop the insult, Darl stands up for Jewel: "Do you think he's afraid to call you that?" The man backs off in the face of the Bundrens united: "Jewel would a whipped him," is how Vardaman sums up their family triumph (231). What began as an expression of disgust at Addie's stinking corpse dragged from pillar to post, common enough in the journey, slides immediately into racial conflict. Jewel is ready to fight the black men but not the whites who have uttered similar sentiments. Yet just as quickly the scene slides out of the racial arena and into conflict between country folk and town fellows. In order to show the Bundrens' willingness to defend and preserve themselves as an entity, whether or not they like each other very much, Faulkner invokes a common southern class conflict; and he does so by creating what Morrison would call a provoking "Africanist presence." Under the influence of Morrison's criticism, we can discover another layer of Faulkner's characterization in the novel: the Bundrens show their colors, as the three black men ease on down the road and out of the text.

Notes

1. In "Eruptions of Funk: Historicizing Toni Morrison," Susan Willis has generalized from these repressed women to Morrison's consistent indictment of "bourgeois reification," or the total commodification of the social world (rpt. McKay 312).

2. For analyses of the relationships between these two films and *The Bluest Eye*, see Gerster, Fick, and Klotman.

3. Gibson reads this dialogue as "introducing the possibility that [Pecola] wanted and needed" Cholly's sexual advances (29).

4. Lynne Tirrell points out that *The Bluest Eye*, while it describes how one becomes an adult by learning to see oneself through the eyes of the community, follows

this "struggle for objectivity" with "another even more difficult challenge," which "demands we not lose our subjectivity in our quest for justification" (124–25).

5. Among the many critics who have commented on Claudia as an artist figure in the novel, Robert Sargent compliments her for her ability to "order experience" (233); Doughty describes her as an "articulate survivor" (43) conforming to the pattern traced by Robert Stepto in *From Behind the Veil.*

6. The substance of "Unspeakable Things Unspoken" and "Black Matter(s)" (Richter 256–68), from which I draw part of my title, appear in revised form in *Playing in the Dark.*

9. UNTOLD STORIES

Black Daughters in *Absalom, Absalom!* and *The Bluest Eye*

Keith E. Byerman

Toni Morrison has repeatedly noted that she undertook the writing of fiction because she felt that she could not find herself in existing literature. For the purposes of this essay, the most important iteration of her position came at the 1985 Yoknapatawpa Conference on Faulkner and Women, where she commented in response to a question, "I sensed that there was an enormous indifference to these people, to me, to you, to black girls. It was as if these people had no life, no existence in anybody's mind at all except peripherally" ("Faulkner and Women" 301). In the same presentation she explicitly rejects any clear influence of the older writer: "I don't really find strong connections between my work and Faulkner's" (297). Certainly Morrison has good reason to disclaim influence, to say nothing of anxiety of influence. After all, Faulkner tends to dominate the space of writing about the South, including race and gender, even if his positions are understood as problematic. And, as John Duvall has noted, criticism itself has followed the "master's" lead: "This belief in a male/female dichotomy in which man as acting subject is opposed to woman as an acted upon object informs not only the corpus of [Cleanth] Brooks's commentary, but also, to a great extent, the discourse of the Faulknerian institution itself" ("Faulkner's Critics" 45). The difficulty only increases if one chooses, as Morrison does, to add race to gender. Dilsey then becomes the touchstone, the measure of black womanhood. Better to distance oneself from such a literary predecessor.

There are, however, good reasons to make the connection that Morrison refuses and to make it in the terms by which she defines her own purpose. One reason to tell the story of the "black girl," and specifically the black daughter, is not because others have been "indifferent," but because they have gotten the story wrong. Through an intertextual analysis of *Absalom, Absalom!* and *The Bluest Eye*, it is possible to see that Morrison is telling the story of the black daughter that Faulkner could not (or would not) tell. Moreover, it is precisely because he defined Clytie as the black daughter that Morrison must revise the narrative. Clytie exists in the text as cipher, as an embodiment of "Sutpenness" without her own identity or agency. Morrison, through Pecola especially, delineates the full implications of such a condition, thus giving voice to the ones most often silenced in Faulkner's saga.

Until very recently, critics of Faulkner have paid relatively little attention to daughter figures in his fiction.[1] Even when they have been acknowledged, as in the cases of Caddy Compson and Addie Bundren, it has seldom been in their roles as daughters. When it comes to black daughters, the attention has been even more limited. In *Absalom, Absalom!*, the center of the novel is Thomas Sutpen, the would-be patriarch of a great southern family; he is the principal concern, in one way or another, of all the narrators. It is his designs and his legacies which they all seek to understand. Critics have followed Faulkner's lead by focusing either on Sutpen, or on the narrative attempts to understand him, or, in good patriarchal fashion, on his sons and their tortured struggles with their patrimony. With important recent exceptions, Judith and Clytie, the two female Sutpens, are virtually ignored in critical discussions. The author again sets the pattern here, since he labels them primarily as Sutpens and little else; they are essentially ciphers who, unlike the sons, have no meaning beyond their status as daughters of their father. Repeatedly, they are said to be inscrutable, silent, and enigmatic. They only make sense to the narrators in their "Sutpenness." As female or, in Clytie's case, black, they cannot be made sense of; or rather, there is no sense to be made because such qualities have no narrative meaning outside the patriarchal context. Each of the narrators finds something more to these two figures, but what that "something more" might be does not exist within the possibilities of the grammar of patriarchy; therefore, it remains enigmatic.

The condition of cipherhood itself is, paradoxically, the marking that defines Clytie and Judith in the text and the context in which they seek to mark themselves. The blankness of Clytie is even greater than that of Judith; this black Sutpen may not even have the right name: "(Yes, Clytie was his daughter too: Clytemnestra. He named her himself. . . . He named them all, the one before Clytie and Henry and Judith even, with that same robust and sardonic temerity, naming with his own mouth his own ironic fecundity of dragon's teeth. Only I have always liked to believe that he intended to name Clytie, Cassandra, prompted by some pure dramatic economy not only to beget but to designate the presiding augur of his own disaster, and that he just got the name wrong through a mistake natural in a man who must have almost taught himself to read)" (*Absalom* 48). Even if Mr. Compson is wrong in his speculation, Sutpen's naming of this black child does at least reflect the convention of slaveowners' marking blacks with pompous and often outrageous names as a means of exaggerating the distance between name and fate in life. Those so designated are not human beings so much as objects of derision. Though clearly a daughter, she lacks even the status of Judith in the family; neither sexuality nor marriage exist as possibilities for her. She is a possession, marked completely by her "Sutpenness": "It was Sutpen face enough, but not his; Sutpen coffee-colored face enough there in the dim light, barring the stairs . . . —the face without sex or age because it never possessed either: the same sphinx face which she had been born with, which had looked down from the loft that night beside Judith's and which she still wears now at seventy-four . . ." (109).

Even Judith, though denied the marking of marriage and expression, has at least the traces of such denial to give her a history and thus a self. Clytie is denied even time itself; because of her race, she exists as almost pure cipher. All of the terms associated with her—"inscrutable," "sphinx," "Cerberus"—suggest not so much a being as a condition entirely outside of time. For all the narrators, she functions, not as a character, but as an indicator of the doom of Sutpen. But unlike Cassandra, she does not speak the fates of anyone; she is herself interpreted as such a mark. Her own voice is insignificant because she serves only to symbolize the situation of others. She is Sutpen, not in the sense of the willfulness of a Judith, but in her role as an extension of the wills of first Thomas, then Judith, then ultimately perhaps, Henry. In her enacting of this will, she is implacable; whatever action she engages in is carried through to its conclusion.

But while such a description suggests the condition of blacks in general, we cannot assume that Clytie is defined by her race, for even that gives her a history and an identity. Just as she is denied age and sex, so her blackness is not a defining characteristic. She herself has no associations with other blacks in the community, and when the mulatto Charles Etienne is brought to Sutpen's Hundred, she is the one who will allow him no such associations. And her own position in the Sutpen household is presented as highly ambiguous by Miss Rosa, herself a marginalized daughter: "*Clytie, not inept, anything but inept: perverse inscrutable paradox: free, yet incapable of freedom who had never once called herself a slave, holding fidelity to none like the indolent and solitary wolf or bear (yes, wild: half untamed black, half Sutpen blood: and if 'untamed' be synonymous with 'wild,' then 'Sutpen' is the silent unsleeping viciousness of the tamer's lash) whose false seeming holds it docile to fear's hand but which is not, which if this be fidelity, fidelity only to the prime fixed principle of its own savageness . . . "* (126). Clytie's position is not determined so much by her race as by her status as sign; such conditions as slave and free are meaningless for a figure who has no being in herself. Slave and free represent limitations and possibilities for the expression of one's own will; Clytie has no such will. And it is precisely this absence of will which gives her such power: she embodies Sutpen energy without any of the limitations of social or sexual qualities. Without mind or will of her own, she cannot be deterred from the course others set, even when they can be.

But it is, paradoxically, that very limiting combination of blackness and womanhood which frees her for such a role. Charles Bon, the black son, has at least sufficient power in his position as son to compel Sutpen to find a way to destroy him. Though Bon himself vainly seeks a sign of his paternity, he is, in the interpretations of the narrators, acknowledged to the extent that his father is forced to take action. Because he has a claim within the patriarchal order, despite his race, he can participate in and shape the Sutpen history and other characters within that history. And Judith, though a daughter, because she is white must at least be acknowledged as a daughter who has a role within the social order. Sutpen must refuse to allow her to marry and thus to be marked by another, which means that she has sufficient value to warrant such a denial. But Clytie has neither claim nor exchange value within a white patriarchal structure. Even the suggestion that she might be the mother of Charles Etienne by Sutpen does not carry for the narrators the implication of incest. Her skin color defines her as outside the realm of social legitimacy and therefore not a daughter in the same sense as Judith, while her sex makes her an object and therefore outside the realm of claims of inheritance. She is, in other words, excess, without a function within the existing order. Her role is defined entirely at the whim of Sutpen; no rules, no systems of law or exchange or discourse limit his authority and authorship of her position.

Even her destruction of the mansion and with it herself and Henry, which could be seen as a deliberate and conscious act of her own will, is in fact merely an expression of her father's self-destructiveness. Those interpretations of this scene which suggest that she acts out of loyalty to the family name and seeks by her action to keep Henry out of jail miss this point. Loyalty and pride imply a self, a substantial being. Clytie is pure sign, existing only to indicate the signified of the tragedy of Thomas Sutpen. Precisely because of her status as sign, she remains inscrutable and sphinx-like; the narrators and readers attempt to read her in the same way as other characters, but her very transparency precludes such reading. Unlike Judith she is not marked, since she herself is the mark. This position makes her always an arbitrary thing, an extraneous existence manipulated to signify that which she can never be.

In *Absalom, Absalom!*, then, Faulkner's black daughter is one of the tools by which the father creates his narrative. In Clytie, Sutpen creates the sign by which he signifies his fate. The implication of such representations is a symbolic incest by which the father begets his true progeny—his story—on the beings and bodies of his daughters.

Faulkner sees the daughter as "inscrutable," beyond explanation; his interest is in the definition of reality undertaken by the father. That rule of order is set over against that of the community, and the similarities and differences are explored. For Morrison, the daughter is the center of attention and what she takes as inexplicable is the order imposed by the Father, whether literal or symbolic.[2] She presents a daughter striving to comprehend the system of signs that both controls her world and that in some way she cannot help but violate. Her effort to construct an order of her own by which to define her relationship to reality is itself taken as a criminal act. Unlike a son, the daughter is not permitted to know the codes by which she must operate; nonetheless, she is held culpable for her inability to interpret them correctly. The end result is that her actions are distortions of the patriarchal order, especially when they deal with matters of desire and power. For Morrison these distortions take the radical form of violence and madness, where distance between patriarchal structure and female desire is shown to be the causative factor.

The Bluest Eye renders problematic the very nature of black female identity. Like Clytie, Pecola Breedlove is not acknowledged as a daughter within the social order, and, as in *Absalom, Absalom!*, the father is responsible. But the situation for Morrison is in this sense more complex, for she understands that the black father himself is not permitted a human identity. It is the symbolic white father, through his control of the sign system of the society, and in particular the emblem of the white daughter, who determines the fates of black daughters and their black fathers. The end result of this dehumanization through marking is, in Morrison, as in other women writers such as Alice Walker, Ntozake Shange, and Gloria Naylor, violence, self-hatred, madness, and death.

While *The Bluest Eye* contains relatively few white characters, whiteness itself is pervasive. It makes itself felt even before the narrative begins, in the "Dick and Jane" epigraph taken from a school reader. This idealized scenario is immediately repeated, first without punctuation and then without word separations. These decreasingly intelligible patterns suggest on the one hand the downward spiral from the orderly white world to the struggle for order of the MacTeer family and then to the chaos of Pecola and the rest of the Breedlove family. At this latter stage the words serve as bitterly ironic chapter titles, since the Breedlove house is a nondescript storefront, the mother abuses her family, the father rapes Pecola, and the "friend" is the schizophrenic other Pecola talks to after going insane.

But this introductory material, while it measures the disintegration of the Breedlove family, also asserts the standard by which they judge themselves and are judged by others. In this sense, there is no motion toward disintegration because this implies an original state of order from which they declined. But this family, as is evident from the chapters on the house and on the parents Pauline and Cholly, has always existed in a flawed condition. They have never had control over the mechanisms of order; they have only been able to see such mechanisms and to compare themselves unfavorably to such an order. Thus, for example, the very means by which they acquire the structure of language, the grade-school reader, reveals to them an idealized world which excludes them. They have no significance in the fundamental system of signification.

Throughout the narrative, the materials of mass culture are used to define the white standard and to preclude any black self-definition. White dolls, Mary Jane candies, movies, advertising, and, most important in this study of daughters, Shirley Temple all embody presence in the text, over against which blackness is an absence. Very early in the story, Claudia MacTeer, the narrator, exposes the real absence at the heart of this powerful presence. After reinscribing the softness and beauty of the doll as hardness and discomfort, she exposes its core: "Remove the cold and stupid eyeball, it would bleat still, 'Ahhhhhh,' take off the head, shake out the sawdust, crack the back against the brass bed rail, it would bleat still. The gauze back would split, and I could see the disk with six holes, the secret of the sound. A mere metal roundness" (21). Claudia literally deconstructs this emblem of white purity, innocence, and beauty to find its meaning; the reality of its defining voice is a cipher, "a mere metal roundness." But this nothing is itself a product, a creation of the symbolic father that through a process of mystification becomes more real than the literal daughter.

What interests Morrison in this novel is less the source of mystification than the effects of it: "There is really nothing more to say—except why. But since *why* is difficult to handle, one must take refuge in *how*" (6). *Why* is in a sense irrelevant to the author's purposes; to explore it requires penetration to the heart of that dominant white patriarchal order which has decided that black children, and especially girl-children, have no status within its structure. But Morrison is concerned with precisely that which the white world has declared marginal and extra. She wishes to speak for that daughter who has no voice and who bears on her mind and body the marks of erasure.

Morrison establishes the strength of mystification by showing us its effects on Claudia, the one who has penetrated to the secret of the artifact. In attempting a more aggressive policy of detection, she begins to attack white girls themselves, trying to uncover the mystery of their success. But this act is intolerable: "When I learned how repulsive this disinterested violence was, that it was repulsive because it was disinterested, my shame floundered about for refuge. The best hiding place was love. Thus the conversion from pristine sadism to fabricated hatred, to fraudulent love. It was a small step to Shirley Temple" (23). Claudia realizes the inhumanity of her position, and like everyone else in the story, turns that shame against herself, which means in effect, turning it into affection for what she is not. She, in effect, denies the truth of her own being and surrenders to the negation of herself that the white world demands. Shirley Temple is the only definition of daughter, and one who cannot be Shirley Temple is refused being at all.

Such self-hatred and the attendant worship of whiteness is especially apparent in the Breedloves: "Except for the father, Cholly, whose ugliness (the result of despair, dissipation, and violence directed toward petty things and weak people) was behavior, the rest of the family—Mrs. Breedlove, Sammy Breedlove, and Pecola Breedlove—wore their ugliness, put it on, so to speak, although it did not belong to them." They do this because "the master had said, 'You are ugly people'" (38–39). For Mrs. Breedlove, this self-perception means finding happiness only in watching white romantic movies and in working faithfully in the kitchens of white people. The houses of whites, whether real or cinematic, serve as emblems of an order which is not possible in her own life. Similarly, her religion serves to validate her hatred of the ugliness of her husband, which is, after all, a version of her own perceived ugliness.

For Pecola, the validation of her ugliness is everywhere about her in the treatment she receives from other blacks, both those who feel that their lighter skins make them superior and those who vent on her the hatred of their own dark skins. It is apparent in the way whites carefully avoid touching her when she comes into their stores. It is also apparent in the way her own mother attacks her when her presence threatens the purity of Pauline's white folks' house. In every moment of her life, Pecola is made to feel that she has been marked as a worthless product of the society. Unlike white daughters, she has no exchange value, and thus has no function in the society. Her only hope, from this perspective, is to re-mark herself as a thing valued. She seeks to do this through her identification with Shirley Temple, by constantly drinking milk from a Shirley Temple cup and by using whatever money she has to purchase Mary Jane candies. Through this mass culture eucharist, she hopes to transubstantiate herself into that sacred image with the blue eyes. She accepts without question the mystery that Claudia sought and failed to expose.

It is through her father, ironically, that she ultimately both succeeds and fails in her perverse quest. But unlike Sutpen, Cholly lacks authorizing power since he himself is the unauthorized son: "Abandoned in a junk heap by his mother, rejected for a crap game by his father, there was nothing more to lose. He was alone with his perceptions and appetites, and they alone interested him" (160). In addition to these failures of parenting, he also suffers humiliation at the moment of sexual initiation; his first experience is interrupted violently by two white men with guns, who force him to continue though he is physically incapable of doing so: "Sullen, irritable, he cultivated his hatred of Darlene. Never did he consider directing his hatred toward the hunters. Such an emotion would have destroyed him. They were big, white, armed men. He was small, black, helpless. His subconscious knew what his conscious mind did not even guess—that hating them would have consumed him, burned him up like a piece of soft coal, leaving only flakes of ash and a question mark of smoke. He was, in time, to discover that hatred of white men—but not now. Not in impotence but later, when the hatred could find sweet expression" (150–51).

Cholly himself has undergone none of the rituals of entrance into society and thus remains a marginal figure. As such he can never function as father, law, or author within the structure. The house he provides for his family is an image of his situation; it is, in fact, not a house at all, but an abandoned store: "The plan of the living quarters was as unimaginative as a first-generation Greek landlord could contrive it to be. The large 'store' area was partitioned into two rooms by beaverboard planks that did not reach to the ceiling. There was a living room, which the family called the front room, and the bedroom, where all the living was done. . . . The kitchen was in the back of this apartment, a separate room. There were no bath facilities. Only a toilet bowl, inaccessible to the eye, if not the ear, of the tenants" (34–35). There is no marginal space here to which to consign a daughter, for the house itself is marginal. Nothing preserves a male or female posterity, for the occupancy by the Breedloves, and all other tenants, is necessarily temporary. Cholly, unlike Sutpen and the whites in this book, cannot lay claim to anything as his own, with attendant rights and responsibilities. He is outside the social order; he cannot build or father a house, but only live in that of someone else. In this sense, he is himself a kind of daughter.

In addition, Cholly can only be an outlaw and outsider who cannot make his daughter into something valued. He can do no more than assure through his marking that she will suffer permanent alienation. Ironically, such an act on the part of this outlaw only confirms the judgment of that society he cannot enter. Adding bitterness to the irony is the fact that Cholly's rape of Pecola is the only act of love that she ever experiences: "If he looked into her face, he would see those haunted, loving eyes. The hauntedness would irritate him— the love would move him to fury. How dare she love him? Hadn't she any sense at all? What was he supposed to do about that? Return it? . . . He wanted to fuck her—tenderly. But the tenderness would not hold" (161–63). To use terms like "love" and "tenderness" in such a context is, of course, a perversion of both language and human emotion, and certainly Pecola does not describe her experience in such terms. But the radical nature of Morrison's insight is that Pecola is so negatively marked by society that only the outlaw Cholly even imagines using the word "love" in reference to her, and his "love" can only be violence and destruction.

Cholly does literally what Sutpen has done figuratively, though it can be argued that Clytie exists because of Sutpen's rape of an unnamed black woman. The crucial distinction is that white men have, through the law, granted themselves permission to engage in acts of sexual violence. And since part of that racial and patriarchal law denies personhood to black women, such acts do not fall in the category of "rape" or "incest." Cholly's physical penetration of Pecola, impermissible within the social order, is his way of defining the daughter's position within that order. The difference is that Sutpen by the facts of maleness and whiteness carries in his being the authority to dictate that position and therefore can exert that authority symbolically; Cholly, having neither name nor law, can only assert himself through a literal impression on his daughter.

The effect of his action, that of an outlaw doing a forbidden thing to an eternally excess being, is to enable Pecola to enter, through a gesture of insane transcendence, the very heart of that world from which she is excluded. After this obscene initiation, followed by another wherein she unknowingly kills another helpless creature, Pecola comes to believe that she has the bluest of eyes. In this completely closed realm of her own mind, she has achieved the status of the white daughter which she (and everyone else, in varying degrees) has sought from the beginning. She, more than Clytie or any of the other daughters, has managed to mark herself. But the marking is, of course, not really hers at all, but that of a patriarchal society which permits only its own labelling of daughters. Claudia recognizes what the entire society, including those who themselves bear the marks of social negation, does to a Pecola: "All of our waste which we dumped on her and which she absorbed. And all our beauty, which was hers first and which she gave to us. All of us—all who knew her—felt so wholesome after we cleaned ourselves on her. We were so beautiful when we stood astride her ugliness. Her simplicity decorated us, her guilt sanctified us, her pain made us glow with health, her awkwardness made us think we had a sense of humor. Her inarticulateness made us believe we were eloquent. Her poverty kept us generous. Even her waking dreams we used—to silence our own nightmares" (205). Making Pecola the scapegoat is the way of evading the reality of the symbolic father in one's own experience; by finding voice in the silence of this victim, it is possible for the community to pretend that its voices have some worth, that its naming carries some meaning.

For Morrison, the refusal to acknowledge the black daughter goes beyond the denial of self-naming by the white daughter; it is an act of fundamental violence: a rape. The suppression of black female identity is in effect a re-enactment of the treatment of female slaves, who were penetrated not because they were valued objects for the creation of progeny, but rather because they could produce additional objects to be used and exchanged. In the case of Clytie, the black woman becomes, for both Sutpen and Faulkner's narrators, merely an extension of the father. Metaphorically, denial of the black female voice is a form of self-aggrandizing violence. In this sense, *The Bluest Eye* can be seen as a commentary on Faulkner's suppression of the voices of Clytie and Dilsey as a means of validating his patriarchal form.

But such suppression is itself a kind of evasion. Thomas Sutpen's very effort to build a self-contained world is itself a reflection of his childhood experience of being turned away from the front door of a plantation house. His own patriarchal construct is a way of being what that wealthy white man was. His marking and refusal to mark his daughters are ways of escaping the meaning of the scars of his own life. The crucial difference between the white father and his daughters is that the very nature of the system grants some validity to the father's pretense of authority but none at all to that of the daughters. The black father, himself marked as outlaw, lacks even the pretense of authorizing power, and his daughter can exist only as negation. Thus, in each case, the daughter serves as a vehicle for expressing the true condition of the father.

Each writer in some sense recognizes this situation. But Faulkner, as the authoring father, assumes that the marks made by the father's refusal to allow anyone except himself to define his daughters are themselves marks that cannot be read. They are an inscrutable hieroglyphic. He refuses to understand those marks as scars and, for this reason, refuses to see them as a text to be narrated. Because he finds no meaningful text, daughters do not require voices to tell the stories of suffering. Morrison, despite her denials, is a daughter literarily defined in some sense by the script of Faulkner, who then seeks to write her own text. She rejects his naming of her (and all black women) as a cipher and turns that naming into a narrative of scarring and voicelessness. The patriarchal presumption of his literary marking must be called by its right name: violence. The marks on the black daughters are for her the most important of all texts.

Notes

1. The work of Minrose Gwin and Diane Roberts is changing this pattern, but though both discuss Clytie extensively, they pay little attention to her status as daughter. See also Davis ("Yoking").

2. If critics have largely ignored the daughters in Faulkner, they have given much of their attention to them in Morrison. See comments on *The Bluest Eye* in Alwes, Byerman (*Fingering*), Kuenz, Pettis, and Sargent.

10. Reading for the "Other Side"

Beloved and *Requiem for a Nun*

Doreen Fowler

At the Faulkner and Yoknapatawpha conference in 1985, Toni Morrison spoke of Faulkner's peculiar and striking gaze: "He had a gaze that was different. It appeared, at that time, to be similar to a look, even a sort of staring, a refusal-to-look-away approach in his writing that I found admirable" ("Faulkner and Women" 297). What is remarkable about Morrison's description of Faulkner is that, consciously or unconsciously, she uses this same image, a "refusal to look away," in the novel she was writing in 1985, *Beloved*. In her novel, the image is used to describe the heroine, Sethe. Sethe is "[t]he one who never looked away": "when a man got stomped to death by a mare right in front of Sawyer's restaurant did not look away; and when a sow began eating her own litter did not look away then either" (12). Startlingly, Morrison endows her character with a quality she finds in Faulkner, drawing together the great-grandson of a white Mississippi slaveholder and Confederate colonel and her own black character, an ex-slave, a character who is arguably a persona for Morrison herself. Both, according to Morrison, share the artist's unflinching determination to see and know what is, no matter how terrible. Both explore the terrain of nightmares, the terrain of the unconscious.

One horror from which both Morrison and Faulkner refuse to recoil is infanticide. In both Morrison's *Beloved* and Faulkner's *Requiem for a Nun*, a mother or mother-surrogate kills an infant, not out of hate, but out of love. In both novels, the murderer-mother is black; in both novels, the infanticide is the central crisis which the novel ceaselessly investigates, casting forward and back for answers, seeking to see and know.

Both *Beloved* and *Requiem for a Nun* read like whirlpools, which circle furiously around a seemingly insane act. In *Requiem*, Temple and Gowan, the bereaved parents, repeatedly describe Nancy Mannigoe's murder of their child as the act of "a nigger dopefiend whore" (119). Thus the murder is represented as the aberration of a deranged mind. Similarly, in *Beloved* Paul D initially describes Sethe's attempt to take her children's lives as an act of barbarism. When he says to her, "You got two feet, Sethe, not four" (165), he casts Sethe as a brute, a creature less than human. In both novels, the slaughter of the innocents, the primal scene of the novels, defies interpretation. In *Requiem* the murder is not dramatically rendered; rather, as in Greek tragedy, the violence occurs off stage. We never see Nancy Mannigoe smother Temple's child; we only hear Temple screaming as she finds her dead infant. Thereafter, Nancy speaks rarely and in monosyllables—language is not her medium—while the voluble Gavin Stevens and Temple endlessly and futilely seek answers. In *Beloved* the carnage in the shed is first seen from the point of view of the white horsemen who have come to take Sethe and her children back to a life of slavery. As Arnold Weinstein writes, "For the whites this scene is unreadable" (274). Schoolteacher's nephew, the one who held her down while the other nephew took her milk, trembles at the sight, without knowing that he is trembling, and he repeats the question that resonates throughout both Morrison's and Faulkner's novels: "What she go and do that for? On account of a beating? Hell, he'd been beat a million times and he was white . . . But no beating ever made him . . . I mean no way he could have . . . What she go and do that for?" (150). The nephew's ellipses are instructive. He cannot say what Sethe has done. Her act is unspeakable, unrepresentable. No more than the nephew can, can either Faulkner or Morrison represent this scene because language, the act of representation, is the product of the symbolic order, and this is an act of another order, an order that precedes symbolic language. Inside the dark shed, the white horsemen are returned to a realm before language and culture, and thus the sheriff, standing in the cool dark beside the bleeding children and the woman who looked like she had no eyes "since the whites in them had disappeared" (150) feels a tremendous desire "to run into the August sunlight" (151). The sheriff longs to be "outside of that place" (151) because within the shed he has stumbled across another place, a place that Sethe refers to as "over there," "through the veil" (163), the dark, buried side, on the other side of consciousness, reason, logic and Law of the Father. Inside the dark shed, the sheriff is returned to a former register of being, the uncharted terrain of the presymbolic, what Lacan calls the imaginary.

The power of the mother is well illustrated by an anecdote in *Beloved* about a rooster. The mean cock, Mister, who whips "everything in the yard" (72), who sports a bright red, oversized comb, and who loves to sit on the tub "like a throne" (72), is a caricature of the ruling male. But, as we learn from Paul D, in the beginning, this representative of male power, like every living creature, was helpless. In Mister's case, the mother hen walked away with her hatched chicks trailing her and left behind one unhatched egg. Neglected by his mother, Mister, the proud cock, would never have been. Had it not been for Paul D, who tapped open the shell, the chick who became Mister would have died before he was born. This anecdote about a cock can be read as a parable about maternal power; it drives home the message that the mother, along with the father, creates and nurtures life. Possibly for this reason, because patriarchal power is threatened by mother-power, in both *Beloved* and *Requiem* motherhood is ceaselessly under attack.

In an early review of *Beloved* Margaret Atwood was among the first to note that Morrison's novel exposes slavery in America as "one of the most viciously antifamily institutions human beings have ever devised" (49). Slavery is indeed anti-family, as Atwood notes, but, above all, slavery is anti-maternal. Slavery, as Morrison realizes it in *Beloved*, institutionalizes the repression of mother-power. The plantation system of the old South deified the power of the master at the expense of the power of the other. Every man, woman, and child on the plantation was ruled by the master, but the slave woman had no rights, nothing: neither her body nor her children were her own. The children she made out of her body belonged to the master to use as he chose. Thus Baby Suggs's first two children are sold before they have their adult teeth, and Baby Suggs only *hears* about their leaving after they are gone: she is not permitted to so much as wave goodbye to them. Seven of Baby Suggs's eight children are taken from her; thereafter, she lives for the last, for Halle, until he too disappears, and schoolteacher enters her yard to take her grandchildren. This theft, and the "rough choice" (180) that Sethe makes in reaction to it, break Baby Suggs's great spirit; she cannot bear that her children are "checkers" in the game of patriarchy: "What she called the nastiness of life was the shock she received upon learning that nobody stopped playing checkers just because the pieces included her children" (23).

Slavery seeks to vitiate the power of the mother. Perhaps nowhere in *Beloved* is this attempt to render the mother powerless more palpably realized than when schoolteacher's nephews take Sethe's milk. One holds her down while the other "suck[s]" (70) her milk from her breasts. Of all the violations Sethe experiences this is the one she repeatedly remarks. And rightly so, for this is a violation of the mother-child bond. The nephews take the milk that belongs to Sethe's child. More, the mother's milk is the outward sign of her life-giving and life-sustaining power, and, when the nephews steal the milk, they sign their desire to divest the mother of her power.

Faulkner's *Requiem for a Nun* takes place almost a hundred years after the abolition of slavery, but a male desire to disempower the mother lives on. In *Requiem* as in *Beloved* the mother-child bond is under attack. Like Baby Suggs, whose children are taken from her, Nancy Mannigoe, a former prostitute, also has been robbed of a child. In the final scene of the dramatic section of *Requiem* we learn of another murdered child, Nancy's child, who was murdered in her womb by a man who may have been the child's father. When Nancy was six months pregnant, a man kicked her in the stomach and killed her unborn child. This brutal act, like the robbing of Sethe's milk in *Beloved*, is a violent attack upon maternal power: its purpose is to destroy maternity, to violate the womb.

This same desire to violate the primal uterus also figures importantly in the novel to which *Requiem for a Nun* is sequel, *Sanctuary*. Indeed the central act of Faulkner's 1931 novel is the violation of Temple Drake's vagina, the gateway to the uterus. Popeye, an impotent thug, rapes Temple with a corncob, an act which speaks his desire both to despoil and to possess the secret dark inner reaches of woman. In fact, it could be argued that the title, *Sanctuary*, is an allusion to Temple's ravaged vagina, for a sanctuary is the holy place within a temple.

Beginning with its title, then, *Sanctuary*, the novel that moved Faulkner to write *Requiem* as sequel,[1] is about female violation. *Sanctuary* documents a patriarchal culture obsessed with a need to assert dominance, particularly dominance over women. Proof of male ascendancy is female subordination; and female subordination is evident everywhere in *Sanctuary*. For example, when Ruby's father shoots her lover, he asserts himself as the dominant male, but he is not satisfied with only killing his rival, he wants to disempower Ruby as well, and his words voice this desire: "Get down there and sup your dirt, you whore" (58), he says to her. And when Ruby attempts to keep Lee Goodwin away from Temple, Goodwin uses the occasion to instruct Ruby in her subordinate status as a woman: "He slapped her again, first on one cheek, then the other, rocking her head from side to side. 'That's what I do to them,' he said, slapping her. 'See?' He released her. She stumbled backward against the table and caught up the child and half crouched between the table and the wall, watching him as he turned and left the room" (95).

I have examined in some detail the indignities suffered by women at the hands of men in both *Sanctuary* and its sequel, *Requiem*, to establish that, although institutionalized slavery no longer existed in America in the 1930s and 1940s, women were and are still victims of the same drive for power that produced slavery. Sethe's and Nancy's acts of infanticide need to be read in the context of a patriarchal culture that seeks to make women abject. Pressed by this culture, Nancy and Sethe are driven to a last desperate alternative. Both women choose death for the child over life in a life-destructive patriarchal culture.

In *Beloved*, Morrison palpably evokes the dehumanized existence under slavery that Sethe repudiates for her child at any cost, even the cost of the child's life; and Sethe graphically describes the fate from which she saves her child: "That anybody white could take your whole self for anything that came to mind. Not just work, kill or maim you, but dirty you. Dirty you so bad you couldn't like yourself anymore. Dirty you so bad you forgot who you were and couldn't think it up. And though she and others lived through and got over it, she could never let it happen to her own. The best thing she was, was her children. Whites might dirty *her* all right, but not her best thing, her beautiful, magical best thing—the part of her that was clean" (251). Sethe will see her children dead before she will allow them to be dirtied in this way. As Sethe explains to Paul D, life "under schoolteacher" is "out" (163); that is, it is unthinkable and intolerable.

Like Sethe, Nancy also professes to be protecting the child she kills. *Requiem for a Nun* dramatizes Nancy's attempt to prevent Temple from leaving her husband to run away with Pete, the brother of Red of *Sanctuary*. Nancy's concern is for Temple's "two little children" (185), she says. As Nancy puts it, Temple is abandoning her children: "You gave up. You gave up the child too. Willing to risk never seeing him again maybe" (185). Running away, Temple intends to leave one child, Bucky, behind with her husband, who doubts that he is Bucky's father. The other child, a six-month-old infant, she will take with her and her lover. As Nancy sees it, Temple is sacrificing her children, surrendering them to the control of menacing patriarchal figures, who will, to apply Baby Suggs's analogy, use the children as checkers in the game of patriarchy. In Nancy's words, Temple is willing to "leave one with a man that's willing to believe the child aint got no father, willing to take the other one to a man that dont even want no children" (189–90). Ultimately, what drives Nancy to her last desperate act is Temple's admission that she is leaving, "[c]hildren or no children" (190). In effect, Temple is abdicating her role as mother.

Arguably, then, both women are acting to prevent a child from being turned over to ruthless and punishing father-figures. However, an important distinction between Faulkner's and Morrison's novels should be noted here. In *Beloved*, the threat that the substitute-father poses to the child is graphically illustrated.

Schoolteacher is fully rendered as an inhuman monster. Sethe refuses to turn over her children to the man who decrees that Sixo should be burned, that Paul A should be hanged and mutilated, and that Paul D should be bridled like a horse. In *Requiem*, on the other hand, the danger that Pete represents to Temple's children is not palpably rendered. While Pete is certainly an unsavory character—he is identified as an underworld figure whose original intention was to blackmail Temple with her letters to his brother—he is distanced in Faulkner's dramatic format. Interestingly, the threat to Temple's children from a particular masculinist culture that asserts ascendancy by degrading the female other needs to be inferred from Faulkner's earlier portrayal of that culture in two closely related works, *Sanctuary* and "That Evening Sun" (1931). The latter work locates Nancy Mannigoe within a racist, sexist culture that seems intent on destroying her.[2] Reduced to prostitution, Nancy becomes pregnant, and her husband threatens to kill her. Her "customer" does not pay her, and, when she publicly exposes him, he knocks her down in the street and kicks her in the mouth to silence her. Nancy is then jailed, where she unsuccessfully attempts to hang herself, and the jailer who cuts her down beats her. I invoke this litany of victimizations from Faulkner's story because, it seems to me, we need to read Nancy's terrible act within a context of the life-repressive culture that Faulkner evokes powerfully in a group of textually related works.

At this juncture I propose to explore the central paradox of both novels—that both women kill a child to protect the child—by introducing Lacan's theory of the development of subjectivity. Seemingly contrary to all reason and logic, both novels assert that Nancy and Sethe were not violating the mother-child bond when they killed a child but rather, in fact, were safeguarding it. Sethe, for example, insists that she did what was necessary to keep her child safe: "I took and put my babies where they'd be safe" (164). And in *Requiem* Gavin Stevens explains that a desire to keep children safe motivated Nancy: "Nancy is going to die tomorrow morning to postulate: that little children, as long as they are little children, shall be intact, unanguished, untorn, unterrified" (211).

This paradox can be read in terms of the central paradox of Lacan's psycho-analytic narrative of identity. According to Lacan, a register of being precedes the world of language and culture. In the beginning, in Lacan's narrative of subjectivity, a child exists in an imaginary dyadic unity with mother. At this early phase of development there are only two, the child and the mother, and the two are one. The child perceives no boundaries and no difference. There is no gender and no identity as we understand identity. The child exists as part of one continuous totality of being, an unbroken mother-child circuit. This original condition of existence identified with the maternal body precedes conscious existence; it also precedes alienation. For there to be individual identity and meaning, there has to be difference. Once we recognize difference we enter into what Lacan calls the symbolic order, the world of language and culture. In the symbolic, the lost mother is gradually replaced by the Law of the Father, a law that decrees our lack.

The central paradox of Lacan's reformulation of Freudian theory is that we gain individual identity and existence in the world of social relations only by virtue of alienation (Lacan's version of Freud's castration). In other words, ego formation is predicated upon lack, and the lacking subject is driven by a desire to restore a former wholeness. But, if we try to restore the lost object and re-fuse with the lost first other, we cease to exist in the world of social exchange. Thus the subject that arises from primary repression is driven by conflicting drives toward ego identity in the register of symbolic (cultural) meanings and toward a loss of subjectivity in the imaginary. In the normal subject the desire for an imaginary totality of being is repressed in obedience to the paternal injunction and the demands of the social order.

Viewed from the perspective of logic, reason, and culturally designated meanings, Sethe's and Nancy's slaughter of the innocents can only be described as acts of barbarism. But psychoanalytic theory provides another perspective, a perspective that is the other of language and logic. Reduced to its essence, Lacan's narrative is about a substitution: an imaginary unity associated with the mother is excluded as the child takes his/her place in a social order defined by alienation and ruled by the Law of Father. Both *Beloved* and *Requiem* can be read in terms of this central Lacanian paradigm. In both novels, mothers are about to be displaced by father-figures, but in these particular historical instances the culture that the child is about to enter is so death-dealing that these women refuse to allow the normal displacement and substitution. Sethe refuses to let her children "live under schoolteacher" (163), and Nancy refuses to let Temple turn over her children to fathers who will use and abuse them. Both choose what they see as the only other option.

Sethe's and Nancy's choice is shocking, unlawful, unreasonable. And Morrison's novel focuses on Sethe's life-long desire to atone, to give back to her child life in the social order. Similarly, in *Requiem* Nancy accepts that she must pay for the death of Temple's child with her own life. At the same time, however, both Sethe and Nancy show signs of a contrary feeling, a feeling that they have not ended a child's life, but rather that the children have been removed from one place and translated into another "where no one could hurt them" (*Beloved* 163). In *Beloved* Morrison appears to realize this place, an unmediated mother-child relation, in the interior monologues. Arnold Weinstein calls these monologues "the ultimate female discourse, the voice of linked women, the gynecocracy that no man can enter" (285), and, locked in this relation, Sethe assures Beloved that "[t]hey can't hurt us no more" (*Beloved* 215). That Beloved does return in the novel, first as a baby ghost, then as a young woman, seems to prove Sethe's contention that her child is indeed "on the other side" (200). Similarly in *Requiem* the possibility of a recovery and return of the lost child is evoked. Nancy, who is sentenced to die for the murder of Temple's child, says she doesn't "know" (280)—cognition is a function of the symbolic order—but she "believes" (280) that she will be reunited with the child she killed and with "the other one" (280), the one she lost when a man, possibly the father of her child, kicked her in the stomach.

Lacan can help us to read this "other side," "through the veil" (*Beloved* 163). The "other side," I propose, is an allusion to the imaginary plane that, according to psychoanalytic theory, precedes conscious existence in the world. James M. Mellard, a Lacanian commentator, writes that the drive "toward love and the imaginary" is always "toward loss of subjectivity," for "the ego loses itself in the loved one" (32). Seen this way, Sethe and Nancy are not choosing death so much as they are choosing the imaginary, the other of the world of language and cultural meanings (which is inseparable from death). Sethe signals her choice of the imaginary for herself and her child by spinning as she attempts to explain to Paul D why she attempted to slaughter her children. She spins because what she is trying to say cannot be put into words: "she could never close in, pin it down for anybody who had to ask. If they didn't get it right off—she could never explain" (163). Words are the medium of the symbolic order, and Sethe's act is of another order, the imaginary. The imaginary precedes the entry into language; it is the realm of the body, and so Sethe uses her body to communicate her meaning: "She was spinning. Round and round the room . . . turning like a slow but steady wheel . . . the wheel never stopped" (159). With her spinning Sethe images a totality of being, a presymbolic wholeness. Her continuous circular motion points to the imaginary, a sealed mother-child circuit, and it points to Sethe, the mother, as an avatar of that original imaginary mother-child relation.

The specter of the preoedipal mother, that is, the mother of the presymbolic relation, casts a long shadow over *Beloved*. For example, when Sethe instinctively gathers up her children and takes them to the woodshed intent on keeping them from schoolteacher, she assumes the aspect of the preoedipal or phallic mother. The mother of this early phase is also called the phallic mother because in the imaginary there is only the mother-child dyad and it subsumes all. The preoedipal mother, Jane Gallop explains, is "the whole" (22). In Greek myth, the inclusive nature of the preoedipal mother is represented by the figure of the Medusa, a female creature whose hair is a mass of writhing snakes. The long snakes, a phallic image on a female creature, designate the union of the opposites, male and female, and the collapse of difference in the imaginary.[3] In *Beloved*, Sethe becomes yet another avatar of the phallic mother of myth when she thwarts schoolteacher. In Lacanian terms, when schoolteacher arrives to assert his ownership of the slaves, he is reenacting the primal rupture, the splitting of the mother-child dyad and the entry into the symbolic order and the rule of the Law of the Father. Read this way, when Sethe foils schoolteacher—"I stopped him" (164), she says—symbolically she is preventing this disruption of the mother-child relation. In other words, she is asserting the primacy of the imaginary, and, in the act of this assertion, she takes on the aspect of the mythic representation of the phallic mother, the Medusa. At this pivotal moment, Sethe pictures herself with a swarm of tiny birds in her hair: "little hummingbirds stuck their needle beaks right through her headcloth into her hair and beat their wings" (163). The hummingbird beaks sticking into Sethe's hair are a phallic image, analogous to the Medusa's snaky hair.

In Faulkner's novel, Nancy, like Sethe, seems to represent the preoedipal mother. But Faulkner's portrayal of this figure differs markedly from Morrison's. In *Beloved*, Sethe's interiority is explored in cryptic, linked interior monologues that seem to attempt to render the not-language of the preoedipal phase, what Kristeva calls the semiotic; in contrast, in *Requiem for a Nun*, Nancy is always seen from the point of view of Temple, who is mystified, and Stevens, who is pointedly referred to as "Lawyer Stevens" (265), as if to underscore his alignment with the Law of the Father. Seen from such a vantage point, Nancy appears inscrutable, and, in the stage directions, she is described as almost sphinx-like: Nancy "doesn't move, stir, not looking at anything apparently, her face still, bemused, expressionless" (278). Above all, Nancy is characterized as an other-worldly figure. On the eve of the day Nancy is to be executed for the murder of Temple's child, Temple and Stevens go to the governor to plead for Nancy's life. But Nancy is through with "hoping" (272). She accepts, even embraces her death. She explains that she severed her connection with the world of courts and law and governors on the night of the murder: "I finished all that a long time back, that same day in the judge's court. No: before that even: in the nursery that night, before I even lifted my hand" (273). Like Sethe, who intended to die with her children and yearned to crawl into the grave beside her dead infant, but stopped herself because her living children needed her, Nancy too always intends to die with the child she killed. Nancy's act, like Sethe's, should be read not as murder but as a joint suicide or *liebestod*, a dying of the ego into the other.[4]

Such a reading would account for Faulkner's title. When directly asked to identify the nun of the title, Faulkner responded, "The nun was Nancy" (*Faulkner in the University* 196), and when asked to explain this curious characterization of Nancy, the child-murderer, as "nun," Faulkner said: " . . . she was just doomed and damned by circumstance to [a life of prostitution]. And despite that, she was capable within her poor dim lights and reasons of an act which whether it was right or wrong was of complete almost religious abnegation of the world for the sake of an innocent child. That was—it was paradoxical, the use of the word *Nun* for her, but I—but to me that added something to her tragedy" (196). Faulkner's use of the word "nun" for Nancy, which he acknowledges is "paradoxical," but "added something to her tragedy," can be read as an unconscious allusion to the presymbolic register. Forbidden, unconscious meanings always return, Freud theorized, but they return disguised so as to avoid conscious censors. Faulkner's identification of Nancy as a "nun," I propose, represents such a disguised return of a refused meaning. A nun is a woman who withdraws from the world of men and social exchange into a community of women. Read for its hidden meaning, the word "nun" may point to Nancy's renunciation of the symbolic order, the world of cultural meaning, in favor of the first community—or communion—of women, the realm of the imaginary, before the appearance of the father.

In Lacan's narrative of identity formation, there is one pivotal moment, the oedipal moment. In that moment, a representative of the paternal metaphor that decrees separation appears, and, under the threat of (always symbolic) castration, the child submits to alienation and becomes a lacking subject in the order of social exchange. Although in both *Requiem* and *Beloved* one reenactment of the moment of crisis stands out—when Sethe and Nancy block the normal transition into the symbolic sphere—in both novels this critical moment is repeatedly reenacted, and each of these repetitions questions and revises Sethe's and Nancy's choice of a return to the imaginary plane. In *Requiem*, for example, the moment of ego formation is symbolically replayed as *Requiem* ends with an affirmation of ego identity in the world of social relations. While Nancy chooses to cease to exist as an "I," Temple elects subjectivity and cultural meanings. *Requiem* ends with the word "Coming," Temple's response to her husband's call. As husband to Temple and father to her children, Gowan Stevens is a representative of the paternal metaphor that ushers the subject into an order characterized by symbolization. His call reenacts the moment of the appearance of the father become Father and the summons to pass beyond the first preverbal stage; and Temple's answer, "Coming," signifies her willingness to take her place in the social order.

Like *Requiem*, *Beloved* also ends with a scene that symbolically reenacts an acceptance of the symbolic order. And before that ultimate submission, the moment of acquiescence to the Law of the Father is repeatedly replayed in *Beloved*. For example, when, at the age of 13, Sethe's sons, Howard and Buglar, who know that their mother just "missed killing" (205) them, flee their mother and go to war, symbolically they reenact the moment of separation, the passage from an imaginary unity identified with the mother to identity in the world of social meanings. Denver describes their feelings: "they rather be around killing men than killing women" (205). And while she loves her mother, Denver, who dreams recurrently that her mother cuts off her head, also fears the specter of the mother that engulfs the child. Denver fears "this thing that happened that made it all right for my mother to kill my sister" (205). From this specter of the mother of the preoedipal phase, Denver expects to be delivered by her father. She secretly harbors the belief that her "daddy was coming for [her]" (207). Denver's obsession with her father speaks her desire for the Law of the Father or paternal metaphor that marks the subject's entry into the world of ego identity and social relations.

In *Beloved*, this all important moment, the constitution of subjectivity and meaning, is restaged again at the novel's conclusion when another agent of the paternal metaphor enters Sethe's yard intent on taking Denver away with him. Like schoolteacher before him, the man wears a black wide-brimmed hat and sits on a horse. The man is of course the abolitionist, Mr. Bodwin, who comes to take Denver to her new job in his home. While Mr. Bodwin poses no threat to Denver, nevertheless, symbolically his coming recreates the oedipal passage. Denver, who had previously lived in a locked relation with her mother, is now about to enter the world of social relations, ushered by a paternal figure. In Sethe's eyes, Bodwin's coming reenacts schoolteacher's: "He is coming into her yard," she thinks, "and he is coming for her best thing" (261). And once again, Sethe attempts to prevent the disruption of the mother-child dyad and assumes the aspect of the Medusa, the mythic representation of the mother before the rise of gender difference: "Little hummingbirds stick their needle beaks right through her headcloth into her hair" (262).

In this moment, the novel revisits its primal scene, the slaughter of Beloved, and, in this reprise, Sethe does not raise her hand against her child. Instead she attacks the representative of the Law of the Father, the Law that decrees difference; and she is stopped by a community of women, the very women whose voices, she recalls, back in the days of the Clearing, "would search for the right combination, the key, the code, the sound that broke the back of words" (261). Morrison seems to allude here to what Julia Kristeva calls the semiotic, the other of speech, the mother-child communication that precedes symbolization. "In the beginning," Morrison writes, "there were no words. In the beginning was the sound" (259). This community of singing women that come to Sethe's door appears to represent the presymbolic order; yet this community prevents her from killing the agent of the paternal metaphor; it accedes to the primary repression that constitutes subjectivity.

The critical moment, the moment of primary repression, is staged yet again in the final pages of the novel. After Denver has successfully entered the sphere of human relations and Beloved has disappeared, Sethe seems to yield once again to the pull toward the disintegration of the "I." Like Baby Suggs before her, who "quit" (177) the world and lay down in her bed and died, Sethe now lies in Baby Suggs's bed, humming lullabies. Finding Sethe in bed, Paul D sees a representation of the mother who subsumes all binary oppositions: "Her hair, like the dark delicate roots of good plants, spreads and curls on the pillow" (271). This spreading, curling hair can be read as another allusion to the Medusa's snaky hair, a symbol for the loss of difference on the imaginary plane. The image heralds Sethe's choice to return, to resume a fused existence in the world. Once again Sethe is choosing death over life, meaninglessness over cultural meanings.

From this dissolution of the "I," Sethe is called back by a father-figure, Paul D, who, when he moves in with Sethe and Denver, takes the place abdicated by Halle. In the final scene of the novel, Paul D asserts the paternal interdiction against a return to a former preconscious fusion. At first, he is "so angry he could kill her" (272), but, then, controlling himself, he recalls Sethe to ego identity: "You your best thing, Sethe. You are" (273), he tells her. And Morrison's novel, which has swung back and forth between the imaginary and the symbolic, between dissolution and affirmation of the separate self, concludes with a tentative, questioning assertion of the "I" separate from the other. The novel ends with Sethe posing the riddle of identity: "Me? Me?" (273).

In both *Beloved* and *Requiem for a Nun*, then, a desire for ego subjectivity in the register of the symbolic competes with a conflicting desire to ravel out in the imaginary. That the presymbolic vies with the symbolic in both novels also seems to be supported by Morrison's and Faulkner's refusal to judge the act of infanticide. Morrison writes that Beloved's death at her mother's hand is "not a story to pass on" (274);[5] similarly, Faulkner also refuses to judge, or "pass on," Nancy's act when, astonishingly, he refers to infanticide with the nonjudgmental phrase, "whether it was right or wrong" (*Faulkner in the University* 196). This refusal to take a stand on an act that, by every rational standard, is so obviously horrific points to another register of being outside of the order we inhabit as social beings. Certainly, in both novels, the social order, as epitomized by the legal system, immediately condemns both Nancy and Sethe. Sethe goes to prison for years, and Nancy is summarily tried, found guilty, and executed. Critics of both novels also have compellingly argued the heinous nature of infanticide.[6] And, from the standpoint of logic, reason, and culturally designated meanings, these critics are inarguably right. But another perspective, a perspective that is the other of language and logic, also infuses both novels.

Notes

1. See, for example, *Faulkner in the University* 96.

2. When asked if there was a connection between Nancy of "That Evening Sun" and Nancy of *Requiem for a Nun*, Faulkner answered, "She is the same person, actually." Faulkner then went on to dismiss the obvious problem that "That Evening Sun" seems to take place nearly forty years earlier than *Requiem*: "These people I figure belong to me and I have the right to move them about when I need them" (*Faulkner in the University* 79).

3. See, for example, Freud's essay "Medusa's Head" (18: 273–74).

4. In *Doubling and Incest/Repetition and Revenge*, John T. Irwin discusses at length the notion of *liebestod*, or love-death, in both *The Sound and the Fury* and *Absalom, Absalom!* (32–47).

5. Morrison's rich phrase is of course open to other interpretations. Alternatively, Morrison's sentence, "It was not a story to pass on" (274) can be interpreted to mean it is not a story to repeat to others; that is, the phrase argues for silence, forgetting, and repression in direct contrast to the represencing of the repressed that takes place in *Beloved*. This construction of Morrison's words is also consistent with my psychoanalytic reading of the novel. For readings of Morrison's expression, see Heinze 181, Arnold Weinstein 267–69, Mobley 196–97.

6. See, for example, Otten 82 and Polk x–xii, 8–11, 61–64, and 194–212.

11. History and Story, Sign and Design

Faulknerian and Postmodern Voices in *Jazz*

Roberta Rubenstein

Throughout their fiction, both Toni Morrison and William Faulkner explore the shifting and unstable relations between *history* and *story*. For Faulkner, the lost, fragmented self is often the central story; in turn, that dislocated self both participates in and mirrors the social history of the South with its deeply rooted conflicts of race, caste, family, gender, and moral purpose. From a different perspective, Morrison also writes of lost, fragmented selves, engaging deeply with African-American experience as it converges with issues of race, caste (determined by skin shade as well as economic circumstance), family, gender, and moral purpose. Constructing the intersections between *history* and *story*, both writers employ a narrative strategy of "deliberately withheld meaning, of progressive and partial and delayed disclosure . . . [for the purpose of keeping] the form—and the idea—fluid and unfinished, still in motion . . . and unknown, until the dropping into place of the very last syllable" (Aiken 138).

Like Faulkner's fiction, Morrison's narratives—particularly her most recent ones—unfold through one or several voices for whom the "facts" are not only unverifiable but less important than the tellers' subjective filterings and interpretive reconstructions of them. In an observation about Faulkner's method that also describes Morrison's, Arthur Kinney proposes that "storytelling and rumor replace observation; judgment and memory displace witnessed knowledge. . . .

The final focus is never on source as it is never on fact, but is rather on the perception of fact or the alternative ways of seeing facts" (7–8).

In this essay, I focus on the ways in which Morrison's novel *Jazz* (1992) suggests Faulknerian correspondences in both structural and thematic dimensions. However, I also contend that Morrison, having assimilated narrative conventions from Faulkner, Woolf, and other modernists, improvises significantly beyond them. Read next to Faulkner's *Absalom, Absalom!* (1936), *Jazz* demonstrates Morrison's intertextual playfulness as she uniquely blends modernist and postmodernist narrative strategies. In both novels, the characters'—and the narrators'—absence of certainty is not only narrative method but a constitutive dimension of meaning. In place of a single authoritative version of events, "facts" and incidents are filtered through several interpreting consciousnesses who are both "outside" and "inside" the events they describe: *outside* because they describe people and circumstances remote from them in time and/or whom they may not know personally; *inside* because, through their imaginative engagement with the narratives they construct out of the stories they have heard, they enter into the psychological reality of their subjects.

Illustrative of the dual focus of Morrison's modernist/postmodernist narrative strategy, the narrating voice of *Jazz*, observing details of the enigmatic "City" in which the narrative is set (never named but understood as Harlem), records a series of "secret messages disguised as public signs": "this way, open here, danger to let colored only single men on sale woman wanted private room stop dog on premises absolutely no money down fresh chicken free delivery fast" (64). The passage may be read not only as an echo of modernist "stream-of-consciousness" but also as exaggerated, self-conscious mimicry—that is, as parody—of that style. The series of signs thus also points to an alternative *mode* of interpretation. According to Linda Hutcheon, in postmodernist fiction, parody functions as an "intertextual mode that is paradoxically an authorized transgression, for its ironic difference is set at the very heart of similarity" (66). Moreover, postmodernism is itself a "contradictory phenomenon, one that uses and abuses, installs and then subverts, the very concepts it challenges . . ." (3).[1] In *Jazz*, "signs" and "trails" figure centrally and also equivocally: both as literal markers and as hints to the reader to heed the fictional assumptions that the text subverts. In particular, several words in the passage quoted above—*this way*, *danger*, and *woman wanted*—function as signs in this dual sense.

As the most "postmodern" of Morrison's and Faulkner's narratives respectively, both *Jazz* and *Absalom, Absalom!* explicitly call attention to their own signs and designs, intentionally resisting a single or unified story or "true" version upon which all of the speculative or incomplete narratives ultimately converge. In *Absalom, Absalom!*, the omniscient narrator is minimally present; the four principal first-person narrators—Quentin Compson and his Harvard roommate Shreve McCannon, Mr. Compson (Quentin's father), and Miss Rosa Coldfield—struggle to articulate and reconcile their understandings of the legendary Thomas Sutpen and his progeny as well as the consequences of his flawed "design." Retellings of events both known and surmised are filtered through the limits and biases of each narrator's perspective, including his or her degree of knowledge and emotional comprehension as well as the relative distance in time between Sutpen's era and the present narrative time of 1909–1910. As Olga Vickery phrases it, each of the novel's narrators, "in accordance with his own experience and bias, . . . works the available facts into what is essentially an aesthetic form" (87).

Jazz also unfolds through multiple narrators: a limited omniscient first-person narrator guides us through the stories of half a dozen major characters—Joe and Violet Trace, Dorcas and Alice Manfred, Golden Gray, and Felice—each of whom speaks partially in his or her own voice and partially through the principal narrator's renderings of their thoughts and actions. Though with the exception of Golden Gray, these voices speak from the same geographical location (the City), their stories, like those of Faulkner's narrators, encompass several periods that precede the present narrative time of 1926. Thus, Morrison adapts to her own purposes the Faulknerian narrative method of telling overlapping but discontinuous stories and of disclosing incrementally her characters' social and emotional histories over time. Both novels employ an oral/aural dimension of narrative to express the centrality of the speaking subject as both mediator and constitutor of the stories and their meanings. Phrased another way, for the characters and (particularly in *Jazz*) for the narrator who presides over their stories, the articulation of their histories is revealed as a *process*; structurally, both *Absalom, Absalom!* and *Jazz* are composed of clusters of stories that are suggestively but inconclusively connected.

On several occasions, Morrison has expressed her view that the closest analogy for this narrative method, developed over the course of her six novels to date, is the improvisational structure of jazz.[2] The musical form originated by African-Americans in the early part of the century functions both structurally and thematically in the novel to which it gives the title, becoming a multi-faceted trope for the social, intellectual, emotional, and sexual turmoil—the up-beat and downbeat—of an entire generation of African-Americans.[3] After *Jazz* was published, Morrison made explicit the analogies she had endeavored to create between the musical form and the narrative structure and voice of the novel:

> Nobody agrees on anything about jazz . . . but everybody thinks they
> know all about it. . . .
> So, when I was thinking who was going to tell this story, the idea of
> 'who owns jazz,' or who knows about it, came up. . . . I decided that the
> voice would be one of assumed knowledge, the voice that says 'I know
> everything.' . . . Because the voice has to actually imagine the story it's
> telling . . . if it's really involved in the process of telling the story and letting
> the other voices speak, the story . . . turns out to be entirely different from
> what it predicted because the characters will be evolving. . . .
> It reminded me of a jazz performance. . . . Somebody takes off from a
> basic pattern, then the others have to accommodate themselves. . . .
> I was trying to align myself with more interesting and intricate aspects
> of my notion of jazz as a demanding, improvisatory art form, so I had to
> get rid of the conventions. . . . (Interview with Angels Carabi 41–2)

In an analysis of the intersections of race and culture in America, Cornel West
suggests a metaphorical meaning of jazz that captures the sense of Morrison's
expressed narrative stance as well as of the unique narrative voice of *Jazz*. He
regards jazz "not so much as a term for a musical art form, as for a mode of being
in the world, an improvisational mode of protean, fluid, and flexible dispositions
toward reality suspicious of 'either/or' viewpoints, dogmatic pronouncements,
or supremacist ideologies" (150).

One of the first literary conventions Morrison discards in order to "align" her
narrative structure with the improvisatory form of jazz is that of the particularized identity of the narrator: the narrating voice of *Jazz* is intentionally "without
sex, gender, or age" (Interview with Angels Carabi 41). In this discussion I will
refer to the anonymous narrating presence as Morrison does, as the "voice."[4]
The enigma of the narrator's identity converges with a different kind of mystery
within the overlapping stories that constitute the narrative. In *Jazz*, as in
Absalom, Absalom!, several narrators attempt to understand and articulate the
meaning of inexplicable tragic events: why did Joe Trace kill Dorcas Manfred,
whom he loved? Why did Henry Sutpen kill Charles Bon, whom he loved? In the
endeavor to resolve these mysteries, each narrator weaves reported or witnessed
events and "facts" together with his or her own speculations, conjectures, and
imaginative constructions.

In *Absalom, Absalom!*, virtually every page of Mr. Compson's narrative is
punctuated with such speculative phrases as "I think," "I believe," "I suppose,"
"I can imagine," "perhaps," "probably," and other qualifiers that reinforce the
conjectural dimension of his narrative. Combining what he knows and what
he thinks he understands about the enigmatic falling-out between Thomas
Sutpen and his son Henry, Mr. Compson nonetheless reaches a narrative

impasse, concluding that his speculations and reconstructions are insufficient to resolve the mystery: "It's just incredible. It just does not explain" (80). In his puzzlement, Mr. Compson also articulates the problematic relationship between the storyteller and the "facts" that derive from events but do not fully yield their meaning. In turn, Quentin Compson, reconsidering the perplexing elements of his father's narrative, speculates with his friend Shreve on details of the Sutpen story that remain open to conjecture because they can never be verified. Even the central matter of Charles Bon's relation to Sutpen remains indeterminate; there is no objective or "true" version of events. Thus, the four "voices" of *Absalom, Absalom!* form a chorus that comes to "know" more of the story of the Sutpens—but only because they collaboratively construct it as they presume to reconstruct it.

Like the several narrators of *Absalom, Absalom!*, the narrating voice of *Jazz* reminds us of the limits of its perspective, frequently qualifying its observations with such comments as "I can imagine," "I like to think," "I don't think," "I can't believe." However, more explicitly than any of Faulkner's narrators in *Absalom, Absalom!*, Morrison's central narrating voice insists upon its equivocal, postmodern relation to the stories it tells, cautioning us that the text we are reading is a succession of speculations that cannot be further verified or authenticated. Nonetheless, the voice advises us that, although it is "risky . . . trying to figure out anybody's state of mind," it is "worth the trouble if you're like me—curious, inventive and well-informed" (137).

Indeed, the narrating voice of *Jazz* paradoxically both observes (as if from inside) and invents (as if from outside) the "action" of the narrative: straddling modernist and postmodernist modes, it imagines/records what it purports to "know" or overhear, even as it authorizes its relation to the narrative to which it gives voice. While Faulkner's several narrators in *Absalom, Absalom!* freely speculate about details that elude verification, the principal narrative voice of *Jazz* explicitly concedes the limits of such speculation. As Morrison explains, "the voice realizes, after hearing other voices, that the narrative is not going to be at all what it predicted. The more it learns about the characters (and they are not what the voice thought), [the more] it has to go on, but it goes on with more knowledge" (Interview with Angels Carabi 42). The stories it tells may be understood not as imaginative *reconstructions* of fact, event, or motive, but as imaginative *constructions*. Admitting, for example, that it does not know much about the life of Violet Trace's grandmother, the voice comments, "it's not hard to imagine what it must have been like" (137). The narrator then proceeds to do precisely that: to imagine the story of True Belle, a black slave woman who was compelled to abandon her own children when she was pressed into service as surrogate mother for the illegitimate child of a planter's daughter.

That child, the most cryptic character of *Jazz*, is the son of a "whitegirl" (148), Vera Louise Gray, who never acknowledged her motherhood, and "a Negro boy out Vienna way" (141) who never knew of his paternity. Typical of white plantation owners in the antebellum South, Vera Louise's father, Colonel Wordsworth Gray—like Thomas Sutpen in *Absalom, Absalom!*—profligately impregnated his female slaves. Re-visiting from an African-American perspective the themes of miscegenation and incest so central to both writers, the narrator hints that Vera Louise's father might even be the father of her own black lover: "realizing the terrible thing that had happened to his daughter made [Colonel Gray] sweat, for there were seven mulatto children on his land" (141). His response to his daughter's pregnancy is to disown her.[5]

Vera Louise, rather than herself abandoning the "mortification" (148) produced by her interracial tryst, keeps the infant because of his exceptional golden skin and hair. She takes with her to Baltimore the so-called "orphaned baby" (139) and a slave mother to share in his care, heartlessly separating True Belle (Rose Dear's mother and later Violet Trace's grandmother) from her husband and two daughters to serve her own needs. Thus, typical of the family dislocations perpetuated by slavery, Rose Dear is separated from her mother at the age of eight.

When the pampered child, Golden Gray—whose first name and surname both encode his boundary-straddling origins—reaches the age of eighteen, he learns from the woman who "lied to him about practically everything including the question of whether she was his owner, his mother or a kindly neighbor" that his father was a "black-skinned nigger" (143). His search for that father, whom he sets out "to find, then kill, if he was lucky" (143), resonates intertextually (if not also ironically) with that of Charles Bon in *Absalom, Absalom!*. Both Bon and Golden Gray are effeminate, light-skinned mulattoes; each, illegitimate and defined by the radical absence of the father who rejected or deserted him, is haunted by the wish to be emotionally legitimized by that father.

Thomas Sutpen's refusal to acknowledge his mulatto son was, in Quentin and Shreve's account, the fatal error that ultimately brought down Sutpen's "design." In their construction of the story, Sutpen never acknowledged Charles Bon as his son because of his "little spot of negro blood" (247) through Sutpen's (also discarded) Haitian wife; his legitimate son, Henry, killed Charles Bon, not because of fear of incest—if his half-brother were to marry his sister Judith— but because of his greater fear of miscegenation. In *Jazz*, Morrison devises a kind of color negative of this tragic scenario: it is the *black* father who repudiates his light-skinned mulatto son (although the fatal gunshot is reserved for a different and later triangular relationship of love and revenge that links Joe Trace, his wife Violet, and his light-skinned lover, Dorcas). Golden Gray's putative father, disclaiming their relationship when they meet for the first time, declares that if the boy wants to claim his black parentage along with his manhood, he will have to surrender the privileges he has acquired by "passing" for white.

While the father's first name, Henry, alerts the reader to the ironic intertextual echoes of *Absalom, Absalom!*, his uncertain surname—"Lestory or LesTroy or something like that" (*Jazz* 148)—signals the narrative's deliberate fictionality: *le story*. Morrison, blending modernist narrative cues with postmodernist strategies that employ displaced or unreliable narrative voices, thus emphasizes the irreducible provisionality—the fictionality—of narrative knowledge. According to Linda Hutcheon, postmodern texts foreground "the challenging of certainty, the asking of questions, the revealing of fiction-making where we might have once accepted the existence of some absolute 'truth' . . ." (48). In *Jazz*, the narrator's understanding is not *prior to* but, rather, *subject to* the unfolding narrative events. Illustratively, at a crucial point in the story of Golden Gray, the presiding voice interrupts, inserting itself to emphasize both the story's artifice and the narrator's own unreliability: " 'What was I thinking of? How could I have imagined [Golden Gray] so poorly? Not noticed the hurt that was not linked to the color of his skin, or the blood that beat beneath it. But to some other thing that longed for authenticity. . . . I have been careless and stupid and it infuriates me to discover (again) how unreliable I am. . . . I have to alter things" (160–1).

Before the meeting between Golden Gray and Henry Lestory takes place, the boy describes his longing for his "phantom father" the way one might describe the uncanny experience of a phantom limb after amputation. The language is the narrative's most explicit representation of the "hurt that [is] not linked to the color of [one's] skin"—the "inside nothing" (37) that characterizes a child's experience of radical emotional absence: "Only now . . . that I know I have a father, do I feel his absence; the place where he should have been and was not. Before, I thought everybody was one-armed, like me. Now I feel the surgery. . . . I don't need the arm. But I do need to know what it could have been like to have had it" (158). In this passage, Morrison reprises an idea that appears throughout her fiction: the imagery of dismemberment as a trope for the incalculable damages inflicted on African-Americans by slavery and its devastating aftermath; remembering—"re-membering"—is understood as a compensatory act that might begin to heal the grievous personal and cultural dismemberments of that history.[6] The passage also resonates (perhaps coincidentally) with images of amputation in *Absalom, Absalom!*. Quentin's father, imagining Henry Sutpen's trip to New Orleans to try to discover the truth about Charles Bon, philosophizes on Henry's relationship with his half-brother as a story of love and its severance or loss: "who knows why a man, though suffering, clings, above all the other well members, to the arm or leg which he knows must come off? Because he loved Bon" (72).

Indeed, the image of emotional amputation and the "phantom" love-object is evocative of the psychologically fragmented lives that both Morrison and Faulkner explore throughout their fiction. It signifies a cluster of resonant emotional issues that I would term *mourning*, whether for the "phantom limb," the phantom parent, or the phantom beloved: mourning for lost possibilities, lost selves, and (for Faulkner) the "lost" South itself. Not only Golden Gray but virtually every character in *Jazz*, whether central or secondary, suffers from early or traumatic separation from one or both parents, the betrayal of the lover, or both.

Similarly, a core image from which many of the overlapping strands of *Absalom, Absalom!* radiate is that of "the forlorn nameless and homeless lost child" (215), Quentin Compson's construction of Thomas Sutpen's vision of his childhood—based, in turn, on what Quentin's grandfather recalled of Sutpen's story. The son of a whiskey-drinking father and a mother who died when he was ten, Sutpen left the South for the West Indies after a youthful humiliation, determined to become a planter in his own right with property, progeny, slaves, and authority. His ambitious "design" ultimately generated a veritable genealogy of orphans of mixed race, including not only the slave woman Clytie but—far more significant with respect to the collapse of Sutpen's grand plan—several successive generations of male mulatto descendants: the "mental and spiritual orphan" (98) Charles Bon, his son Charles Etienne de Saint Valery Bon, and, lastly (and most orphaned of all), *his* son, the idiot Jim Bond.

As Quentin and Shreve hypothesize a critical turn in the Sutpen story, what Charles Bon most wanted was a sign from his father acknowledging his paternity. They imagine him wishing for the sign of "indisputable recognition" (255) that would pass between them: *"He would just have to write 'I am your father. Burn this' and I would do it. Or if not that, a sheet a scrap of paper with the one word 'Charles' in his hand, and I would know what he meant and he would not even have to ask me to burn it"* (261). In *Jazz*, Morrison's Joe Trace is driven by a similar powerful ache to have his parental bond validated through some gesture of acknowledgement. He pleads with his long-absent mother, "Give me a sign. . . . You don't have to say nothing. Let me see your hand. Just stick it out someplace and I'll go; I promise. A sign" (178). But apparently no such sign was given by either Charles Bon's father or Joe Trace's mother.

Joe determines to act upon another kind of sign, tracing what he believes is the actual trail of his mother in the Virginia woods. Although he never finds the woman referred to only as "Wild"—both a name and a condition—he discovers the den-like home of the feral woman who, many years before, had abandoned her newborn baby; the "simple-minded woman" was "too brain-blasted to do what the meanest sow managed: nurse what she birthed" (179). Joe's quest for even a trace of his lost mother may be understood as the wish to neutralize the experience of her absence that continues to disrupt his emotional life even into middle age; what the narrator calls the "inside nothing" is constituted by profound yearning for what has been irrecoverably lost but whose traces are "everywhere and nowhere" (179). One icy January day, Joe, driven by the feeling he associates with his phantom mother, sets out to find his lover, Dorcas: "I tracked my mother in Virginia and it led me right to her, and I tracked Dorcas from borough to borough. . . . I wasn't looking for the trail. It was looking for me . . ." (130).

Not consciously intending to injure the young woman he loves, Joe stalks Dorcas the way he has stalked his absent mother, but this time carrying a gun in a concealed bag. Locating her at a party in the City, he is angered when he discovers her preference for the younger man with her, pointedly named Acton; Dorcas's abandonment of him, recalling his mother's abandonment years before, literally triggers Joe's impulsive, destructive act. "[I]f the trail speaks, no matter what's in the way, you can find yourself in a crowded room aiming a bullet at her heart, never mind it's the heart you can't live without . . ." (130). Shooting Dorcas, he acts out what may be understood as an ambivalent wish both to connect with and to hurt the woman who, like his mother many years before, has deserted him: "I had the gun but it was not the gun—it was my hand I wanted to touch you with" (130–1). Dorcas bleeds to death from that "touch."

Morrison has revealed an even more provocative context for the circumstances that culminate in Joe Trace's precipitate action. Like Faulkner, who narratively revived the character of Quentin Compson *after* having ended his life with suicide (the publication of *The Sound and the Fury* preceded that of *Absalom, Absalom!* by seven years), Morrison extends the fictional life of one of her most vividly realized characters. Pointing out that "the dates are the same" for Sethe's daughter's disappearance near the end of *Beloved* and Joe Trace's birth in *Jazz*, she suggests that "Wild is a kind of Beloved. . . . You see a pregnant black woman naked at the end of *Beloved*. It's at the same time . . . back in the Golden Gray section of *Jazz*, there is a crazy woman out in the woods. The woman they call Wild . . . could be Sethe's daughter, Beloved. When you see Beloved towards the end [of *Beloved*], you don't know; she's either a ghost who has been exorcised or she's a real person who is pregnant by Paul D, who runs away, ending up in Virginia, which is right next to Ohio" (Interview with Angels Carabi 43). Thus employing the same kind of speculative, even teasing, storytelling mode that she grants the narrating voice of *Jazz*, Morrison intimates that Joe Trace's mother may be none other than Beloved herself. Her revealing (and surprising!) comment underscores the figure of the *beloved* as the radically unavailable embodiment of a primary emotional attachment, whose absence persists as a haunting, idealized presence.

One of the most obvious departures from Faulkner's modernist narrative method in *Absalom, Absalom!* is Morrison's shaping of the primary narrator's role in *Jazz*. In Faulkner's novel, the omniscient narrator is a neutral, minimal presence, functioning primarily as the facilitator for Quentin's extended conversations with Shreve; in Morrison's novel, the limited-omniscient narrator functions far more centrally and less neutrally (as it finally reveals itself), confessing that it has "imagined" each of the stories that constitute the narrative. Moreover, the stories the voice articulates may be understood as representations not only of the characters' longings but of the narrator's own yearning for an idealized love. The voice admits that it is not Joe Trace's confusion but its own that initially led it to imagine that Joe was seeking Dorcas rather than his mother. "All the while . . . I thought he was looking for [Dorcas], not Wild's chamber of gold. That home in the rock. . . . *I want to be in a place already made for me, both snug and wide open.* . . . I'd love to close myself in the peace left by the woman who lived there and scared everybody. . . . She has seen me and is not afraid of me. She hugs me. Understands me. Has given me her hand. I am touched by her. Released in secret" (221, my emphasis). The language suggests a nostalgic fantasy, originally expressed through Joe Trace's quest, for reunion with or return to the beloved/mother/womb.

Through this congruence between the narrator's own longings and those of the characters it has invented, Morrison also emphasizes the provisional, improvisational relation of the narrative voice to the stories it articulates. Alongside of its construction of particular lives there are, implicitly, other (unarticulated) stories that may contradict the ones we've been told. Indeed, the voice admits it had assumed a different *denouement* than the one that unfolds: "I was sure one would kill the other. I waited for it so I could describe it" (220). Instead, the story of Joe and Violet Trace and Dorcas Manfred concludes not with another murder but with a reconciliation and a revision. Dorcas's friend, Felice, brings the Traces (and, implicitly, the story's other "traces") together through her revelation that Dorcas "let herself die" (204) by bleeding to death. That revelation releases Joe from full responsibility for his young lover's death.

In acknowledging the limits of its control over the outcome of Joe and Violet's story, the voice concedes, "I thought I knew [the people] and wasn't worried that they didn't really know about me. Now it's clear why they contradicted me at every turn: they knew me all along. . . . They knew . . . that when I invented stories about them—and doing it seemed to me so fine—I was completely in their hands. . . . Busy, they were, busy being original, complicated, changeable—human, I guess you'd say, while I was the predictable one . . ." (220). This confession on the narrator's part is Morrison's literary approximation of the spontaneity and riskiness of jazz: as the musician willingly surrenders control to the medium itself, so the narrator of *Jazz* relinquishes its power over the lives of the characters it has created. As Morrison explains, "It's very strange, but I like it because it's risky. But jazz unsettles you. You always feel a little on edge. 'Did I catch it?' You're not in control. It was this assumption of control, the reader's control, the book's control—all of these had to be displaced, so no one's in control" (Interview with Angels Carabi 42).

Morrison also reveals that, to convey the sense of a story "telling itself," she attempted to make the deliberately ageless, genderless narrative voice of *Jazz* embody not a person but the *book itself*: "the voice is the voice of a talking book . . . but few people read it like that. . . . I deliberately restricted myself using an 'I' that was only connected to the artifact of the book as an active participant in the invention of the story of the book, as though the book were talking, writing itself, in a sense" (Interview with Angels Carabi 42). The "talking-book" narrator of *Jazz* admits that it has surrendered its authority not only to the characters but to the medium—the language itself—and to the reader who engages with it. Indeed, in seductive language, the voice of *Jazz* proposes that the real love story—the culminating act in the quest for the beloved—is "the love song of a book talking to the reader" (Interview with Angels Carabi 42): *"I have loved only you, surrendered my whole self reckless to you and nobody else. . . . I want you to love me back and show it to me. . . . I love the way you hold me, how close you let me be to you. I like your fingers on and on, lifting, turning. . . . If I were able [to say that aloud] I'd say it. Say make me, remake me. You are free to do it and I am free to let you . . ."* (*Jazz* 229, italics in original). In the final words of *Jazz*—"Look where your hands are. Now." (229)—Morrison explicitly places in the reader's hands the responsibility for constructing the meaning of her text, affirming the imaginative collaboration between narrator and reader that might secure the presence, rather than the absence, of love. Reminiscent of Italo Calvino's playful reversal of the self-reflexive relationship between reader and book in *If on a winter's night a traveler*, Morrison grants the narrating voice of *Jazz* its ideal reader, who literally holds the book that contains its articulations; words and meanings achieve life beyond the page only through the reader's willing collaboration.

Morrison manages to have it both ways in *Jazz*: on the one hand, a series of overlapping stories in the tradition of Faulkner and other modernists that draw readers into the psychological dimensions of her characters; on the other, a postmodern narrative that cancels that involvement, intentionally contesting the illusion that we can "know" either characters or their stories by calling attention to their absolute fictionality. These complementary modes of representation are captured in an image early in *Jazz* that expresses the shifting relationship between surface and depth. Naming as "cracks" in Violet Trace's normalcy the disruptive actions that reveal her underlying emotional disarray, the narrating voice further describes these "dark fissures in the globe light of the day": "The globe light holds and bathes each scene, and it can be assumed that at the curve where the light stops is a solid foundation. In truth, there is no foundation at all, but alleyways, crevices one steps across all the time. But the globe light is imperfect too. Closely examined it shows seams, ill-glued cracks and weak places beyond which is anything. Anything at all" (22–3). The globe light may illuminate "consciousness," that primary subject for Faulkner and other modernists.[7] At the same time, it also exposes the "cracks and weak places" that, in the postmodern sense, betray the absence of a "solid foundation" and permit the narrator to create "anything"—either a continuous or a discontinuous world—for the reader to ponder. Morrison slyly alludes to that bifurcated vision, the deliberately discrepant "signs" of her novel, through her central character, Joe Trace, who has "double eyes. Each one a different color. A sad one that lets you look inside him, and a clear one that looks inside you" (206).

As *Jazz* straddles modernist and postmodernist modes, the narrating voice situates itself "midway between was and must be" (226). Through that double focus, Morrison blends *history* with *story*, granting her readers a unique and unconventional relation to her narrative. Similarly, in a statement that implicitly illuminates his view of the relationship that exists between history and story, Faulkner contended that "there is no such thing really as was because the past is. It is a part of every man, every woman, and every moment. All of his and her ancestry, background, is all a part of himself and herself at any moment" (*Faulkner* 84). Through each writer's complex representation of the intersections between past and present, story and teller, book and reader, sign and design, the reader is invited (or obliged) to collaborate in the text's intentional equivocations, its refusal to cohere around a single truth or core story. Assimilating but also inventively improvising beyond Faulknerian narrative method, Morrison has devised a vocal medley of jazz riffs: voices that signal but do not exhaust the alternative possibilities imaginable in their interrelated stories.

Notes

1. See also Brian McHale, *Constructing Postmodernism.*

2. Morrison remarked, in a 1983 interview with Nellie McKay, "Jazz always keeps you on the edge. There is no final chord. There may be a long chord, but no final chord. And it agitates you. Spirituals agitate you, no matter what they are saying about how it is all going to be. There is something underneath time that is incomplete. There is always something else that you want from the music. I want my books to be like that—because I want that feeling of something held in reserve and the sense that there is more—that you can't have it all right now" (Interview with Nellie McKay 429).

3. Mark S. Harvey proposes that modernism and jazz express deep cultural correspondences. As he phrases it, "Jazz from its inception has been perceived as an exemplary expression of the modernist impulse in American culture." The first phase of jazz (before "Bebop") began "at about the turn of the century through the 1920s when jazz most explicitly carried the modernist spirit here and abroad and when its innovations challenged the old order of Western music and culture . . ." (128).

4. Denise Heinze speculates that the narrator of *Jazz* "must be African-American, given the authority, almost arrogance, with which she portrays black characters and the uncertainty with which she characterizes whites; and feminine since her method of narration begs for the distinct feminine desire for connectedness and shared knowing" (182). Paula Gallant Eckard makes an interesting case that the voice of the novel is jazz itself, expressed in both male and female, singular and multiple forms. As the "essential narrator of the novel" (13), jazz "improvises on itself, utilizes the language of music and syncopated rhythms, and sings classic blues themes of love and loss" (11). Eckard shares my view that *Jazz* is "a post-modernist novel which blends modernist themes and subject" (11), though this observation is not further elaborated in her essay.

Proposing correspondences between jazz and poetry, Charles O. Hartman focuses on the suggestive connotations of *voice*, observing that "voice seems to be not self but the going outward of the self, a going that can be indirect or redirected" (3).

5. See my discussion of the incest theme in Morrison's fiction 146–8.

6. See my discussion of the recurrent imagery of dismemberment in Morrison's fiction 125–59 and 232–3.

7. Virginia Woolf's important manifesto of Modernism provides an interesting intertextual echo of the passage from *Jazz* quoted above: "Life is not a series of gig lamps symmetrically arranged; but a luminous halo, a semi-transparent envelope surrounding us from the beginning of consciousness to the end. Is it not the task of the novelist to convey this varying, this unknown and uncircumscribed spirit, whatever aberration or complexity it may display, with as little mixture of the alien and external as possible?" 150.

III *ABSALOM, ABSALOM!* AND *BELOVED*

12. BUILT ON THE ASHES
The Fall of the House of Sutpen
and the Rise of the House of Sethe

Michael Hogan

In *The Poetics of Space*, Gaston Bachelard asserts that when we engage a text, we " 'read a room' or 'read a house.' Thus, very quickly, at the very first word, at the first poetic overture, the reader who is 'reading a room' leaves off reading and starts to think of some place in his own past" (14). Although I am not certain that we "leave off reading" whenever we encounter a fictional house (if so, then we've been missing quite a bit of narrative action that authors happen to locate indoors), I do think Bachelard accurately describes how we spatially orient ourselves in constructing our own text and how the fictional house often functions as a primary tool in this process. American literature resonates with such houses. As Marilyn Chandler has noted, "In many of our major novels a house stands . . . as a unifying symbolic structure that represents and defines the relationships of the central characters to one another, to themselves, and to the world and raises a wide range of questions starting with Thoreau's deceptively simple 'What is a house?' " (1).

In a famed 1858 speech, Abraham Lincoln dramatically echoed a popular contemporary phrase, "A house divided against itself cannot stand" (426). Lincoln's house was, of course, the union, and the source of division was the institution of slavery. Scholars have read William Faulkner's *Absalom, Absalom!* in the context of these words, seeing the fall of the house of Thomas Sutpen as a metaphoric playing out of Lincoln's prophecy.[1] In Toni Morrison's *Beloved*, we again encounter such a "house," *possibly* divided against itself and certainly, like Sutpen's, a dwelling disturbed by the legacy of the American South. Both Faulkner's and Morrison's fictional homes assume significance because they are our primary sites of narrative action, the stages upon which we observe both character (the inhabitants) and setting (the community).

And yet unlike the "House of Sutpen," we do not speak of the "House of Sethe." Why not? As much as Faulkner's novel, *Beloved* recalls the double meaning of "house": both dwelling place and family. And Sethe, like Sutpen, is a monumentally proud and tragic character; Morrison is right in claiming that African-American communal tales—like hers—reproduce the conditions of "Greek tragedy . . . the heroic struggle between the claims of community and individual hubris" ("Unspeakable" 2). Surely, Morrison's tale is not Faulknerian tragedy written small.

In part, we can account for the absence of the "House of Sethe" because 124 Bluestone Road is *not* Sethe's house. Though undoubtedly a woman's place, it is owned by Edward Bodwin, an abolitionist. Additionally, Morrison's fictional house is a much more ambiguous dwelling than Faulkner's, refusing—until the very last—to reveal whether or not it is indeed a house divided. It is a site riddled by paradox: both white house and black house, safe house and slaughterhouse. It is home to both priestess and pariah. Not until the final pages of the narrative do we recognize that the house of Sethe will not go the way of Sutpen's house: both structure and family have endured.

In that same speech, Lincoln went on to assert that "[the house] will become *all* one thing, or *all* the other." Focusing upon Sutpen's mansion and 124 as fictional manifestations of Lincoln's American "house," and reading both houses as spaces defined by individual and communal identity as well as by gender, this essay seeks to explore how Sutpen's mansion and 124 fulfill Lincoln's prophecy. I will argue that the textual construction of each house is shaped largely by the identity and gender of its inhabitants as well as by each house's place within its community. The degree to which Sutpen and Sethe are part of—or alienated from—broader social structures is reflected in their dwellings. Consider, for example, how the fate of each house pivots upon the response of Sutpen and Sethe to each community's charge of pride. While Sutpen refuses to acknowledge the arrogance of his "design," Sethe's selfless actions at the end of *Beloved* reconcile her with her community. Consequently, both Sutpen's mansion and 124 mirror the fate of their respective inhabitants: Sutpen's home is destroyed by fire, but 124 perseveres, seemingly welcomed back into the black community that had shunned and abandoned it for eighteen years.

Moreover, the contrast between Sutpen's Hundred and 124 Bluestone Road is deepened if we consider the two houses as gendered spaces; that is, if we read Sutpen's Hundred as a patriarchal site and 124 as a matriarchal one. Sutpen's mansion, an icon of patriarchy and slavery, burns; 124 Bluestone Road, an emblem of female strength and freedom, endures. In this way, Sutpen's house becomes "all one thing," and Sethe's "all the other."

Constructing Self

Both *Absalom, Absalom!* and *Beloved* are spatially fragmented, shifting place both within and without the American South. Despite this fragmentation, both narratives always let us know not only *where* we are—in the Clearing with the freed slave Baby Suggs, or in Quentin and Shreve's chilly dormitory room—but *why* we are there. The authors use physical geography to orient us narratively; specific places become, accordingly, textual signifiers.

Although Faulkner recognized that his "little postage stamp of native soil was worth writing about," in constructing *Absalom, Absalom!* he kept largely to the topographic fringe of his Yoknapatawpha map, specifically the northwest quadrant containing Sutpen's Hundred (*Lion* 255). This marginalization foregrounds the isolation of the house. Sutpen's Hundred is characterized as a "desert island" with which the town of Jefferson has merely "assumed armistice rather than accepting and assimilating" (*Absalom* 79).

The relationship between place and self in *Absalom, Absalom!* and *Beloved* is distilled in the question that Justice Jim Hamblett puts to Charles Etienne de Saint Valery Bon: " '*What are you? Who and where did you come from?*' " (165). As we know from Quentin's anguished protestations to Shreve in the final lines of *Absalom, Absalom!*, where one comes from has much to do with who one is. Identity is rooted in issues of place; perhaps the most vivid characterization is Faulkner's description of Quentin: " . . . his very body was an empty hall echoing with sonorous defeated names; he was not a being, an entity, he was a commonwealth. He was a barracks filled with stubborn backlooking ghosts still recovering, even forty-three years afterward, from the fever which had cured the disease . . ."(7). When Quentin removes himself to Harvard, the stubborn backlooking ghosts join him: Faulkner's South is as moveable (though hardly as ebullient) as Hemingway's Paris. Quentin's identity is so fully fused with the American South that when he denies Shreve's assumption in the question "Why do you hate the South?", we feel as though Quentin is fighting for his self, his identity (303).

The interplay between place and self in these texts also manifests itself on a much finer scale than that which weighs North against South. Blurring the distinction between person and place, Morrison's narrator begins each of *Beloved*'s three sections with a statement personifying the house by characterizing its mood: "124 was spiteful." "124 was loud." "124 was quiet." Accordingly, the inhabitants of 124 recognize it as much as a person as a place. Sethe's daughter Denver regards the house "as a person rather than a structure" (29), and Sethe's two sons, Howard and Buglar, have "crept away from the lively spite the house felt for them" (3). Until Beloved arises from the stream and physically moves into the house, 124's spirit is that of a petulant but powerful child.

Consider too how Faulkner's metaphoric prose constructs Miss Rosa Coldfield's identity as much as describes her house: "it was of two storeys—unpainted and a little shabby, yet with an air, a quality of grim endurance as though like her it had been created to fit into and complement a world in all ways a little smaller than the one in which it found itself . . ." (6). The room in which Rosa and Quentin speak is "a dim hot airless room with the blinds all closed and fastened for forty-three summers," possessing a "dim coffin-smelling gloom" and "the rank smell of female old flesh long embattled in virginity" (3–4). Passages such as this do more than merely evoke the feel of the place; they help to define the identities of the inhabitants of that place. Rosa's house has assumed her temperament—or perhaps it is the other way around. Bachelard notes, "The house, even more than the landscape, is a 'psychic state' " which "bespeaks intimacy," suggesting that houses—even more than geographic place—are capable of revealing character (72).[2]

"124 was spiteful." "124 was loud." "124 was quiet." It seems odd that the two-story gray and white house on Bluestone Road is always and only referred to by its number. Just as there is something dehumanizing about referring to persons merely by number—it suggests the branded flesh of African slaves, or more recently, the inky tattooed forearms of Nazi camp survivors—so too the narrator's bald repetition of "124" abstracts the dwelling. It is not Baby Suggs's home, or Sethe's place: it is 124. Emily Miller Budick notes that "124" is a broken numerological sequence (i.e., 1, 2, [3], 4), perhaps signaling Beloved, Sethe's missing third child (131). And Morrison asserts that she chose to call the house simply 124 because numbers, which have "no posture of coziness or grandeur" about them, nevertheless "constitute an address, a thrilling enough prospect for slaves who had owned nothing" ("Unspeakable" 31). Sutpen too names his house with a number. Yet in prefacing the number with his own name, one senses his "posture" of "grandeur." Written out as a word, Sutpen's number indicates not an address but the size of the plantation in square miles; it emphasizes his ownership, his possession of the place. More than anything else, "Sutpen's Hundred" reflects Sutpen's ersatz pedigree, his spurious claim to be part of the southern gentry.

Morrison states that she began her novel with the simple naked number in order to reproduce the sense of deracination experienced by slaves sent to America: "I wanted that sudden feeling of being snatched up and thrown into that house, precisely the way they were. They were picked up from anywhere, at any time, and removed without resources, without defenses, without anything, naked. . . . Snatched just as the slaves were from one place to another. . . . And the house into which this snatching—this kidnapping—propels one, changes from spiteful to loud to quiet, as the sounds in the body of the ship itself may have changed" ("Unspeakable" 32). Thus, "124" signifies the uprooting of millions of black slaves while Sutpen's Hundred stands as one white man's furious, failed attempt to establish roots. Still more ironic is the fact that Sutpen has, of course, built his house with the labor of such slaves, whom he has uprooted from Haiti and shipped to Mississippi.

But we know that Thomas Sutpen did not always live within a plantation house. When his father uproots the family from their West Virginia mountain cabin, moving them "toward a place they had never seen and had no conception of, let alone wanted to go to" (182), young Sutpen apprehends the move surreally; as the land floats past, he realizes that he is lost: "He didn't know where they were. For a time, during the first days or weeks or months, the woodsman's instinct . . . kept him oriented so that he could have (so he said) found his way back to the mountain cabin in time . . . [Now] he knew neither where he had come from nor where he was nor why" (183–4). This profound deracination—a displacement of both self and geographic place—is mitigated by the boy's dim perception of his new locus: the plantation where his family has settled. But this reorientation is not fully realized until Sutpen, sent by his father to deliver a message, approaches the front door of the plantation's big house. Even before he is rejected—told by the black house slave never to come to the front door again—Sutpen seems to apprehend his own presence at the door as both literally and metaphorically liminal: " . . . before the monkey nigger who came to the door had finished saying what he did, he seemed to kind of dissolve and a part of him turn and rush back through the two years they had lived there like when you pass through a room fast and look at all the objects in it and you turn and go back through the room again and look at all the objects from the other side and you find out you had never seen them before . . ." (186). What transpires here—and what the boy cannot fully articulate—is Sutpen's moment of self-recognition. How he is perceived from the other (more privileged) side of the threshold informs how Sutpen later treats his own slaves. The "objects" that young Sutpen sees and then re-sees in the plantation mansion are moments of memory that now assume new epiphanic meaning: the "speculative antagonism" with which the white plantation workers look at the slaves (186), his father's exultation at participating in the beating of a plantation slave (187). As these images, these "objects," surface and dissolve in the boy's psyche, they are contextualized in terms of Sutpen's emergent subjective self, defined literally at the threshold of the big house.

Sutpen describes this moment of subjective awareness as "an explosion—a bright glare that vanished and left nothing" (192). His rejection at the front door triggers a psychic split: the boy describes two voices arguing inside his head, one still "innocent" and genuinely perplexed by the rejection, the other poised for retribution. It is this second voice that propels the boy to self-alienation: "when it said *them* in place of *he* or *him*, it meant more than all the puny mortals under the sun" (192). Sutpen's self-alienation is nearly self-deification; it demands a privileging of self over community.

Sutpen ponders his rejection for several hours before returning to his family's cabin. It is this return home—the juxtaposition between the big house and his own meager dwelling—that completes Sutpen's formation of selfhood in the context of a larger, grander world: "And then he said he began to think *Home. Home* and that he thought at first that he was trying to laugh and that he kept on telling himself it was laughing even after he knew better; home, as he came out of the woods and approached it, still hidden yet, and looked at it—the rough partly rotten log walls, the sagging roof whose missing shingles they did not replace but just set pans and buckets under the leaks, the leanto room which they used for kitchen and which was all right because in good weather it didn't even matter that it had no chimney since they did not attempt to use it at all when it rained . . ." (190). Thus, from the threshold of the Tidewater plantation's big house to his family's shoddy cabin, Sutpen experiences a sort of psychic introduction to self. His juxtaposition of the two dwellings leads him to define how he must physically manifest his design: "to combat them you have got to have what they have that made them do what he did. You got to have land and niggers and a fine house" (192). The equation is, at least for Sutpen, complete. His "design" is a perverse rendering of the American Dream which, as Marilyn Chandler notes, frequently manifests itself in the hope of owning a house, "which to many remains the most significant measure of the cultural enfranchisement that comes with being an independent, self-sufficient (traditionally male) individual in full possession and control of home and family" (1–2). Chandler notes too that the ideal expression of this dream is for the individual to have designed and built the house himself; the house therefore becomes "a direct extension of that self into the enduring media of wood and stone" (2). Identifying the plantation house as a site of rejection, young Sutpen conceives a house that will become not a site of communal acceptance, but only a house where "*he* would never again need to stand on the outside of a white door and knock at it" (210; emphasis added).

Building Community

Like Faulkner, Morrison locates her tale in marginal space: Bluestone Road sits several miles outside Cincinnati. 124 is both geographically isolated—we learn from Edward Bodwin that the house is surrounded by eighty acres of land— and, because of the unexpiated evil that has transpired there, isolated also by the surrounding community. The neighbors avoid 124 as if it is . . . well, as if it is haunted. Horse riders passing the house accelerate into a gallop, and until Sethe finds Paul D—a fellow slave from the Sweet Home plantation—sitting upon her porch, 124 has apparently received no visitors in eighteen years.

And yet 124 is a vivid contrast to Sutpen's mansion. Situated in a free state, peopled by black women, it is a small house: two rooms up, two down. Unlike Sutpen's mansion, which testifies to an unfulfilled future, a brick manifestation of Sutpen's doomed design, 124—in Baby Suggs's hands—functions as a two-story Promised Land. Those who cross the Ohio River to reach the house are literally rewarded with selfhood. Until Sethe arrives at 124, she is defined not as a person but only as commodity: "property that reproduced itself without cost" (228). Even at Sweet Home, the garden ideal of the plantation home—an Edenic hell, so to speak—the slaves are not fully invested with a sense of self; Paul D wonders why their first master, Garner, "called and announced them men—but only on Sweet Home, and by his leave. Was he naming what he saw or creating what he did not?" (220). Baby Suggs has Paul D's answer: although Sweet Home is an improvement over ordinary plantation life, as an agency of dehumanization it too denies selfhood to slaves. Baby Suggs observes that while at Sweet Home, her body was merely a "desolated center where the self that was no self made its home" (140).

Morrison's text counters Sutpen's megalomania with a dwelling characterized by tolerance and fellowship, whose inhabitants privilege community over self. The wonder—and the danger—of 124 is that it represents freedom. Sethe, arriving at the house after her successful escape from Sweet Home, experiences the rush of independence. Telling Paul D that her newly found freedom felt "Good and right . . . and deep and wide" (162), Sethe's sense of self, like Sutpen's, is realized literally at the threshold of a house. But while Sutpen's liminal moment at the big house is one of alienation, Sethe's experience at 124 is characterized by a communal love. As she tells Paul D, "when I got here, when I jumped off that wagon—there wasn't nobody in the world I couldn't love if I wanted to. You know what I mean?" (162). Paul D knows precisely what Sethe means: to love anything one chooses, "well now, *that* was freedom" (162). Sethe's moment of self-recognition—in its embracing of emotion over bare logic, and in its appeal to community rather than alienation from community—represents a wholesale inversion of Sutpen's.

And yet 124 is dangerous because it promises what it cannot provide: refuge for its inhabitants. As a free-standing American house, it promises protection; as home to African-American slaves, the disenfranchised and dehumanized, it cannot possibly deliver. As Baby Suggs asserts, "Not a house in the country ain't packed to its rafters with some dead Negro's grief" (5). And Paul D recognizes that the only thing that Sethe had "wanted for her children was exactly what was missing in 124: safety" (164). In a sequence evoking the biblical book of Revelation, four white horsemen—including "Schoolteacher," the clinically vicious master of Sweet Home plantation—arrive at 124. Their trespass subverts any sense of 124 as a safe haven for the community and specifically threatens Sethe and her children's claim to be "free"—legally or otherwise. It also triggers 124's devolution from safe house to slaughterhouse. Sethe's desperate act—the murder of one of her children—is a reaction to the white men's transgressive appearance at 124's threshold. As Baby Suggs articulates over and again to Stamp Paid, "I'm saying they came in my yard" (179). Her words do not exonerate Sethe, but they assuredly condemn the four white men for trespassing upon her place.

Clearly, much of the black community's attachment to place in *Beloved* can be understood as a psychological reaction against slavery. Paul D, who is emblematic of slavery's dislocating and deracinating effects, recalls that during his years of fleeing, "he could not help being astonished by the beauty of this land that was not his" (268). He remembers slaves on the run and homeless ex-slaves, sleeping in trees by day, hiding in caves, pursued by the Klan, by war veterans, and by posses, but unable to reach safety, because they had no place to go (66). But while Sutpen's uprooting from his West Virginia cabin initiates his progressive alienation, the ex-slaves in *Beloved* respond to their deracination by establishing communal bonds. When Stamp Paid discovers that Paul D, displaced from 124, has been sleeping in a church basement, he is outraged; for such behavior implies a breakdown within the fragile black community. He apologizes to Paul D, then affirms the communal strength of the black Cincinnati people: "Stay around here long enough, you'll see ain't a sweeter bunch of colored anywhere than what's right here. Pride, well, that bothers em a bit. They can get messy when they think somebody's too proud" (232). In its selfishness, its privileging of one's own needs over those of the group, pride is perhaps the least pardonable transgression within this marginalized community.

As in *Absalom, Absalom!*, the sin of pride functions as the trigger for tragedy in *Beloved*. It is Baby Suggs's pride which first "bothers" the community. There is the sense among these people that Baby Suggs, "who had probably never carried one hundred pounds to the scale. . . . Who had never been lashed by a ten-year-old whiteboy as God knows they had. Who had not even escaped slavery—had, in fact, been *bought out* of it by a doting son . . . ," has somehow not suffered sufficiently as a slave (137). Having failed to pay her dues, she is not fully a member of the ex-slave community. And the day of Sethe's tragedy (the day following a feast held at 124), the black Cincinnati community is "furious" at what they perceive as the "uncalled-for pride" and "reckless generosity on display at 124" (137). After Sethe murders her child, she, too, is perceived as proud. As she is led away by the sheriff, the community gathers, asking themselves, "Was her head a bit too high? Her back a little too straight?" And they answer: "Probably" (152).

After Sethe's act, 124 is inhabited by a presence, at first the ghost of Sethe's slaughtered child, then replaced by the mysterious appearance of the young girl Beloved. The three generations of women at 124 each respond differently to the presence. As Chandler has suggested, Baby Suggs, Sethe, and Denver "represent successive stages in emergence from enslavement and endangerment" (309). Furthermore, their lives mark a cycle of acceptance, isolation, and re-acceptance for 124 within the black Cincinnati community. Baby Suggs, the community's spiritual leader and agent of healing who has transformed 124 into a haven for the free and fleeing, is unable to "approve or condemn Sethe's rough choice" (180); after the arrival of the ghost, she simply shuts down, defeated. Baby Suggs spends her remaining years in bed, contemplating colors, a lonely activity for the community's former caregiver, but one which she has chosen because it is "something harmless in this world" (179).

Prior to Baby Suggs's death, Sethe and Denver wage "a perfunctory battle against the outrageous behavior" of 124 (4). After, they seem to arrive at a truce with the familiar. Though she justifies the killing of her child, Sethe seems to endure the venom of 124's ghost as a self-imposed penance. She is outraged when Paul D suggests that she and Denver move from the house, "as though a house was a little thing," because it would signify an abandonment of the ghost (22). But when Beloved appears bodily at 124, she upsets the house's balance of power. Sethe's beliefs concerning "rememory" do allow her to live with the past; as she tells Denver, "If a house burns down, it's gone, but the place—the picture of it—stays, and not just in my rememory, but out there, in the world" (36). But Sethe's beliefs do *not* prepare her to face (literally) her most painful rememory as part of her constant present. As Karla Holloway notes, Beloved denies Sethe and Denver "their space in a secure and memory-less present" ("*Beloved*," in *Callaloo* 520).

Yet it is Beloved's incarnation that nearly destroys, but ultimately redeems, Sethe. Sethe's moment of redemption comes, appropriately enough, at 124's threshold. With 124 as her stage and thirty neighborhood women as her audience—and with Edward Bodwin cast unaware as Schoolteacher—Sethe is seemingly driven to replay her infanticidal role from eighteen years before. This time, however, Sethe chooses not her daughter—she leaves Beloved standing alone at the threshold—but Schoolteacher (Bodwin). Beloved's subsequent departure from 124 not only means the end of psychic and physical torment for Sethe, but it also signals that Sethe's choice—attempting *this* time to attack the white man, the threat against her family—was the right one. In attacking the white man, Sethe offers herself—rather than her child—for sacrifice. It is a decision that conveys Sethe's selflessness, rather than her pride, to the thirty women watching and allows Sethe to re-enter their community.

The neighborhood women who appear at 124 do so largely because of the efforts of Denver, whose transformation at 124 is no less remarkable than that of her mother. Like Clytie in *Absalom, Absalom!*, Denver perceives the house as her fortress. 124 represents "all the world she knew or wanted" and when she is driven by her mother's illness to seek help within the community, "she stood on the porch of 124 ready to be swallowed up in the world beyond the edge of the porch" (101; 243). Throughout Denver's transformation—from the sensitive, house-bound child to the young woman who helps her family re-establish itself as part of the community—her innocence remains remarkably intact. The significance behind Baby Suggs's boarding up of 124's back door (the only door accessible to slaves) is lost on Denver; she merely thinks it a nuisance to always enter 124 by the front. And when she knocks on the white Bodwin's front door, their housekeeper chides her for not knowing to go to the back; "But Denver only half heard" (253) the scolding, a reaction radically different from that of young Sutpen at the big house. Unlike the other inhabitants of 124, Denver's frame of reference—her own "rememory"—does not include slavery: she was born during Sethe's escape from Sweet Home. It seems fitting, then, that Denver will inherit 124 and bring it one generation further away from slavery. Like Faulkner's Clytie, Denver is black and female; but in Morrison's text, she is also the legitimate heir. Along with Sethe, Denver ushers 124 back into the community, bringing the house full circle.

The significance of 124 also extends beyond its female inhabitants to encompass the surrounding black society. The eighteen years—1855–73—of 124's isolation frame, of course, the Civil War and the Emancipation Proclamation, events which radically re-defined concepts of identity and community for newly freed slaves.[3] The history of 124 is, then, a history of these quasi-free people, the fragile black community set on the periphery of Cincinnati, literally at the geographic threshold between slavery and freedom. Finally, it is their sense of fellowship that sets 124 apart from Sutpen's Hundred. 124 is a forgiving and forgiven place, one that—following its years of isolation—witnesses its inhabitants re-entering the ex-slave community.

What also distinguishes the house of Sethe from the house of Sutpen is how each house responds to the community's charge of pride. Sutpen, of course, never does, telling General Compson that the only possible flaw in his design was his own "innocence" (178). But Mr. Compson rightly characterizes Sutpen's attitude, in the carrying out of his design, as one of "utter disregard" for the Jefferson townspeople (56). Sethe, by attempting to harm Schoolteacher (Bodwin) instead of her child the second time a white man "threatens" her family, is poised to re-enter her community. Also, that the women of the neighborhood gather at 124 to protect Sethe reflects *their* affirmation of communal bonds: "the personal pride, the arrogant claim staked out at 124 seemed to them to have run its course" (249).

Gendered Spaces

Morrison's and Faulkner's fictional homes differ not only in the relationship that their inhabitants establish with their communities, but also—and more simply—in the gender of their inhabitants. Both Sutpen's mansion and 124 might be read as gendered space, which in turn informs the fate of the houses. When Henry, Thomas Sutpen's son and heir, accompanies Charles, his half-brother (and non-heir), to New Orleans, the architecture of the home there is described as "femininely flamboyant and therefore to Henry opulent, sensuous, sinful" (87). By contrast, the house of Sutpen is founded in a bitter, patriarchal, southern Puritanism, "a granite heritage where even the houses, let alone clothing and conduct, are built in the image of a jealous and sadistic Jehovah" (86). In building his mansion, Sutpen and his slaves "overrun suddenly the hundred square miles of tranquil and astonished earth and drag house and formal gardens violently out of the soundless Nothing," a description which not only evokes the biblical creation story but also suggests Sutpen's transgressive violation of the (feminine) earth (4). Thomas Sutpen's mansion is a "halfacre gunroom of a baronial splendor," a place "without any feminised softness" about it (30). The naming of the house and surrounding plantation as "Sutpen's Hundred"—which I have argued is a sort of self-titling—also enables Sutpen to legitimate himself within the southern *male* nobility. Moreover, the plantation's function—supporting the patriarchal institution of slavery—emphasizes its maleness.

In contrast to Sutpen's mansion, 124 is a matriarchal place. Edward Bodwin feels "something sweeter and deeper about the house" than about its surrounding property (259). Bodwin associates the house with images of domesticity, and recalls its female history, remembering "that women died there: his mother, grandmother, an aunt and an older sister before he was born" (259). Defined as a matrilineal site, the house passes into the hands of Baby Suggs, who shapes it into a "cheerful, buzzing house" where ex-slaves were "fed, chastised and soothed. Where not one but two pots simmered on the stove; where the lamp burned all night long. Strangers rested there while children tried on their shoes" (87). Under Baby Suggs's guidance, 124 evolves into a vibrant stop on the underground railroad—a combined message center, aid station, community kitchen and gathering place for the free and fleeing.

While Baby Suggs's 124 welcomes male and female alike, women are routinely commodified and animalized in the house of Sutpen. For nearly five years, Thomas lives without a wife "just as he had [lived with] no furniture in his house and for the same reason: he had at the time nothing to exchange" for either piece of property (48). Among the "wild niggers" who accompany Sutpen to Yoknapatawpha are two women, chosen by him "with the same care and shrewdness with which he chose the other livestock—the horses and mules and cattle" (48). When Charles Etienne de Saint Valery Bon moves his pregnant wife onto the plantation, he "kenneled her" in a "ruined cabin" (167). And when Milly—the granddaughter of Wash Jones, a squatter on Sutpen's property— gives birth to Sutpen's child on the very day that his mare foals, Sutpen tells her, "Well, Milly; too bad you're not a mare too. Then I could give you a decent stall in the stable," an insult whose vicious misogyny epitomizes the place of women in the house of Sutpen (229). Women may cross Sutpen's threshold only by virtue of birthright (Clytie and Judith) or because they are necessary components of his design, i.e., "breeders" (Ellen, Rosa, and Milly Jones).

Although he tells General Compson that "acquiring" a wife is only "inciden- tally" part of his plan, in order to effect his design, Sutpen must through marriage acquire the social legitimacy that the house lacks (212). Ellen Coldfield exchanges both "pride and peace" for the house (10); corrupted through her marriage to Sutpen, she is powerless in his house. Mr. Compson's wry speculation that Ellen "might have risen to actual stardom in the role of the matriarch arbitrating from the fireside corner of a crone the pride and destiny of her family" not only ridicules Ellen, but also mockingly subverts the possibility of a matriarchy within the existing southern culture (54). Even in Sutpen's absence, the females in *Absalom, Absalom!* are unable to effectively "displace" him. When Sutpen leaves for the war, his presence remains "as though houses actually possess a sentience, a personality and character acquired not from the people who breathe or have breathed in them so much as rather inherent in the wood and brick or begotten upon the wood and brick by the man or men who conceived and built them—in this one an incontrovertible affirmation for emptiness, desertion; an insurmountable resistance to occupancy save when sanctioned and protected by the ruthless and the strong" (67). After Ellen's death, the "trium-feminae" comprising Judith, Clytie, and Rosa (a three-woman household that prefigures that of Sethe, Denver, and Beloved) is left to maintain the house. But the women assume a limbo life, their identities defined only in relation to their *lack* of Sutpen: "So we waited for him. We led the busy eventless lives of three nuns in a barren and poverty-stricken convent. . . . We kept the house, what part of it we lived in, used; we kept the room which Thomas Sutpen would return to . . ." (124–25). When he does return after the Civil War, Sutpen furiously undertakes the restoration of his house, for it is his *sine qua non*. But the plantation has been reduced to "Sutpen's One" (136), and his attempts to produce a male heir—including both his suggestion to Rosa that they "breed together" and his de facto rape of fifteen-year-old Milly Jones—also prove futile, ultimately leading to Sutpen's own destruction. After Wash Jones kills him, the mansion eventually becomes the House of Clytie, the illegitimate mulatto daughter, and, as Chandler puts it, the "passing of the house into feminine control parallels the gradual fading of the 'white' power in the household into 'black'" (266). The fall of the house of Sutpen resonates with such tremendous irony because its passing into Clytie's hands inverts all that the white patriarchal world of Sutpen has privileged.

While men are not commodified or brutalized at 124, they do routinely fail there: Baby Suggs's son Halle never arrives to join his wife and children and her grandsons Buglar and Howard abandon the house. Schoolteacher comes to retrieve his human property but leaves empty-handed. And after Stamp Paid fails for the sixth time to muster enough will merely to knock at the front door, he acknowledges his lack of strength at 124: "Spirit willing; flesh weak" (173).

Paul D also fails at 124. Asking Sethe "What kind of evil you got in here?" as he crosses the threshold, Paul D develops an uneasiness about the house that he is unable to shake off (8). His triumphant exorcism of the poltergeist is no triumph at all; she is merely incarnated in a more powerful form, one which quickly displaces Paul D himself. Moved further and further away from Sethe's bedroom, Paul D thinks he is having "house-fits" until he finds himself sleeping in the cold house, an outdoor shed. When Beloved comes to Paul D, ordering

him to "call me my name" and "touch me on the inside part," he submits.
His inability to resist shames him, humiliates him. Yet with humiliation often
comes humility, which leads Paul D, like Sethe, to reconcile with the Cincinnati
ex-slave community.

That Toni Morrison creates such a nurturing, welcoming house here is
certainly informed by her broader aims in *Beloved*, and yet her impulses may
extend well beyond any single narrative. When asked in a 1976 interview to
comment upon the sense of place in her writing, Morrison replied: " . . . I
think some sense of it is just a woman's strong sense of being in a room, a place,
or in a house. Sometimes my relationship to things in a house would be a little
different from, say my brother's or my father's or my sons'. I clean them and I
move them and I do very intimate things 'in place': I am sort of rooted in it,
so that writing about being in a room looking out, or living in a small definite
place, is probably very common among most women anyway" ("Intimate" 213).

The sins of Sethe and Paul D—sins of emotion, sins of the heart—stand in
sharp contrast to Sutpen's sin, his icy rational disregard for others. As Sutpen
says to General Compson: "You see, I had a design in mind. Whether it was a
good or bad design is beside the point" (212). Yet it is Sutpen who misses the
point. And since the houses in both texts function as synthesizing symbols of
their inhabitants and the surrounding communities, Sutpen's Hundred falls as
the doomed temple of a monomaniacal patriarch. Finally, the matrilineal 124
is a more forgiving place—to male and female alike—than Sutpen's mansion,
enduring because of the communal female strength of ex-slaves.

Notes

1. For a full analysis of Sutpen's house as an analogue for the Union during the
Civil War, see Sundquist 96–130.
2. Bachelard discusses how psychologists, by studying drawings of houses made
by children, can determine certain traits of those children. One characteristic of a
relatively happy child's depiction of a lived-in, functional dwelling is the presence of
door-knobs and windows. Curiously, Sutpen's house stands for three years "without
a pane of glass or a doorknob or hinge in it" (*Absalom* 44).
3. Charles Scruggs notes, too, the significance of the Fugitive Slave Law of
1850, which provided the services of federal law-enforcement agents to southern
slave catchers. "A United States marshal, for instance, could now *compel* whites
to cooperate with the slave catchers by deputizing a *posse comitatus* in his district"
(102).

13. A Postmodern *Absalom, Absalom!*, a Modern *Beloved*

The Dialectic of Form

Catherine Gunther Kodat

I have a title for it which I like, by the way: ABSALOM, ABSALOM; the story is of a man who wanted a son through pride, and got too many of them and they destroyed him. . . .
—William Faulkner

I don't know if that story (of Beloved*) came because I was considering certain aspects of self-sabotage, the ways in which the best things we do so often carry seeds of one's own destruction.*
—Toni Morrison

It may seem ironic to open a paper concerned with formal issues in *Beloved* and *Absalom, Absalom!* with epigraphs that apparently set the tone for a discussion of thematics. But since irony—both the Western "high modernist" definition of irony and the uniquely African-American survivalist sensibility called "signifying" (see Gates, *Signifying*)—will be an item under discussion here, it is perhaps not a bad way to start. I want to begin my examination of *Beloved* and *Absalom, Absalom!* with a brief foray into matters of content in order to underline the notion that formal issues are important *precisely because* our approach to the literary subject is so thoroughly mediated by structure, diction,

181

and tone. There is, of course, the sad history of Cold War formalist criticism in the United States, which saw undue (and ideologically vested) emphasis on this mediation; certainly, we have all learned that the excesses of the old New Criticism are traps to be avoided. By the same token, however, contemporary efforts to discuss a text's content and context that treat issues of literary technique as givens run the risk of a different sort of ahistoricizing move, one that fails to read how an author's approach to formal problems *is likewise* grounded in history and social context. So I back into form via content in order to point out that, in addition to many striking similarities (the deployment of the Gothic in describing a family tragedy, the use of a family tragedy as synecdoche for the larger social scene, the effort to represent this country's slaveholding past via historic romance), *Absalom, Absalom!* and *Beloved* share a theme; Morrison identifies it in the opening epigraph as "self-sabotage," which she elaborates as "the ways in which the best things we do so often carry seeds of one's own destruction" ("Toni" C17).

Tracking Morrison's comments about *Beloved* as it was being written (and even in the few weeks after it was first released in the early fall of 1987) reveals that the historic, lived experience of slavery first appeared to her not as planned subject but at most as a *backdrop* for the (seemingly) larger question of what she calls, in one interview, "self-murder" (Interview with Melvyn Bragg). It is worth remembering that Morrison initially envisioned *Beloved* and *Jazz* as one novel, inspired by two bits of historic flotsam uncovered through her editing duties at Random House.[1] A 1985 interview with Gloria Naylor, given as Morrison was in the midst of writing *Beloved* (and, importantly, when she still saw *Beloved* and *Jazz* as one work), helps us identify the impulse responsible for the novel's shift in emphasis from the "universal" to the historic particular:

> What made those stories connect [Margaret Garner's history and the 1920s Harlem murder that became the basis for *Jazz*], I can't explain, but I do know that . . . both of those incidents seem to me, at least on the surface, very noble . . . generous, wide-spirited. . . . And I thought . . . the best thing that is in us is also the thing that makes us sabotage ourselves. . . . So . . . I just imagined the life of a dead girl which was the girl that Margaret Garner killed. . . . I just imagined her remembering what happened to her, being someplace else and returning, knowing what happened to her. And I call her Beloved. . . .
>
> I have about 250 pages and it's overwhelming me. There's a lot of danger for me in writing it, which is what I am very excited about. The effort, the responsibility as well as the effort, the effort of being worth it, that's not quite it. The responsibility that I feel for the woman I call Sethe, and for all of these people; these unburied, or at least unceremoniously buried, people made literate [*sic*] in art. But the inner tension, the artistic inner

tension those people create in me; the fear of not properly, artistically, burying them, is extraordinary. (Interview with Gloria Naylor 584)

Imagining the dead girl gives rise to a sense of responsibility and a fear of not "properly, artistically" burying those summoned forth in the service of the "larger" theme. It is in the effort to *embody* the theme of self-sabotage—to flesh out the ghost, to give form to the idea—that Morrison confronts the specifics of her "responsibility." It is in this dialectic of content and form that the moment of historical consciousness emerges for Morrison.

Recalling the more thoroughly reported details of the writing of *Absalom, Absalom!* shows us that this dialectical model holds for Faulkner, as well. Indeed, the search for a proper form in which to express an historical content is explicitly dramatized in that novel, as the effort to reconstruct the Sutpen saga replaces the saga itself as the work's central concern; Joseph Blotner notes that it was "not the events in the lives of Sutpen and his children, but how to relate and interpret them" that "perplexed [Faulkner] from the start" (890). Keeping this dialectic uppermost in mind is what enables the production of a formalist criticism that remains deeply engaged in questions of historical context and content. And Theodor Adorno's notion of a negative dialectics, wherein the dream of synthesis is always blocked by some residue, some surplus, some haunting, has enormous ramifications for a text like *Absalom, Absalom!*, in which, finally, the ledgers don't balance out. For Adorno, this "sense of nonidentity" in the dialectical moment, of something left over and unaccounted for, is in some ways constitutive of thought itself (*Negative* 5); the modernist turn arrives, he believes, with the recognition and explicit acknowledgment of this truth. In Faulkner's high modernist text, the acknowledged inassimilable surplus is African-American history itself; first invoked as a necessary adjunct to the story of Sutpen, it gathers force and momentum, sweeping all else before it by the novel's conclusion.

It is this remainder haunting the mediation of form and content that makes it possible to read *Absalom, Absalom!* and *Beloved* together and helps to explain the similar effects the texts have on their readers. Both novels force us to struggle with what is most resistant to expression (the nature and purpose of Beloved herself, the ultimate ramifications of Sutpen's design) and which, in its resistance, fuels some of the novels' most breathtaking technical accomplishments. Morrison and Faulkner do this by adopting formal strategies that invite us to hear "unspeakable thoughts, unspoken," that offer tales of telling which are "true enough" yoked to others which are clearly impossible (Sutpen's Haiti adventure, for example [see Godden]), and that make narrative choices scarred by "*the lost irrevocable might-have-been*" (*Absalom* 109). For Faulkner, this meant producing a postmodern text that, to paraphrase Frederic Jameson, draws its power from its effort to represent the attempt to think historically in an age that believes it has forgotten how to do so (ix). *Absalom, Absalom!* figures this effort to think historically as a dialectical residue in the work's *content*: Jim Bond remains at large in the novel's conclusion, where the remembered anguish of his howling sets Quentin to shuddering in his Harvard dormitory bed. Morrison, on the other hand, produces a narrative that deposits its excess in the realm of *form*: *Beloved* critically deploys high modernist techniques in order to reveal the Africanist remainder at the center of modernism's enterprise. Thus, *Absalom, Absalom!* and *Beloved* not only represent African-American history artistically: they comment upon the history of artistically representing African-Americans. While it is possible to arrive at these observations by examining each text independently, it is only through reading them together that we gain a historical perspective on the importance of African-American *forms* in the emergence of American literary modernism. ("Forms" here has a double charge, indicating both those African-American aesthetic practices that have influenced American modernism, and the bodies of African-Americans themselves, so often invoked as characters or symbols in modernist works.) Reading the two works together also opens up a way toward thinking of the distinction between modernism and postmodernism as a phenomenon of reader reception—in which an examination of the social, political, and aesthetic uses to which texts are put becomes an important factor—rather than as a question of "formalist" periodization.

If there is resistance to reading American literary modernism as deeply indebted to both Africanist aesthetics and the strategies of indirection born out of the enslaveds' responses to slavery, it is because we have been trained to read a haunted space as an empty place. The period that gave us the New Criticism and the humanist Cold War Faulkner (Lawrence Schwartz has superbly described the symbiotic relationship between the two) also gave us the dominant ideological reading of modernism, in which various strategies of indirection—difficult syntax, highly stylized structure, and ruptures in narrative sequence—were held to serve the overall aim of making, to paraphrase Joseph Frank, history ahistorical. In this view, the empty horror at the center of industrialized life fueled an effort on the part of modern literary artists—Frank selects James Joyce, Marcel Proust, T. S. Eliot, and Djuna Barnes as his primary examples—to transform "the time world of history into the timeless world of myth" (Frank 60). Allen Tate seconded Frank's formulation when he argued that literary modernism sought to "arrest the naturalistic flux of experience at an instant of time that . . . [has] neither temporal antecedents nor temporal consequences"

(Tate ix). It is this idea of modernism as a flight from history that has fueled much of the Left's criticism of the movement, starting with Georg Lukács and continuing up to Houston A. Baker, Jr. (see especially Baker's *Modernism* xv–xvi).

Yet modernist strategies appear forcefully in *Beloved*, when, in the novel's middle section, Morrison offers the reader four chapters of direct discourse in which Sethe, Denver, and Beloved give voice to their histories, fears, and desires, first singly, and then together. Starting with Sethe's recollections of her childhood, her life at Sweet Home, and the murder of her daughter, the chapters become progressively more technically challenging and culminate in a dense fugal interplay of all three voices that achieves its effects through liberal use of verbal compression, fragmentation, and juxtaposition. Before this choral moment, each woman speaks her past directly to the reader; Sethe and Denver reveal their personal pasts, already partly shown in the novel, while Beloved's section reveals the hitherto hidden "deep past" of the Middle Passage. The eight pages comprising Beloved's speech and the ensuing chorus with Sethe and Denver are perhaps the most technically dazzling and reader-resistant pages in all of Morrison's work. What most concerns me here is *why* Morrison decided to shape this language as she did, and why she chose to use a fragmented narrative method overall: given *Beloved*'s effort to reclaim a lost history, why would Morrison decide to use a technique so closely identified with the effort to escape history?[2]

Morrison's many pronouncements on how she would like to be read and critiqued are enough to give pause to anyone attempting to place her work next to that of a white, Western, male author, but she herself, in fact, provides some precedent for reading *Beloved* with *Absalom, Absalom!*. In her Master's thesis on Faulkner and Virginia Woolf she writes, "It can be inferred from contemporary literature that a great part of the uniqueness of our time has its roots in the widespread concept of man as a thing apart, as an individual who, if not lost, is impressively alone" ("Virginia" 1). Morrison concludes that for Woolf "isolation is inevitable but, because of the world's disorganization and despair, it can be an advantage" (2), while Faulkner, on the other hand, "believes it possible to establish complete harmony between man and his position by a return to the old virtues of brotherhood, compassion and love. He believes, too, that man has a responsibility to the future and must be reconciled to it. Alienation is not Faulkner's answer" (3). It seems clear from this and other remarks Morrison has made about Faulkner that it would be fair to characterize her view of his work as a patient, even perhaps a sympathetic, one; certainly, her discussion of Faulkner is more admiring than her discussion of Woolf, whose very style, Morrison argues, "suggests . . . that by isolating oneself into the fragmentary experiences and sensations as they come, the dread of time eating at the edges of life can be avoided. One can live outside time, as it were" (23). For Morrison, though, living outside time is ultimately undesirable: "In death only the alienated find freedom and refuge from time—a solution Virginia Woolf may well have believed in to end her life as she did in 1941" (23). Morrison's examination of Faulkner comes on the heels of this dismissal of Woolf's vision, in which (Morrison seems to say) one type of modernistic style emerges out of an escapist, nihilistic, and finally unacceptable world vision. Morrison uses Faulkner's Nobel Prize speech to argue that he repudiates Quentin's self-involved alienation and final suicide as a "victory without hope and worst of all without pity or compassion" (35).

Morrison concludes her thesis by noting that Faulkner and Woolf have "approaches to isolation [that] differ greatly, [but] they have this important value in common: each treatment is an effort to discover what pattern of existence is most conducive to honesty and self-knowledge, the prime requisites for living a significant life" (39). Morrison rejects one modernist approach—what she describes as Woolf's belief that "isolation . . . [provides] the means for acute self-analysis"—while embracing another that, in her formulation, emerges as a dialectical negation of the Woolf view: "William Faulkner's Quentin Compson never attains self-knowledge *because* he is alienated" (39; emphasis added). Alienation is cast as both a product of modern life and as an obstacle in the effort to live a "significant" life in the modern period. It is thus simultaneously an injury and a defense mechanism, and—to the extent that a modernist literary practice treats it as such—an indictment of the material conditions from which it emerges.

While it would not be fair to characterize Morrison's mature view of Faulkner as progressing unchangingly from one formed when she was 24 years old, it is clear, in this conclusion to her thesis, that she already is viewing literary modernism with a careful eye, sifting its themes and techniques and selecting for praise those that seem more likely to contain within themselves some seed of self-critique. And if we look closer to the present day, we find Morrison again talking about Faulkner in sympathetic (if somewhat more guarded) tones. Morrison appeared at the 1985 Faulkner and Yoknapatawpha Conference at the University of Mississippi and read from *Beloved*, then a work in progress. Before she began reading her fiction, Morrison offered these brief remarks about Faulkner: "I have to say, even before I begin to read, that there was for me not only an academic interest in Faulkner, but in a very, very personal way, in a very personal way as a reader, William Faulkner had an enormous effect on me, an enormous effect" ("Faulkner and Women" 295–96).

After her reading, Morrison accepted questions from the audience, and she was asked what effect reading Faulkner had had on her writing. This was her reply:

> Well, I'm not sure that he had any effect on my work. . . . But as a reader [I found that] there was in Faulkner this power and courage—the courage of a writer, a special kind of courage. My reasons, I think, for being interested and deeply moved by all his subjects had something to do with my desire to find out something about this country and that artistic articulation of its past that was not available in history, which is what art and fiction can do but sometimes history refuses to do. . . . And there was something else about Faulkner which I can only call "gaze." He had a gaze that was different. It appeared, at that time, to be similar to a look, even a sort of staring, a refusal-to-look-away approach in his writing that I found admirable. . . . (296–97)

In the midst of writing her first historical novel, Toni Morrison found that what she had been drawn to in Faulkner "as a reader" was an "admirable . . . refusal-to-look-away," an approach to representing "an era" that exemplified for her "a special kind of courage" in an "artistic articulation of [this country's] past that was not available in history," something that only "art and fiction can do." While denying Faulkner any direct influence on her work, Morrison does find that he had attempted something similar to her current project, and that his effort produced something worthwhile—if also, perhaps, incomplete.

Past efforts to read *Beloved* in the context of the white Western canon largely have focussed on the text's relationship to nineteenth-century romance, and especially on its relationship to *The Scarlet Letter*. *Beloved*'s engagement with that prior text, it has been argued, produces, among its effects, a revision and rearticulation of the notion of literary mastery (Stryz); a challenge to Hawthorne's cultural authority (Woidat); a criticism of contemporary criticism (Lewis); or a realization that both it and the nineteenth-century text remind us how "that which the past has taken from us no present or future reality can restore" (Budick 135).[3] All of these judgments are inestimably useful to any effort to read Morrison in and against the white American canon; but reading these critiques, and then turning to Rafael Pérez-Torres's essay on *Beloved* as a postmodern novel, would lead one to believe that, as far as contemporary scholars are concerned, *Beloved*'s relationship to twentieth-century modernism is a non-issue, a dead end, a nothing.[4] But just as Morrison seeks, through her novel, to reclaim a lost history—to "call them my people, which were not my people; and her beloved, which was not beloved"—so, it seems to me, she seeks to reclaim an entire artistic movement, to uncover "the ghost in the machine" ("Unspeakable" 11) of modernism by pointing out the ways in which that movement owed its emergence to what she has elsewhere called "a dark, abiding, signing Africanist presence" (*Playing* 5). In a 1988 speech, Morrison remarked that she was "always amazed by the resonances, the structural gear-shifts, and the uses to which Afro-American narrative persona and idiom are put in contemporary "white" literature. . . . The most valuable point of entry into the question of cultural (or racial) distinction, the one most fraught, is its language—its unpoliced, seditious, confrontational, manipulative, inventive, disruptive, masked and masking language. Such a penetration will entail the most careful study, one in which the impact of Afro-American presence on modernity becomes clear and is no longer a well-kept secret" ("Unspeakable" 11).

This emphasis on the language (rather than on the "story") is, I would argue, an effort to direct the excavation of the "Afro-American presence on modernity" along formalist lines. Four years later, Morrison made her point (and claim) again, this time drawing a parallel between American political habits and American literary conventions: "It has occurred to me that the very manner by which American literature distinguishes itself as a coherent entity exists because of this unsettled and unsettling population. Just as the formation of the nation necessitated coded language and purposeful restriction to deal with the racial disingenuousness and moral frailty at its heart, so too did the literature, whose founding characteristics extend into the twentieth century, reproduce the necessity for codes and restriction" (*Playing* 5–6).

For the purposes of exploring a historically sensitive refashioning of modernist formalism in *Beloved*, I would like to draw attention to Morrison's assertion that the creation of the American nation depended on "coded language and purposeful restriction." In addition to being an exact description of white America's legal and social relationship to its Africanist roots, it is also a strikingly apt and economical description of the formal properties of literary modernism *and* of the African-American rhetorical practice, signifying, that Henry Louis Gates, Jr., has seen as a paradigm for African-American literary expression.[5] The difference between signifying and high modernism lies in the intensely reflective nature of the Africanist literary practice: it reads both itself reading (the usual modernist turn) *and* the dominant culture's effort to read it (as it reads itself). Morrison's modernism is both of the earlier Anglo-American movement and apart from it, a relationship established through a critical turn on double consciousness that, in *Beloved*, underscores the vested nature of the desire to forget at the center of western modernity. In its fragmented and recursive narrative, *Beloved* dramatizes the *survivalist desire* to forget and, through this critical yet critically interested dialogue with literary modernism, forces a reconsideration of the charge that modernism, in its flight from history into myth, seeks to "naturalize" social injustice.

Morrison's effort to connect Africanist values and modernist values comes to the fore in *Beloved*, where knowledge that we have all "forgotten" comes back to haunt us and demand some reckoning; in Morrison's novel, Faulkner, the apotheosis of American literary modernism, and *Absalom, Absalom!*, the crowning achievement of that apotheosis, become the chief targets for exhumation and reburial. Before *Beloved*, one could argue, *Absalom, Absalom!* was a text whose *content* appeared dis(re)membered and scattered throughout Morrison's work: Clytie revised as Circe in *Song of Solomon*, Charles Bon as Son in *Tar Baby*. In *Beloved*, Morrison realizes that the real target for revision and reclamation is not the author's use of individual black characters, but the very literary language itself. *Beloved* remembers that prior text's most striking formal properties—its recursive use of multiple voices, its fragmentation, even its acknowledgement that some stories never can be properly told or forgotten—in order to respectfully, but nonetheless thoroughly and without regret, bury the notion of a "pure" white American modernism. Reading *Beloved* through *Absalom, Absalom!* helps us to see how, in her novel, Morrison "properly, artistically," places the Africanist body in that grave where "*we had no corpse*" (*Absalom* 123); *Beloved* suggests that modernism's "empty hall echoing with sonorous defeated names" ultimately housed not many ghosts, but one (*Absalom* 7).

Morrison's notion of "purposeful restriction" would seem to coincide philosophically with Tate's "arrest" and Frank's "timeless world of myth," insofar as it implies a concerted effort to refuse narrative entry to certain (undesirable) elements. I would like to approach the notion of "purposeful restriction" in another sense: how it describes what an author does in seeking to transmute "content" into "form." Morrison's approach to *Beloved* is perfectly suited to this inquiry, since the seed for the novel was the true story of Margaret Garner, a fugitive slave who, finding herself in imminent danger of being returned to slavery, chose to kill one of her children rather than see the child re-enslaved. In the many interviews given upon the publication of *Beloved*, Morrison was careful to point out that the book was only *inspired* by Garner's story; it was not an effort to retell it:

> I was amazed by this story I came across about a woman called Margaret Garner who had escaped from Kentucky, *I think*, into Cincinnati with four children. . . . And she was a kind of cause célèbre among abolitionists *in 1855 or '56* because she tried to kill the children when she was caught. She killed one of them, just as in the novel. I found *an article* in a magazine of the period. . . .

> Now, I didn't do any more research at all about that story. . . . I did
> a lot of research about everything else in the book—Cincinnati, and
> abolitionists, and the underground railroad—but I refused to find out
> anything else about Margaret Garner. I really wanted to invent her life.
> ("Toni" C17; emphasis added)

Morrison's remarks here are representative of claims she made whenever she
was asked about the genesis of the story of Sethe, complete with the hedging ("I
think," "1855 or '56") and the emphasis on a minimal amount of research (*one*
article in a magazine, not three or four). But in fact, Morrison knew quite a bit
about Margaret Garner's story, as one interview shows. When, in a conversation
published in the March 1988 issue of *The Women's Review of Books*, Marsha Jean
Darling wonders "what difference it would have made if Halle had been there
the day that the white men came across the yard to get Sethe," Morrison replies:
"In fact it didn't make a difference, because in fact Margaret Garner escaped with
her husband and two other men and was returned to slavery." When Darling
follows up this response by asking, "Despite the fact that she killed the child,
she was returned?", Morrison replies,

> Well, she wasn't tried for killing her child. She was tried for a *real* crime,
> which was running away—although the abolitionists were trying very hard
> to get her tried for murder because they wanted the Fugitive Slave Law to
> be unconstitutional. They did not want her tried on those grounds, so they
> tried to switch it to murder as a kind of success story. They thought that
> they could make it impossible for Ohio, as a free state, to acknowledge the
> right of a slave-owner to come get those people. . . . But they all went back
> to Boone County and apparently the man who took them back—the man
> she was going to kill herself and her children to get away from—he sold
> her down river, which was as bad as was being separated from each other.
> But apparently the boat hit a sandbar or something, and she fell or jumped
> with her daughter, her baby, into the water. It is not clear whether she fell
> or jumped, but they rescued her and I guess she went on down to New
> Orleans and I don't know what happened after that. ("In the Realm" 6)

In response to Darling's rather vague question, Morrison reveals a strikingly
thorough knowledge of the particulars of Margaret Garner's sad history, including a familiarity with the legal maneuvers employed by the abolitionists
in order to use Garner's infanticide as a test case for the Fugitive Slave Law.
That Morrison even remembers the name of the Kentucky county from which
the Garner family fled (Boone County, named nowhere in *Beloved*) indicates a
familiarity with the history born of some research more thorough than a brief,
emotionally bedazzled reading of a single magazine article. Morrison doesn't
know what happens after Garner's accident on the river boat not because she

chose to cut off her research, but because the historical record itself, in fact, fails to tell us what became of the woman.[6]

I bring this up not to complain that Morrison has misrepresented the process by which she came to write *Beloved*, but to examine how she chose to exercise a "purposeful restriction" in fitting Margaret Garner's story to her artistic project. In shaping her story, Morrison was confronted with a conflicting series of accounts in both the popular press and scholarly journals; the very way in which the child died remains unclear. But there is enough agreement in the general outlines of the event to highlight those points at which Morrison chose to depart from the historic record.[7] In these accounts, Garner was not alone with her children in the early summer in a woodshed behind a house situated at the outskirts of Cincinnati, but in the city home of a free kinsman in the middle of January (the fugitives walked across the frozen Ohio to freedom); the Garner family was not owned by a single slave-holder, but split up between the owners of two plantations in Boone County (one man owned Garner's husband and his parents, another owned Margaret and the children). The fugitives were recaptured within hours of their escape, rather than one month later as in *Beloved*. And, as Morrison tells Darling, Margaret Garner was never tried for the murder of her daughter. A federal judge remanded the slaves back to Kentucky; efforts to try Garner for murder under state statutes were rendered superfluous when she was sold down the river in spite of pledges from Kentucky officials that she would be held to stand trial in Ohio.

Nearly all of the areas of disagreement in the historical record appear—not surprisingly—in the realm of the act itself and the slaves' reactions to it. Some reports stressed that all four adults were in the room at the time of the murder and that the men "began to scream" when Garner attacked the child; others emphasized that the men were elsewhere in the building, armed and, in a desperate, manly effort to protect their women and children, shooting at (and wounding) the slave-catchers. One report claims that, when Margaret asked her mother-in-law to " 'help me to kill the children' . . . the old woman began to wail . . . and ran for refuge under a bed" (Yanuck 52); another states that the mother-in-law "neither encouraged nor discouraged her daughter-in-law,—for under similar circumstances she would have probably done the same" (Middleton Harris 10). Finally, according to one account, the murdered child was not "thunder black and glistening" (*Beloved* 261) but "almost white" (Coffin 563).

There are two ways of looking at Morrison's "purposeful restrictions," and both of them are pertinent to a discussion of the novel's relationship to *Absalom, Absalom!*. The first is Morrison's belief—expressed both in interviews and in the novel—that the historical record cannot be trusted to offer a true appraisal of slave history. As Morrison tells Christina Davis, "the reclamation of the history of black people in this country is paramount in its importance because while you can't really blame the conqueror for writing history his own way, you can certainly debate it. There's a great deal of obfuscation and distortion and erasure, so that the presence and the heartbeat of black people has been systematically annihilated in many, many ways and the job of recovery is ours" (Interview with Christina Davis 142).

The trail of newspaper clippings, the articles in historical journals written out of those clippings—in the last analysis, none can be trusted to tell Margaret Garner's story, because they are, to greater and lesser degrees, historically grounded in a racist enterprise. In *Beloved*, Morrison puts it this way:

> [T]here was no way in hell a black face could appear in a newspaper if the story was about something anybody wanted to hear. A whip of fear broke through the heart chambers as soon as you saw a Negro's face in a paper, since the face was not there because the person had a healthy baby, or outran a street mob. Nor was it there because the person had been killed, or maimed or caught or burned or jailed or whipped or evicted or stomped or raped or cheated, since that could hardly qualify as news in a newspaper. It would have to be something out of the ordinary—something whitepeople would find interesting, truly different, worth a few minutes of teeth sucking if not gasps. (155–56)

This rejection of the notion that "realist" descriptions of events are suitable to the effort to recover African-American history leads to the second way of looking at Morrison's revisions, one that sees her strategy as a reclamation of exactly those modernist methods of telling deployed in *Absalom, Absalom!*. As first Rosa Coldfield, then Mr. Compson, then Rosa again, then Shreve and Quentin all strive to tell the story of the fall of Sutpen and the murder of Charles Bon, the reader is forced to recognize the ways in which each character invests his or her own psychological needs in the story. Thus the enraged, embittered Rosa Coldfield presents a nostalgic, Old South view of the tale, emphasizing romance and a Manichean ethics. The cynical, alcoholic Mr. Compson prefers a detached, ironic reading that suggests the cause of the fall of Sutpen in Bon's exoticism, Henry's prudish (yet voyeuristic and homoerotically charged) sexuality, and Sutpen's lack of breeding, but that collapses into paradox: "It's just incredible. It just does not explain" (80).[8] In their turn, Shreve and Quentin seek to wrest a meaning from this history for themselves, first clearing a space for "play" that will permit their search for a deeper truth in "love, where there might be paradox and inconsistency but nothing fault or false" (253). But even in their play Shreve and Quentin (and we) make use of what has gone before; their "overpassing" must launch itself from the scenes of those deeply vested versions of the story that they have heard. Faulkner thus simultaneously beckons toward and abjures a notion of narrative transcendence; however much it may be desired, there is no "overpassing" that does not start (and end) in some specific place.

In writing *Beloved*, Morrison was faced with a choice: to creatively deploy a "realist" narrative discourse so that its complicity with racial terror became clear, or to enter into a dialogue with "psychological" modernism that would complete the gesture begun in *Absalom, Absalom!* by exploring the ways in which modernism simultaneously inscribes and unmasks its complicity in social injustice. In fact, Morrison does both: revising realism through *Beloved*'s content (especially through the figure of Schoolteacher, the sadistic scientific racist) and modernism in its technique and form. And by invoking and repudiating past printed accounts of Margaret Garner's story, Morrison, like Faulkner, warns against a too-easy transcendence of a confusing, painful history. What she has given us, after all, is not a story to pass on.

This brings us to the conclusions of the two novels and back to the question of irony. As Quentin and Shreve settle for sleep in their dormitory room, Shreve describes the telling of the Sutpen story as a scene of incomplete compensations:

> "So it took Charles Bon and his mother to get rid of old Tom, and Charles Bon and the octoroon to get rid of Judith, and Charles Bon and Clytie to get rid of Henry; and Charles Bon's mother and Charles's Bon's grandmother got rid of Charles Bon. So it takes two niggers to get rid of one Sutpen, dont it?" Quentin did not answer; evidently Shreve did not want an answer now; he continued almost without pause: "Which is all right, it's fine; it clears the whole ledger, you can tear all the pages out and burn them, except for one thing. And do you know what that is?" Perhaps he hoped for an answer this time, or perhaps he merely paused for emphasis, since he got no answer. "You've got one nigger left. One nigger Sutpen left. Of course you cant catch him and you dont even always see him and you never will be able to use him. But you've got him there still. You still hear him at night sometimes. Dont you?"
> "Yes," Quentin said. (302)

All of the past tellings—the fragmented circumlocutions and desiring displacements, the embracing and rejecting in turn of nostalgia and paradox as avenues of explanation—that have gone into this "overpassing," and the "overpassing" itself, stop dead at the agonized, howling remainder present in the figure of Jim Bond. He is what the novel cannot overpass, that lived and living piece of Sutpen history that prevents Quentin and Shreve from clearing the ledger and burning the pages. His presence reduces Shreve's smug amazement to an ironic anthropological fantasy—ironic in light of what we know about civilization perhaps having, indeed, "sprung from the loins of African kings" (302). It renews in Quentin the gnawing, unreconciled nature of his own feelings toward the South. If the narrative project of *Absalom, Absalom!* has been to show that nothing is ever told once and is finished, Jim Bond serves as the (racial, historical) sign of remainder that fuels the repetition. "You will never be able to use him," Shreve says, in an odd formulation that recalls the use to which blacks were put in slavery. "But you've got him there still." If the Africanist body is the nothing at the center of Faulkner's text, then there is literally nothing that can be done with Jim Bond.[9] Faulkner's novel closes with Jim Bond's howling ringing in Quentin's (and the reader's) ears. Quentin's response to Shreve's question (" 'Why do you hate the South?' 'I don't hate it,' Quentin said . . . 'I dont hate it,' he said. *I dont hate it* he thought . . . *I dont. I dont! I dont hate it! I dont hate it!*" [303]) represents a feeble attempt to silence that howling through paradox.

This reading of the narrative project and conclusion of *Absalom, Absalom!* has been more suggestive than definitive, but it puts us in a position to see the second—and, I would say, more radical—way of viewing Morrison's recuperation of modernism via Faulkner's novel. *Absalom, Absalom!* is haunted by the ways in which an unfree Africanist presence conditions the modernist enterprise, and it shows us how irony and paradox may be deployed in an effort to contain that remainder. *Beloved*, too, is haunted by this presence, and Morrison, too, deploys irony and paradox in the conclusion of her novel. Having pieced together the story of the murder of Sethe's child; having followed the disembodied haunting and consuming embodied presence of that child, and the final dis(re)membering and scattering of that body; having made the imaginative links between the spirit of Beloved and those of all Africans lost in the Middle Passage; having done all this, the readers of *Beloved* are unequivocally told at the end of the novel that what they have just read "is not a story to pass on" (275). Many critics have decided that Morrison simply can't really mean this, and have pointed to the fact that the story has, in fact, been passed on—through the novel.[10] James Phelan argues that Morrison's insistence on *Beloved*'s "stubbornness" in yielding up its meaning serves to uncover the reader's own desires for interpretive "mastery and possession" (721). Phelan's reading offers a fruitful way of exploring *Beloved*'s relationship to modernist paradox in general and *Absalom, Absalom!* in particular—a text about a master, by a (modernist) master, that in many ways owes its continuing aesthetic life to its readers' attempts to master its hidden meanings. To borrow terms from digital audio technology, Morrison samples and remasters Faulkner's text— both by critically redeploying its method and by reinhabiting the history it simultaneously evokes and abandons—and thus places into question the very notion of literary mastery.

But the conclusion of *Beloved* also reflects quite literally on the problems Morrison confronted in writing the novel. As she has remarked in several interviews, she was repeatedly surprised by how much slave history had been silenced—not only by the masters but also by the enslaved. "There was something untold, unsaid, that never came down," Morrison said in one post-publication interview. "There was some deliberate, calculated, survivalist intention, to forget certain things. [For example], there was almost no reference to the ships . . . I know no songs about it. I know no stories about it" (Interview with Melvyn Bragg). But while the story of the Middle Passage was not "passed on," it was not truly forgotten. As Morrison tells Paul Gilroy, "the struggle to forget, which was important in order to survive, is fruitless and I wanted to make it fruitless" ("Living" 179). The irony lies in knowing how some things are not "passed on" yet remain unforgettable; now our "weather," Beloved will be with us forever (*Beloved* 275).

Reading *Beloved* as a modern postmodern text and *Absalom, Absalom!* as a postmodern modern text raises the question, finally, of just what these terms—modern, postmodern—practically mean. It seems to me that examining the social, political, and aesthetic *uses* to which texts are put is perhaps a better approach to what frequently has been seen as a question of periodization. A brief discussion of the public response to *Beloved* and *Absalom, Absalom!* opens the way toward thinking about modernism and postmodernism as phenomena of reception. Thus, as we began this discussion of form with content, let us end with context.

Over and over again, in the first reviews of *Absalom, Absalom!*, critics remarked (usually complaining, sometimes marvelling) on the forbidding surface of Faulkner's text. Clifton Fadiman's infamous comment that "one may sum up both substance and style by saying that every person in 'Absalom, Absalom!' comes to no good end, and they all take a hell of a time coming even that far" (62) represents an extreme view, but it is representative: Harold Strauss remarks that the novel is "strange chiefly because of the amazing indirectness with which Faulkner has managed to tell a basically simple story" (7), and William Troy observes that "through neither the form nor the style do we escape from the closed universe of his intensely personal vision" (524). In these reviews, Faulkner's form was all; this remained the dominant view even after his reputation was rehabilitated in the Cold War period. In the 1930s, Faulkner was rejected because his forbidding style marked him as an author uninterested in, if not absolutely opposed to, the current effort to enlist the arts in building an equitable society. In the 1950s, Faulkner was embraced because his forbidding style seemed to confirm the then-ascendant notion of the modern "heroic" artist, whose merit derived solely from the completeness with which he realized his own (intensely personal, socially disengaged) aesthetic vision.

Today, Faulkner is being read for his history—particularly for the ways in which his texts reveal how the southern modernist desire to "forget" history arises as much from the white ruling class's effort to remain in power during a period of social upheaval as from any individualistic psychosexual trauma.[11] This view of Faulknerian texts corresponds with notions of the postmodern outlined by both Jameson and Linda Hutcheon: it is the engagement with history, contrasted to the modern flight from history, that marks the postmodern text. Certainly, much of this new Faulkner arises from his texts; but more than a small portion of it—in fact, a rather large portion of it, if the grounds for my project here have warrant—arises from the interaction of Faulkner's novels with works like *Beloved*, which force us to go back to the older author with new eyes and new ears.

From its first appearance, *Beloved* was hailed as an historical, politically engaged, redemptive novel. In the conclusion of his review, Thomas R. Edwards asserts that, "I would suppose that in *Beloved* Morrison means to help thoughtful black people, especially women, to create or re-create an imagination of self that 'white history' or 'male history' has effectively denied them" (19). Margaret Atwood remarks that the novel invites us to "experience American slavery as it was lived by those who were its objects of exchange" (49); even Stanley Crouch, in his notorious dismissal of the work, latched onto its historic reach in order to enter the complaint that "*Beloved*, above all else, is a blackface holocaust novel." (40). This attention to history is appropriate, if complemented by a reading of the novel's formal strategies that is itself also historical. The notable exception in this rush toward history is Judith Thurman's review, in which she observes, "Despite the richness and authority of its detail, 'Beloved' is not primarily a historical novel. . . . [Morrison] treats the past as if it were one of those luminous old scenes painted on dark glass—the scene of a disaster, like the burning of Parliament or the eruption of Krakatoa—and she breaks the glass, and recomposes it in disjointed and puzzling modern form. As the reader struggles with its fragments and mysteries, he keeps being startled by flashes of his own reflection in them" (175).

Thurman comes to this view because she reads *Beloved* in companion with other texts, starting with "The Cosby Show," continuing with Shakespeare's *The Tempest* and Mary Shelley's *Frankenstein*, and finally concluding with selected insights drawn from Sigmund Freud and Frederick Nietzsche; putting the postmodern *Beloved* in a historical cultural context leads Thurman to consider its "modern" impulses. This seems to me to indicate that, though we have made good postmodern use of Morrison's novel (reading it helps us think historically when we believe we have forgotten to do so), we do well to attend to the ways in which that use is predicated upon modernist assumptions that *Beloved* simultaneously distances itself from and fulfills. For some time now, literary modernism itself seems to have been the nightmare from which we have all been trying to awaken; *Beloved* and *Absalom, Absalom!* both remind us how it is the undigested histories that stick around to haunt us.

Notes

1. In almost every interview given at *Beloved*'s publication, Morrison discusses her discovery of Margaret Garner's story while editing *The Black Book* (the news clipping about the case appears at the top of page 10 of that anthology, published in 1974); see Middleton Harris. For two representative examples, see the interviews with Melvyn Rothstein and with Marsha Jean Darling. The inspiration for *Jazz* came from a photograph in *The Harlem Book of the Dead* (Morrison "Foreword"), which featured photographs by James Van der Zee, poetry by Owen Dodson, and an interview of Van der Zee by Camille Billops. Morrison edited this project, and wrote the book's foreword, in 1978; the photograph of the woman who was the model for Dorcas appears on page 53.

2. Linda Krumholz correctly identifies Morrison's use of modernist technique in this section (396), but she does not explore why Morrison would decide that a modernist method was particularly suitable there.

3. Two important exceptions to this trend toward reading *Beloved* with or against *The Scarlet Letter* are Duvall ("Authentic") and Moreland (" 'He wants' ").

4. Indeed, Pérez-Torres's essay (inadvertently, I believe) casts modernism as exactly a huge nothing out of which *Beloved* arises: "The narrative emerges, then, at the point at which premodern and postmodern forms of literary expression cross" (690). Modernism thus becomes a gigantic hole, a ghost, as it were, haunting the scene of its emergence.

5. Important companions to Gates's work for any consideration of the conjunctions of African-American expressivity and Western modernism are Gilroy (*Black Atlantic*), North, and Lott.

6. For a thorough examination of Margaret Garner's story, see Yanuck. Another likely source for Morrison would have been Levi Coffin's *Reminiscences*. Yanuck's essay cites scores of articles from various newspapers that covered the Garner case, any one or more of which Morrison could have perused.

7. Some newspaper accounts describing the murder say the child died a gruesome, lingering death, in which the mother "hacked" repeatedly at the girl's throat with a butcher knife (Yanuck 52). Levi Coffin claims that the child was killed mercifully, "with one stroke" (560). All the accounts, however, agree that the murdered girl was

three years old—not almost two, and thus in a preOedipal phase of development, as in Morrison's novel. Rendering Beloved as a preOedipal infant is certainly crucial to Morrison's artistic project and has been remarked upon by many critics of the novel. See, for instance, Wyatt, Moreland (" 'He wants' "), and Horvitz, and, in this volume, Fowler.

8. I am partly drawing here on Moreland's reading of the novel in *Faulkner and Modernism*, in which Rosa and Mr. Compson are seen as Faulkner's efforts to work through and critique the two dominant methods available to his effort to "tell about the South": a backward-looking nostalgia and an ironic detachment.

9. For a discussion of the European and Euro-American trope of African blackness as blankness, see Gates (*Figures* 21–24).

10. See, for example, Budick and Homans.

11. For one example of how Faulkner's psychology is being mined for its history, see Matthews ("Rhetoric"). Godden also combines psychoanalytic and Marxist insights in its reading of Haiti in *Absalom, Absalom!*.

14. SIGNIFYING SILENCES

Morrison's Soundings in the Faulknerian Void

Phillip Novak

Any attempt at aligning Toni Morrison's work with that of others—particularly if the other happens to be an earlier white male writer—confronts her cautionary remark that "I am not *like* James Joyce; I am not *like* Thomas Hardy; I am not *like* Faulkner, I am not *like* in that sense" (Interview with Nellie McKay; rpt. Taylor-Guthrie 152). For her remarks here—grounded as they are in concerns about assimilation—insist that criticism of her work attend, not just to the aesthetic, but to the political implications involved in establishing intertextual relations. What *are* the consequences of citing affinities, tracing out affiliations, establishing connections? What does it mean to say that one text is *like* another? On the one hand, I do want to suggest that Morrison's *Beloved* and Faulkner's *Absalom, Absalom!* can be brought into meaningful relation without effacing distinctions between them or, more significantly, without assuming the priority of the earlier novel—without, that is, simply assimilating Morrison's literary production to a stylistics, and thus a mode of conceptuality, determined in advance. On the other hand, I also want to acknowledge at the outset that there are difficulties, a certain resistance, to be not so much overcome as accounted for in arguing that *Beloved* plays with and plays off of, repeats and revises, simultaneously recites and (as it were) re-sites Faulkner's text.

For Morrison's novel not only appropriates many of *Absalom*'s central themes but replays and implicitly replies to its strategies of narrative articulation as well.

Like *Absalom*, *Beloved* is designed to produce or represent a series of marked absences—the absence of a narratable meaning, of a history that can be fully experienced or adequately known—around which is then allowed to circulate a deep sense of loss. But whereas in Faulkner this sort of recuperative deconstructive technique is associated thematically with Western cultural traditions and with what Faulkner conceives to be a universal—and therefore supremely valuable—human suffering, in Morrison it is deployed in order to validate a history that Western cultural traditions managed to suppress (the history of American slaves written from the subject position of the slaves themselves) and to acknowledge a form of suffering that is historically specific. Morrison thus revises Faulkner, not simply in order to punch holes in a Western tradition perceived to be simultaneously inescapable and exhausted, but also in order to bring to the surface—in the openings thus provided—a countertradition that Faulkner's work pointedly ignores.

The surface similarities between the two novels are striking. Both texts, for example, are preoccupied with antebellum southern history and with history as an idea—indeed, at their most basic level, both are *about* the meaning and the possibility of history. Both are concerned with constructing monuments, memorials, to the past—and in both the acquisition and erection of headstones function as figures for that concern. Both narratives turn around the repressed memory of an interfamilial murder (in one case infanticide, in the other fratricide) that must be brought to the surface, resurrected and confronted, in order to be worked through—and both question the possibility of such a confrontation and such a release. Generically, both novels are ghost stories, in which haunted houses figure prominently—and in both cases the haunting is invested with cultural, political, and aesthetic significance.

Perhaps the most important measure, however, of these two texts' relation has to do, not with any of the particulars of repetition and recall, but with the novels' basic attitudes toward the idea of narration, the singlemindedness with which both work at questioning the narratological grounds on which they stand. My point is not simply that *Beloved*, like *Absalom*, can be described as openended, or that the novels strive to achieve a kind of generalized indeterminacy of effect. Indeed, Faulkner's and Morrison's texts are specifically set up to *exceed* at a certain point the limits presupposed by the idea of ambiguity. Both in fact move beyond merely problematizing meaning to the more radical position of questioning the very possibility of narrating, of relating a history, of making events speak. The aim in the case of both novels is not, thus, a proliferation of significations, but a kind of articulated, deeply meaningful silence. And it is precisely by attending to the timbre of their signifying silences, to the sound of their quiet difference (a difference in which can be traced the arc of historical transformation) that one can best catch the resonance, hear the call and response.

In the case of *Absalom*, the narrative's movement toward silence is effected mainly by a confounding of location—the dissolution or dispersal of the site of the utterance. Faulkner's novel resolutely refuses mooring. It places itself *between* two distinct and incompatible stories: the story, on the one hand, of the narrative's own telling (its investigation into problems of perspective, narrative authority, and narrative transmission); and the story, on the other hand, of that which is told (the troubled meditation on the rise and fall of antebellum southern culture). Again, certain distinctions need to be drawn: for in arguing that *Absalom* marks itself as a kind of *trace* in the Derridean sense, I do not mean to suggest that the narrative is simply subsumed in a chain of subjective impressions. Nor am I saying that *Absalom*, like much recent fiction, functions on two different narrative "levels" simultaneously. The narratological problems *Absalom* poses cannot be resolved by this sort of appeal to the layering of narrative meaning: the layers in this case are simply too antagonistic, too systematically aimed at a sort of mutual exclusion that effectively effaces them both.

Beloved poses similar sorts of difficulties; for here again the central questions the novel raises have to do, not with what the story signifies, but with whether it can signify at all. And again the narrative is marked by a kind of radical blurring of narrative focus. On the one hand, and most obviously, there is the story of Sethe and her family, which emphasizes the value and the necessity of acknowledging and incorporating the shame, guilt, and sorrow of history. And at this level, from the standpoint defined by this tale of time's passage, of the emergence of a new generation, which brings with it the hope, however attenuated, of *regeneration*, *Beloved* absolutely insists on the need for closure, the need to work through (and past) the past, to lay history to rest. On the other hand, however, and up to the very close of the novel, there is the story, the figure, of Beloved, through which Morrison's text insists just as stridently that history can be neither effectively recuperated nor entirely left behind. From the point of view located by and within this image of the traumatic and traumatized past itself, no closure is *ever* available: because the past makes demands on the present that the present can never hope to meet, history remains at once an irrecoverable loss and a perpetually open wound, an alien presence in the present that can never be quite assimilated—a type of haunting.

Like *Absalom*, *Beloved* thus situates itself in the flickering movement between two perspectives that are somehow simultaneously present yet inherently incompatible; it presents itself in the form of a trace. Both novels are in fact marked by a particular and rather peculiar double movement, an odd sort of folding of the text back on itself aimed ultimately at an equally odd form of self-cancellation. And in the case of both novels this folding of the text is directly related to how they conceive the possibility of *un*folding a history.

For all of *Absalom*'s relentlessness, for example, in attempting to destabilize character and event, the narrative nonetheless strains to present itself as a gradual unveiling, painfully achieved, of a determinate historical reality—the "truth" of the Sutpen family saga. The text's most obvious generic alignments, for instance, are the detective fiction/murder mystery, whose defining feature is a deliberate, almost fetishized, uncovering of the real, and the ghost story, whose most striking and consistent thematic concern is the necessity of confronting and atoning for the sins of the past. Merging these generic interests, *Absalom* grounds itself in the mysteries surrounding a moment of historical trauma—a trauma that it identifies with the story of Thomas Sutpen, and by extension the history of the South, and that it attempts to heal by means of a process of (psycho)analysis, engaged at the level of the culture as a whole and effected by proxy. The actual nature of the events the novel seeks to uncover and confront thus becomes vitally important. And as *Absalom* proceeds, as it moves from Rosa's lyric diatribe, through Mr. Compson's fatalistic musings, to Quentin's and Shreve's impassioned collaboration, there are repeated suggestions that the narrative is drawing ever closer to a direct confrontation with the set of historical circumstances from which it arises. During the course of Quentin's and Shreve's collaboration on the story, for example, they reach a moment in their narrating when language seems suddenly to give way, seems somehow to give rise to a more immediate kind of communication, a moment when all mediation seems somehow to cease: "They were both in Carolina and the time was forty-six years ago, and . . . now both of them were Henry Sutpen and both of them were Bon" (280). Quentin and Shreve here enter into direct contact not only with each other, but with the rather elusive object of their mutual interest and inquiry. For them, through them, through a kind of excess of sympathy that collapses the distinctions between subject and object, self and other, history starts simply to unfold, to narrate itself, to make itself known.

That history, of course, as it comes to be revealed, is as viciously expressive as an actual lynching—as Sundquist succinctly puts it, Henry "murder[s] Bon not as the 'brother' but as the 'nigger' who is going to sleep with his sister" (126)—and the process of its unveiling is accompanied by profound anxiety. The well-known exchange between Quentin and Shreve that closes the novel, for instance, presents itself as the accomplishment of a profound recognition, the transformative moment in a melodramatic psychoanalysis invested with cultural meaning. And in order for it to be effective either as analysis, or as scene, in order for it to avoid just seeming silly, this recognition requires historical grounding, needs to be accepted as in some sense "real."

As has often been noted, Morrison's *Beloved* is similarly rooted in history. Indeed, given the circumstances surrounding the novel's inception—that Morrison "discovered" the basis for her story while doing research for *The Black Book*—the text's connection to history is in some sense integral, a point Morrison makes emphatic in the novel. For the clipping Stamp Paid shows to Paul D in order to inform him of the murder of Beloved, and that Paul D in turn takes to Sethe, is a fictional analog of the newspaper article from which *Beloved* itself originates. By representing the clipping *in* the novel, Morrison not only creates a point of contact between the history *Beloved* tells and the history of its own construction; she sets up as well an analogy between the various confrontations with and reconstructions of the past that the characters are engaged in and those that the novel itself works to effect. History, in that sense, is the very warp and woof of Morrison's text. But history is as much in the foreground of *Beloved* as it is a part of the novel's grounding. The domestic concerns that are the narrative's primary focus of attention are necessarily intertwined with larger historical issues: the Fugitive Slave Bill, the Settlement Fee, skin voting, the Dred Scott Decision—all of which are specifically mentioned in the text, as are such clear historical markers as Frederick Douglass's *North Star* and the travels of Sojourner Truth. Because, in the lives of slaves and former slaves, the domestic *is* the political, the individual actions of the characters inevitably carry historical weight.

Beloved thus mirrors *Absalom*'s concern for history—mirrors in many ways, in fact, that history itself. The framing of the two texts, both in temporal and cultural terms, is strikingly similar. Both novels involve, for example, a post-Civil War reflection on antebellum southern culture, and in both cases the site of this reflection is a socially and politically charged geographical space in the North (in *Beloved*, Ohio; in *Absalom*, Massachusetts). Moreover, the principal events in both novels all take place in the same general time period (roughly 1830–1880), with most of them tightly focused in the period just prior to and during the war. It is a measure, for instance, of the two novels' interconnection that Baby Suggs, who would be about twelve years older than Sutpen, dies the same year in which Henry kills Charles Bon.

But if *Beloved* functions as something of a mirror of Faulkner's novel in this regard, it does so only in the sense that a mirror reverses the image that it reflects.[1] For while *Absalom* undoubtedly does work to engage America's troubled past, this engagement is presented entirely, perhaps inevitably, from the perspective of the whites who owned—or, as is the case with Sutpen's father, felt themselves to be in competition with—America's slaves. The slaves themselves are fairly studiously confined to the position of setting. Thoroughly objectified, generally silent, they are depicted, not as subjects engaged in history, but as part of the material through which the processes of history are seen to work. Like Bon's mistress, "the magnolia-faced woman" (157), who is "taken at childhood, culled and chosen and raised more carefully than any white girl, any nun, than any blooded mare even, by a person who gives them the unsleeping care and attention which no mother ever gives" (93), and who is thus "saved" from a life of abject misery by being born into prostitution, they remain nameless. Or they are wholly reduced to the mere sound of their names, to the status of interchangeable examples: "Send me Juno or Missylena or Chlory" (87). They are anonymous, inscrutable, and quietly violent, like Sutpen's "band of wild niggers" (4). Or they are purely functional, counters in a class struggle waged between white men, like "the monkey-dressed nigger butler" (187) who rebuffs the adolescent Sutpen at the door of the plantation house. Thus, paradoxically, for all of *Absalom*'s sensitivity to issues of race, and despite its desire to stage a direct confrontation with the criminality and fatality of the South's slaveholding past, the novel so generalizes and objectifies slave experience that it effectively writes that experience out of the history it is attempting to relate.

In *Beloved*, the task Morrison sets for herself is to write this experience back into the record, to reconstruct history, as Linda Krumholz has put it, "through the acts and consciousness of African-American slaves rather than through the perspective of the dominant white social classes" (395)—a task in which the narrative succeeds with a kind of uncanny comprehensiveness. Like Whitman, that is, Morrison "contains multitudes," and in the process of unfolding Sethe's story she manages to present an almost encyclopedic account of the varieties of slave existence: detailed descriptions of life on small farms and large plantations, in prison camps and private homes; portraits of slaves in the field and of those engaged in domestic service; sketches of the movements of the underground railroad; catalogs of concretely imagined particular incidents designed to render a host of individual lives. "[T]hrough painstaking research into the historical record," as Carol E. Schmudde has noted, Morrison thus provides "an imaginative re-creation of slave experience with an immediacy and credibility unparalleled in American literature" ("Knowing" 135).

Needless to say, this experience is frequently filled with tragedy and is often trauma-based. In the histories of the principal characters—or in the novel's frequent summaries of a kind of collective, communal history—*Beloved* paints a portrait of lives literally shattered by the difficulties endured under, or in the aftermath of, slavery; lives broken, like Sethe's is, into discrete parcels of experience that resist interpretation, that fail to cohere. Indeed, all of the characters whose lives we see in detail here have been so scarred by their histories (and in a gesture typical for the novel, the cliche is often literalized) that they have, by the time we first see them, fallen out of history into what Sethe—in a particularly Faulknerian turn of phrase—thinks of as the "no-time" of simple endurance (*Beloved* 191). Too fragile to allow themselves the hope of a future, simultaneously locked into and cut off from pasts that they actively refuse to confront, they abide a dissociated, fugue-like existence in flight from the present, which they experience as an emptiness, as an unsatisfiable longing related to grief. And all are starved (again the cliche is literalized) for some sense of meaningful connection. Like Beloved, they are all "looking for the join" (213).

Most obviously, this sense of destitution and voracity is reflected in Sethe's and Beloved's and Denver's triangulated desire. Painfully, poignantly, Denver feeds on the returned glance of Beloved—who can always, indeed mostly does, look away. Sethe can always, and ultimately must, *go* away from Beloved, whose exigency, like Denver's, is thoroughly uncompromising and who can therefore, like Denver, never quite get enough of the attention she craves. Sethe too, for her part, is consumed (again almost literally) by her desire, her longing for some sign from Beloved that she has been forgiven, that she no longer needs to try to explain. One of *Beloved*'s central concerns is thus the regular iteration, the almost compulsive playing out of a certain mode of felt incompletion—an incompletion the novel registers, not only thematically, in the lives of the characters, but structurally as well.

What is most interesting here, however, is that this acute sense of longing, this experience of the present as being marked by an absence, leads both the novel and its characters inexorably to the past, to a kind of continuous reproduction or reliving of the trauma from which this sense of divestiture seems somehow to spring.[2] For the characters, the past is meaningful precisely because it *is* traumatic, because it is invested with the sort of felt significance that the present so perfectly lacks. Thus Denver fixates on the story of her own rather harrowing and improbable birth and dotes on Beloved, the embodiment of her feelings of loss and isolation. Thus Beloved endlessly replays—both literally, in the form of a kind of neurotic compulsion, and figuratively, in the form of her musings—the two critical moments of her mother's disappearance.[3] Thus Sethe and Paul D are drawn, despite their best efforts at resistance, to memories of Sweet Home, which on one level, they both recognize, was neither "sweet" nor "home"—as Paul D puts it (14)—but which they nonetheless persistently recall with an odd, sharply ironized wistfulness.

As is the case with *Absalom*, this compulsive return to—or of—the past is part of the narrative's deepest structure. And, like *Absalom*, *Beloved* presents itself at once as a ghost story,[4] a murder mystery, and a process of psychotherapy— perhaps even of exorcism—carried out at the cultural level. From the first brief evocations of Sethe's fragmentary memories of Sweet Home, *Beloved* struc- turally retraces *Absalom*'s steps by moving inexorably toward an increasingly immediate presentation of the horrifying history that is simultaneously the text's clearest subject and its most guarded secret. Frequent, elliptical references to the haunting of the house on Bluestone Road in the opening pages of the novel hint at the violence done there. Equally sketchy allusions to the "tree" on Sethe's back suggest but do not quite tell the story of her whipping. Slowly, circuitously, the story unfolds: in a kind of narrative "channeling," Denver "remembers" Sethe's arduous escape from Sweet Home, her meeting with Amy Denver, her giving birth; Paul D finally recalls and fully recounts his painful experiences in and flight from the prison in Alfred, Georgia. And when Sethe eventually "recognizes" Beloved, when she finally hears the "click" of the pieces of the past "settling . . . into places designed and made especially for them" (175), and when she and Beloved, as a consequence, enter into a kind of fused dialogue concerning the past, Morrison's novel, like Faulkner's, stages a direct confrontation with history. From *Beloved*'s opening sentence, with its evocation of the resentful, unappeased, and unintegrated past, the narrative has been driving toward just such a moment of joyous psychic fusion. For here that hunger for connection that is the novel's thematic preoccupation seems finally to be satisfied. Not only do past and present communicate here without mediation, they speak with a single voice. Relations here are defined and acknowledged, explanations offered and apparently accepted, reconciliations seemingly achieved.

The scene replays in striking ways the climactic encounter in *Absalom* between Quentin and Henry, that odd confrontation, late in the novel, between an awed and apprehensive present and the desiccated body of a still living past. As a form of mystery, even as a ghost story, *Absalom* requires this meeting, for it is the only moment in the narrative when the mysteries the text has generated can actually be solved, the only moment when the past can finally be laid to rest. Even those scenes that function as formal anticipations—such as the passage alluded to earlier in which the novel attempts to effect an "unmediated" presentation of the past—work to make this ultimate unveiling not unnecessary but more urgent. For they stage the *possibility* of connecting with history but at the same time suggest that the kind of connection Shreve and Quentin make through their narrating is somehow suspect, perhaps simply delusional. Here, in contrast, there can be no question of the encounter being *merely* imaginative. As in *Beloved*, but here just for an instant, at the close of the novel, we are offered a glimpse of the *kind* of scene needed to hold *Absalom* together as a story, precisely the kind of scene of discovery that the narrative has from the beginning suggested it will provide, and—strikingly, ostentatiously—nothing happens.

As Peter Brooks has pointed out, the brief passage that "represents" Quentin's encounter with Henry is, in terms of form, something of a palindrome (306); and in terms of content it is virtually empty: it "says" nothing.[5] More importantly, it prevents the novel as a whole from saying anything either—prevents it from narrating meaning, or from responding meaningfully to the actual history of the South. Indeed, in staging as it does the failure of connection between the past and the present, the narrating and the narrated, in raising the possibility of disclosure and simultaneously refusing to produce it (in producing instead a parody of disclosure) the passage creates a kind of permanent slippage, an inescapable "something is missing," that essentially "hollows out" the novel, that drains it of meaning. Or, to put the point in slightly more positive form, the passage at once establishes the novel as a narrating of meaning's absence and identifies the absent of the novel—the something that has *always* been missing—as meaning, as content, as that which might hold the story together.

Granted, to say that *Absalom* aims at impasse, that it is a text designed to frustrate "reading" is to say nothing that the novel doesn't in some sense tell us itself (at times quite explicitly). "It's just incredible," Mr. Compson notes, for example, during one of the novel's most obvious, and most famous, self-reflections, "It just does not explain. . . . [S]omething is missing. . . . [Y]ou bring [the ingredients] together . . . but nothing happens" (80).[6] Mr. Compson's is but one voice, of course, in a novel constructed out of disparate and often dissonant voices—and it possesses no special authority. But there *is* an analogy to be drawn here. We *are* meant to see a resemblance between our own interpretive efforts and the various attempts at reading represented in the novel, to see our struggle to wrest meaning from the fractious and refractory materials of the text as related to, as somehow prefigured in, the characters' struggles to understand the story they are severally trying to tell, to see ourselves as caught up in a kind of chain of hermeneutic striving. And although Mr. Compson's description of both the Sutpen story and the processes involved in its interpretation no doubt reflects a personal bias, there is in fact nothing in the novel which suggests that that description is in any way inadequate.

Mr. Compson is not, after all, the only narrator in the novel to have difficulty identifying the "thread" of his own narration. Indeed, all of the individual narratives that go into *Absalom*'s making arise out of and revolve around some basic conceptual or imaginative impasse;[7] and they all bear witness to some fundamental *inability* to explain—to some feeling on the part of each of the narrators that somehow "something is missing." Miss Rosa's famous "demonizing" of Sutpen, for example, serves throughout her narrative as a means of marking the limits of her own comprehension, as a way for her text to register wonder, to call attention to that which it does not, which it cannot, account for. And unlike Mr. Compson, Miss Rosa is a central character in, as well as the narrator of, her story. She was actually "there" in that past that the reader, along with Quentin and Shreve and Mr. Compson, is forced to confront throughout the novel. And yet for her, too, the story is enigmatic, deeply mysterious—even more mysterious, perhaps, than it is for Mr. Compson. For the central mystery in Rosa's case lies not outside, in the realm of external circumstance, but inside, in Rosa's own motives and actions. Having seen all the suffering and destruction Sutpen's very existence seemed to have wrought, how, Rosa asks herself, could she ever have agreed to marry him? This is the puzzle, the problem that generates her telling. And she too, in her own, way insists that the story "just does not explain."

In *Beloved*, in the story of Sethe's possibly fatal attempt to come up with an adequate account of her actions, Morrison similarly foregrounds the difficulties involved in trying to "explain." Like *Absalom*, Morrison's narrative arises out of and is propelled by the need to elucidate a central traumatic event—the killing of Sethe's "crawling-already? baby" mirroring, in this structural sense, the killing of Charles Bon. And like *Absalom*, *Beloved* moves gradually toward immediate contact with its initially veiled point of origin: indeed the text fairly quickly establishes the *aim* of the narrative as the discovery or disclosure of the narrative's own source. As is the case with Faulkner's novel, however, the very process that provides the text's direction ultimately serves to expose that aim as futile. For the narrative—a sort of Derridean postcard—never quite manages to arrive at its destination, insists in fact that the origin/aim of the discourse lies outside the realm of narratability. "[I]f she'd only come," Sethe says to Denver early on in the novel—referring of course to the ghost, Beloved—"I could make it clear to her" (4). Then Beloved *does* come to join her mother and her sister at 124 Bluestone—and Sethe's effort at explanation becomes, not just interminable but life threatening. If Sethe's attempt to explain the killing ends at all, it can only end at/in her death.

This general protracted failure on Sethe's part to justify the murder of Beloved is reiterated and reinforced, in a sense encapsulated, when Paul D confronts Sethe with the newspaper account of her imprisonment. Though

Sethe struggles to find the words that will help her make sense of her experience, she acknowledges during this encounter something that her response to the returning Beloved seeks to deny—that the killing of her baby in some way defies explanation. The motives for her actions, the event, its meaning, remain incommunicable. There are only her own impressions of the time of the killing, which can be registered solely by means of an appeal to a private, and extremely ambiguous, symbolism. To the extent that she can explain her motives at all, she explains them entirely in terms of negation: "No. No. Nono. Nonono." The truth is simple, she thinks; but it is also irrational, cannot in fact be rationalized. And Paul D, whose sympathetic understanding is his most marked trait of character, a gift of heroic proportions, simply doesn't understand—must work his way back to Sethe, in fact, through processes of acceptance and love that supersede reason, that obviate the need for explanation.

Ultimately, Sethe's attempt to account for the past in this scene is paradigmatic, not only of her ongoing struggle to come to terms with her personal history, but of the novel as a whole; for the narrative itself duplicates Sethe's circling of the subject.[8] Like her, it cannot quite pin the event down, cannot render an account of the past that will make the past fully "make sense." Indeed, and again as is the case with *Absalom*, the climactic action of Morrison's novel, that event whose clear delineation would serve to tie the various strands of the text together, remains to the end unpresented, a vacuum out of which the story arises, toward which it ceaselessly returns.

Morrison quite insists on the point. As I have said, from the very outset of the novel, *Beloved* presents itself as the unfolding of a mystery, as an effort at historical investigation associated structurally and thematically with psychoanalytic recovery. As the story progresses, the text thus sets up a pattern of incremental revelation, marks itself as moving toward a moment of complete disclosure, where the mystery whose existence the narrative continuously predicts will at long last, and of necessity, be resolved. And yet that moment of seemingly inevitable revelation is never quite allowed to arrive. For when the novel finally does come to the day of the killing, the narrative strains to continue to conceal the event in the very process of describing it:

> The slave catcher dismounted then and joined the others. Schoolteacher and the nephew moved to the left of the house; himself and the sheriff to the right. A crazy old nigger was standing in the woodpile with an ax. You could tell he was crazy right off because he was grunting—making low, cat noises like. About twelve yards beyond that nigger was another one—a woman with a flower in her hat. Crazy too, probably, because she too was standing stock-still—but fanning her hands as though pushing cobwebs

out of her way. Both, however, were staring at the same place—a shed.
Nephew walked over to the old nigger boy and took the ax from him.
Then all four started toward the shed.

   Inside, two boys bled in the sawdust and dirt at the feet of the nigger
woman holding a blood-soaked child to her chest with one hand and an
infant by the heels in the other. (149)

As is almost always the case in *Beloved*, the scene is rendered from the perspective
of characters involved in the action. The crucial difference here, however, is that
the perceptual filter Morrison employs in this particular instance happens to be
white: first the slave catcher, then Schoolteacher, later the nephew, later still the
sheriff. At no other point in the novel are we asked to bear witness to events in
quite this way.

   The issue is complex. On the one hand, this brief opening onto the attitudes
of those who seek to return Sethe and her family to bondage does shed a sort
of oblique light on the immediacy and violence of her reaction to their arrival.
Given the way these men think, Sethe's visceral and complete rejection of the
situation, her elliptical and enigmatic "No. No. Nono. Nonono," becomes in a
way profoundly expressive. On the other hand, by describing the scene of the
murder from the perspective of those least equipped to empathize or understand,
Morrison nonetheless manages to keep the event at a kind of representational
distance. To the extent that we see the killing of Beloved at all, we see it entirely
from the outside, from the only available perspective that can render the scene
while at the same time rendering it essentially opaque. Moreover, the scene itself
is never fully rendered; for at the crucial moment of the novel's closest contact
with the killing, the narrative quietly sinks the event in a kind of interstitial
space. In the movement from paragraph to paragraph, in the passage quoted
above, the story leaps forward—not dramatically, almost imperceptibly—but
just far enough to elide the very action the text has identified as its aim: the
four white men move toward the shed where Sethe has retreated with her
children; the paragraph breaks; the story continues, inside the shed now, with
Sethe already clutching the corpse of her child to her chest. As is the case with
Absalom, Absalom!, we are always already located in the aftermath of the killing,
always already struggling with a series of consequences whose cause remains
obscured, absented.

   In setting itself up as the unveiling of a mystery that it nonetheless refuses to
disclose, *Beloved*, thus, like *Absalom*, presents itself structurally as the production
of an absence, as the marking of a loss. And, like *Absalom*, Morrison's novel
makes use of the ghost figure as a means of representing, of literally embodying,
the particular loss involved. The ghosts serve to recapitulate at the thematic

level that presencing of absence which is both novels' most striking structural peculiarity. Faulkner, for his part, makes use of a number of ghost figures—the spectral Henry Sutpen, the disembodied Jim Bond. Principally, however, in *Absalom, Absalom!*, there is the elusive Charles Bon, who, like the circumstances surrounding his murder, functions as a kind of opening, an absence the text attempts to define. Of the novel's many narrators, for example, only Sutpen can be said to have seen him; and in his own narration Sutpen never mentions Bon. For Mr. Compson, Bon is "completely enigmatic" (74), "a myth, a phantom" (82). And although Rosa falls in love with Bon, she "*never saw him . . . never even saw him dead . . . never even heard his voice, had only Ellen's word for it that there was such a person*" (117). Indeed, the only concrete evidence of Bon's existence is the letter he sends Judith—which mainly serves to duplicate the ambiguity surrounding his history—and the headstone marking the site of his grave.

This monument—with its improbable specificity—is perhaps the most fitting image of Bon the novel provides, and it functions on two different narrative levels simultaneously. First, it serves as a reminder of the novelistic tradition quietly being displaced in *Absalom*, a tradition built on the possibility that meaning might be made of such specificity, that such details might in fact be made to signify. Here they are simply irrelevant, and the allusion they obliquely make to the kind of concrete particularity associated with the novel as a form is at once ironic and profoundly wistful. Second, the monument as a site of mourning underscores the role Bon plays from beginning to end. For he is not so much a character in the narrative as he is a focus for feelings of longing and loss, a register of failed possibilities.

Beloved serves a similar function in Morrison's novel; for, like Bon, she is consistently presented as enigmatic. She seems for example—as Mr. Compson says of Bon—to arrive on the scene "apparently complete, without background or past or childhood" (*Absalom* 74). She "[j]ust shot up one day sitting on a stump" (234), Paul D tells Stamp Paid, who, priding himself on "know[ing] everybody" (232), nonetheless fails to recognize Beloved. And although the text eventually offers up the fragments of a vaguely remembered past for her, it suggests early on that her "clearest memory . . . was [simply] the bridge—standing on the bridge looking down" (119). Aside from her unmanageable and astonishing desire, Beloved is in fact almost wholly without attribute as a character; she is more a mode of functionality than a personality, a kind of cipher in the text.

Indeed, to the extent that Beloved's story is provided at all, it is provided as conflict, as paradox. She is at once a ghost and a traumatized runaway slave; she is simultaneously the child Sethe killed and the mother Sethe lost; she is both a witch, a "devil-child," and an image or idol of a goddess of fertility ("Thunderblack and glistening, she stood on long straight legs, her belly big and tight. Vines of hair twisted all over her head. Jesus. Her smile was dazzling" [261]).

The effect of this proliferation of possibilities is not I think—as James Phelan has suggested—that the reader experiences Beloved as somehow fully present in each of her roles. The effect, rather, is that the text ends up realizing precisely the kind of fragmentation that Beloved herself so poignantly fears: "Beloved, inserting a thumb in her mouth along with her forefinger, pulled out a back tooth. . . . Beloved looked at the tooth and thought, This is it. Next would be her arm, her hand, a toe. Pieces of her would drop maybe one at a time, maybe all at once" (133). The scene is persuasive enough in terms of the psychology it represents: having been stripped of her identity, Beloved worries not only about her psychic but her physical integrity. But the scene also dramatizes or epitomizes a process of disintegration the novel itself ultimately enacts. For during the course of the story's development, Beloved as a character is not so much incrementally fleshed out as she is progressively attenuated, subjected to a form of systematic dispersal. At the point of her departure, in fact, she comes to be seen, not so much as a woman, but as an idea, an "it": "It had taken the shape of a pregnant woman . . ." (261); "Paul D doesn't care how It went or even why" (267). And by the novel's concluding pages, Beloved has been translated almost wholly into the realm of the mythic: "Everybody knew what she was called, but nobody anywhere knew her name. Disremembered and unaccounted for, she cannot be lost because no one is looking for her. . . . In the place where long grass opens, the girl who waited to be loved and cry shame erupts into her separate parts" (274). Dismembered and disremembered, Beloved thus becomes a form of evanescence, a disapparition: "So they forgot her. Like an unpleasant dream during a troubling sleep" (275). And she goes without leaving a trace. Yet, as in the case of the forgotten dream, whose effects linger long after waking, Beloved nonetheless remains—precisely *as* trace, in the Derridean sense of the term, as the traceless source of a sense of loss.

Thus, in tracing the history of Beloved—this history that is a trace yet leaves no trace—Morrison retraces in detail the structure and thematic content of Faulkner's text. Yet this repetition, as I stated at the outset, is also a reinscription. And it is precisely in the way Beloved's disapparition replays the absencing of Charles Bon that Morrison's reply to Faulkner is most clearly delineated. For Faulkner, that is, Bon's history is exemplary in the most general of senses, an almost allegorical expression of a universal truth: although Bon functions in *Absalom* as a figure for the loss of history—a form of deprivation that has at least the potential for a certain specificity—the loss of history as it is articulated in the novel is itself a figure for the loss of meaning as such. Thus, Faulkner's construction of Bon as absence does not so much point *to* the loss of history as it points *through* it, to what Faulkner clearly considers larger, more significant philosophical and epistemological concerns. And *Absalom* addresses those concerns in a host of other ways. The novel is filled, for example, with representations of dissolution, and it focuses from the outset on the ephemeral, the intangible, the unexpressed. It is a novel dominated by images of vapor, smoke, shadow, a novel *peopled* by ghosts: characters who, once they have died, seem never to have lived, who leave no trace of their existence; characters who, while they are living, seem more unreal than the dead. It is a novel built around unrealized possibilities—stories that are started only to unravel; consummations that are proposed, if not promised, but that consistently fail to take place. Bon, in short, is simply the most elaborate—undoubtedly the most poignant— expression of an idea everywhere encoded in Faulkner's text. Because his history is so purely paradigmatic, because it is merely one means among many of locating meaning as lost, the historical specificity of his particular situation is ultimately turned into an irrelevance.

For all its seeming interest in history, in other words, *Absalom* is essentially ahistorical: for although the meaning the novel memorializes is consistently associated with the past, and although the loss of the former therefore *seems* to be related to our inability to recover or to connect with the latter, this inability itself is persistently universalized—a kind of ongoing proof that the meaning so ardently desired is not actually *in* the past, was never there in fact, has always already been lost. While the text, like the monuments that figure so prominently in it, is designed to serve a commemorative function, what it commemorates is the loss of a conception of meaning shorn of any historical grounding. Primarily the past is an empty placeholder for the sheer desire for coherence—a means, in the face of what is perceived to be an overwhelming sense of meaninglessness, of holding on to the idea of meaning.

In *Beloved*, in contrast, history is never generalized in this way, is never pushed to the point of becoming monolithic, an abstraction—and not simply because what interests Morrison in the novel is not history as such but African-American history, for one can imagine that history, too, being turned into an idea, a sign for something else. At first flush, after all, *Absalom*'s chief concern also seems to be a historically specific experience. In *Beloved*, however, history—the history of America's slaves before, during, and immediately following the Civil War— is multiform, variegated. And parts of that history *can* be recounted. Denver eventually breaks out of the near autism produced by her traumatic childhood, gains a measure of self-assurance, and moves toward meaningful engagement with the world. Paul D lets go of the anxieties he has been harboring concerning his manhood, accepts in himself the kind of vulnerability that makes love both necessary and possible, and returns to Sethe, whose vulnerability *and* strength he can now finally accept as well. Whereas in Faulkner, *all* the stories the novel tells eventually unravel—including, most significantly, the story of Quentin's and Shreve's attempt to stage a confrontation with history—many of Morrison's stories do hang together.

Moreover, the fragments of history presented in *Beloved* are not, as they are in *Absalom*, subjected to systematic undercutting. All here is not merely construction, retrojection, the imaginative recreation of a past. The fragments in this case are real, concrete, reliable in ways they never are, or are never allowed to become, in Faulkner's text. For in *Absalom* history can never be anything but a collection of provocative, ultimately incomprehensible fragments. The issue, Faulkner insists, is determined in advance by the nature of subjectivity, the nature of human experience. Incoherence is a kind of inevitability, the mark of a theoretical limit built into the structure of human consciousness as it goes about the unceasing, important, but necessarily quixotic, business of striving to encounter the real. In *Beloved*, on the contrary, the fragmentation of history— the fragmentation, specifically, of African-American history—far from being a theoretical necessity, is itself a consequence of determinate historical events.

And these too are part of Morrison's text. For although her primary concern in the novel is to provide an account of slavery from the perspective of the slaves themselves, the very process of narrating those experiences serves to record the actions, attitudes, and policies of the dominant culture as well. The story of Baby Suggs's loss of her children, for example, is told entirely from the inside, from her own point of view. And the principal aim of that story is to provide a persuasive rendering of the subjective experience of that kind of loss. But the story also serves—and not simply incidentally—as a means of registering the effort made by the slaveholding South to destroy the cultural memory of slaves by severing lines of cultural transmission. Similarly, when the narrative takes up Paul D's memories of the life he was forced to live in prison in Alfred, Georgia, its primary concern is his private struggle to contain these memories. But in the process of attending to the issue of presenting Paul D's complex and compelling subjectivity, the narrative also provides a telling examination of the lengths southern slaveholders would go in their effort to strip slaves of any stable sense of identity. In contrast to *Absalom*, in short, where individual and cultural fragmentation are simply a given, the products of an unrecorded— and therefore presumably timeless—catastrophe, a catastrophe at the origin of time, at the origin of meaning, *Beloved* represents both the fragmentation *and* its causes.

The fragmentation is real, however, and the losses are considerable. Histories have unfolded without benefit of record. Traditions have been forgotten. Individual and collective memories of particular events have been permanently erased.[9] And these myriad of losses, both public and private, are in some sense unpresentable, "unspeakable" (to use a term the novel itself employs), for the deprivation is absolute. To the extent that they can be represented at all, they can be represented only *as* loss, as a form of evanescence, as an evocation of grief. And this is how *Beloved*'s deconstruction ultimately comes to function in the text: as the pointed representation and poignant commemoration of a loss that can never be transcribed as such but only, profoundly, felt—like the almost imperceptible pulsing in the air after the sound that caused the pulsing has long since died away. Beloved: "She reminds me of something," Paul D says shortly before her disappearance. "Something, look like, I'm supposed to remember" (234). But of course he can't. Neither Paul D, nor the rest of the Bluestone community in fact, can remember Beloved after she is gone, because there *is* nothing there to remember. There is only the ache, the felt knowledge that something important once was—and was lost. Such knowledge can only be passed on in the form of a passing, can only be presented in terms appropriate to grief.

Notes

1. I owe this image to Sundquist, though he uses it in an entirely different context (105).

2. Much of the critical commentary on the novel deals with the intertwined issues of trauma, memory, repetition, history. See, for example, Mobley, Holloway ("Revisions"), Guth, Krumholz, and Rushdy ("Daughters" and " 'Rememory' ").

3. Beloved's mother "leaves" her first when the two of them are captured, then again when the mother opts for suicide rather than slavery and jumps from the transport ship. This dispossession is re-enacted symbolically when Sethe runs from Beloved near the end of the novel.

4. For extended discussion of *Beloved* as ghost story, see Horvitz, House, Krumholz, and Schmudde ("Haunting").

5. See also, on this point, McPherson 443 and Ross 232–233.

6. Understandably enough, this passage has gradually come to represent the novel in critical discussions of the text. Miller offers an extended reading of the passage, and McHale (*Postmodernist*) uses it to set up a discussion of the difference between modernist and postmodernist fiction.

7. This is Kartiganer's basic thesis (in *The Fragile Thread*), but Kartiganer discusses these aporia solely in terms of psychology, see 71–72. It is my contention here that we need to take a broader, more narratological view of the problem.

8. For further discussion of the paradigmatic aspects of this scene of telling, see Page.

9. On the necessity of recovering African-American history, and on the difficulties involved in this project of reclamation, see Morrison's interview with Christina Davis: "[T]he reclamation of the history of black people in this country is paramount in its importance because while you can't really blame the conqueror for writing history his own way, you can certainly debate it. There's a great deal of obfuscation and distortion and erasure, so that the presence and the heartbeat of black people has been systematically annihilated in many, many ways and the job of recovery is ours" (142).

Coda

15. FAULKNER IN LIGHT OF MORRISON

Patrick O'Donnell

The title of Toni Morrison's Massey Lectures at Harvard is laden with the implications of shadow, game, liminality, jazz, the interplay of black and white, the serious play of racialized figures that emerge from the repressed and hidden racisms of our "classic" literature. The very playfulness of Morrison's title is suggestive of the extent to which the journey to enlightenment about matters of race in America has barely begun. Shrouded in obscurity and in the bankrupt ideology of "American innocence," in Morrison's view, the dark background upon which white identity is screened is barely visible, or only visible *as* background. Morrison's stirring lectures issue a call for visuality, for illumination, but perhaps not that wholly ironic illumination of darkness visible that one sees at the end of *Invisible Man*, where the stolen white light shed on the narrator's dark figure only brings his invisibility into relief. Rather, the visibility that Morrison endorses and brings to her work might be called the light of intersubjectivity, the critical light that exposes the degree to which "blackness" and "whiteness" are interdependent. Morrison's project in *Playing in the Dark* is to show the extent to which the relation between figures in black and white—which are figures of writing, identity, and the intertwined historical experiences of domination and slavery in America—is shot through with raciality.

As Morrison writes in *Playing in the Dark*:

> Deep within the word "American" is its association with race. . . .
> American means white, and Africanist people struggle to make the

term applicable to themselves with ethnicity and hyphen after hyphen
after hyphen. . . . The American nation negotiated both its disdain and
envy [of Africanist people] . . . through a self-reflexive contemplation of
fabricated, mythological Africanism. For the settlers and for American
writers generally, this Africanist other became the means of thinking about
body, mind, chaos, kindness, and love; provided the occasion for exercises
in the absence of restraint, the presence of restraint, the contemplation
of freedom and aggression; permitted opportunities for the exploration
of ethics and morality, for meeting obligations of the social contract, for
bearing the cross of religion and following out the ramifications of power.
(47–48)

For Morrison, the American national identity, which is raced as "white" and,
for the most part, gendered as "male," is constructed—to use her phrase—"as
a means of thinking" about "blackness"; or more precisely, what grounds the
American identity is a displacement of both anxiety and desire upon that which
is constituted as other by means of this displacement. Deploying an existentialist
terminology inflected by Hegel and Sartre, Morrison writes that the American
conception of freedom is bound over to constraint, to the restraining of and
aggression against African-Americans that continues to be part of our common
historical experience. Implicitly, in this experience, the highly-touted freedom
of the American individual is known only through its negation in slavery, only
by what it is not. In this scenario, the Africanist presence—a presence that is
repressed *as* presence—is background, playing field, cast shadow.

The figures for this (non)identity vary, but, to take one which has a rich
history in African-American literature, that of the shadow: in itself, it is nothing,
but those who do not cast shadows in the light of day are phantoms, figuratively
lacking the identity that the shadow signifies and outlines. All of the "spooks,"
"zombies," and wide-eyed, open-mouthed, ghost-ridden stereotypes of the
Western racist imagination speak to the phantasmic status of black identity
in America from the perspective of those who can only see their light, white
identities when screened against blackness. Struggling with this metaphor of
repression as the imposed sign of their non-identity in American culture and
"white writing," African-Americans, Morrison explains, have metonymically
hyphenated themselves in the effort to write a proper name in the margins
of American culture. As Derrida suggests, the hyphen in writing—like all
textual "gaps" ("bars . . . dashes, numerals, periods, quotation marks, blanks,
etc.")—marks a space where one form of writing is grafted onto another in the
"heterogeneity of different writings [that] is writing itself" (356). The hyphen
signifies, among other things, a rupture in the smooth linearity of language
or cultural narrative; to use another Derridean term, it is a form of "spacing"

in writing that—itself lacking content—limns the content of the vocabulary that it spaces out. So too, for Morrison, the seemingly endless hyphens that indicate African-American ethnicity serve to establish it in American discourse as a gap within and a diacritical marking of this discourse—the language of a culture that has repressed and has been framed or marked by the paradox of an Africanist "presence."

The interdependency of black and white figures that Morrison sketches in *Playing in the Dark*—their intersubjectivity—does not indicate the equivalencies that "intersubjectivity" in the liberal view usually connotes, where the term is deployed to indicate the fantasy of a wholly democratized dialogism that sublimates race, or the fantasy of a "color-blind" cultural discourse. Instead, for Morrison, the intersubjective relation (and, as I will suggest, the intertextual relation) is one of differentials. As in the always unequal relation of background to foreground, or shadow to body, each term acquires definition in terms of the other; but the latter (foreground, body) acquires its specific definition as that which is *not* the former (background, shadow). The terms suggest that the white body, the foregrounded identity, arises out of the background to cast the dark shadow that proclaims the body's substance and the shadow's lack. The figure of Joe Christmas as he emerges into the glare of oncoming headlights in Faulkner's *Light in August* captures the interdependent ratio of white and black figures that Morrison describes:

> He stood with his hands on his hips, naked, thighdeep in the dusty weeds, while the car came over the hill and approached, the lights upon him. He watched his body grow white out of the darkness like a kodak print emerging from the liquid. He looked straight into the headlights as it shot past. From it a woman's shrill voice flew back, shrieking. "White bastards," he shouted. "That's not the first of your bitches that ever saw. . . . . . ." But the car was gone. There was no one to hear, to listen. It was gone, sucking its dust and its light with it and behind it, sucking with it the white woman's fading cry. He was cold now. It was as though he had merely come there to be present at a finality, and the finality had occurred and now he was free again. (108)

In this white light, Christmas's racial identity—a source of confusion throughout the novel—appears as a reified presence that gains its substantiality only in relation to the darkness from which it has emerged and to which it will return. In the failed call and response that occurs between the white woman and Christmas, where misogynist and racist stereotypes are conflated as he ventriloquizes the differential conception of how a black man "thinks" of white women, Christmas is seen as a dark figure made white, visible, while his rejoinder is lost to the sound of the car rushing past and that, like a black hole, sucks all light and air into itself. Faulkner's racial figure in this instance is one of radical contradiction—a contradiction to which Morrison replies as she replays it—in that Christmas appears to be both absent and present, racially indeterminate, his "blackness," the sign of the shadow, emerging in the passing light as "whiteness," the sign of identity. This presencing of a negation serves as a form of "finality"—the construction and enactment of identity—that demarcates Christmas's "freedom." But this is the ironic and self-contradictory "freedom" of the abject, the non-figure, the non-identity, the non-raced: that is, the figure of blackness precisely as it is constructed within the white light of the American cultural imaginary, a figure that is all too easily assimilated into a view that would wish to forget race.

Morrison writes: "the habit of ignoring race is understood to be a graceful, even generous, liberal gesture. To notice is to recognize an already discredited difference. To enforce its invisibility through silence is to allow the black body a shadowless participation in the dominant cultural body. According to this logic, every well-bred instinct argues *against noticing* and forecloses adult discourse" (*Playing* 9–10). In *Playing in the Dark*, Morrison's effort is to renegotiate figures of blackness in white writing so that we may learn how to read them in a different light and to see them as figures *of* difference that can tell us a great deal about the extent to which the "dominant cultural body"—to use Morrison's phrase— has constituted itself through these figures. The effects of this renegotiation can be seen in returning anew to the image of Joe Christmas running into the headlights of a passing car, which is often read in Faulkner criticism— like Christmas's character *tout court*—as, alternatively, nihilistic, apocalyptic, radically free, radically determined, scapegoated, abject. This multivalence of character is perfectly consistent with the figure of an ambiguous racial body blacked into whiteness—an ambiguity that demarcates a crucial intertextual *difference* between Faulkner and Morrison.

While Faulkner's figure stresses the fundamental indeterminacy of racial identity that (pursuing the metaphor of the photograph that informs this scene) develops in the "fixing solution" of the social into a specific racialized object, Morrison, in *Playing in the Dark*, stresses the seemingly contradictory, determinative quality of black (non)identity as the definitional screen of white identity. This play of difference—this contradiction—of indeterminacy and determinacy is crucial to the racist articulation of "black identity," which must be available to any construction placed upon it, and yet, once "located," must be securely anchored to a specific site on the map of the cultural imaginary. In the critical intertextual relation I am drawing between Faulkner and Morrison, what Faulkner dramatizes, Morrison critiques. While, for Faulkner, identity is, "at the beginning," indeterminate (non-raced), and then only becomes racially specific in the tragedy of socialization that is played out in Joe Christmas's life and "apotheosis," for Morrison, black identity is *determinately non-existent*; it is merely the backdrop upon which the specificity of white identity can be located. For her, there is not what one might call the existential luxury of Christmas's tragic situation, which presupposes an identity to be confused about and, eventually, to be constructed and abased by others. Between Faulkner and Morrison, then, in their intertextual figural relation, there is projected the utter contradiction of the void of black identity that acquires definition as void or absence only to the extent it is illuminated by white light—a "light" that, in turn, gains *its* power and definition from the darkness it illumines. It is in the differential of this relation that the gap between and, yet, conflation of humanist and constructionist versions of racial identity are revealed in Morrison's view of black identity as the negative upon which white identity is screened.

As we have seen, for Faulkner, the protagonist of *Light in August* is this "negative" of white identity which can be scandalized by the sight of an emerging, naked black body and, thus, horrified at the apprehension of "black" sexuality. Being scandalized, being horrified, is the basis for the construction of a disciplinary social identity that depends upon laws, boundaries, and taboos structured according to dominant cultural binaries (black and white, among others) for its constitution. In order for this identity construction to "make sense," there must be something to be horrified at and scandalized by. Hence, Joe Christmas, though it is crucial to remember, once more, that there is no biological certainty about Joe's racial make-up. Playing out the relation of indeterminacy and determinacy that exists both within Faulkner's novel (but bounded by the fixed parameters of tragedy and the fatalism that adheres to Christmas's character) and between Faulkner and Morrison, we can see that the social construction of Joe Christmas as "black," an activity in which both he and others conspire, takes place upon the body, which is merely a cipher—a palimpsest—over which abjection and desire are written. Christmas's body, read through Morrison, is merely the indeterminate background upon which is screened the specific, determinate racisms (Christmas's lust for white women; his attraction to crime; his laziness) that Faulkner integrates into the logic of a novel that dictates the annihilation of a "black" body consecutively with the birthing of a white body in Lena's child. There is, literally, no body in the scene of Christmas's apparition, just as for Morrison, in the American cultural imaginary, the black body has been ciphered, symbolized, hyperbolized, and vilified, a process that is co-dependent with the historical employment, exhaustion, and annihilation of black bodies in slavery. Indeed it is precisely the gap between actual historical experience and the symbolization of that experience—and the elision of this gap—that constitutes for Morrison the intersubjectivity of black and white figures in the culturally dominant expressions of white writing.

I have cited this passage from Faulkner's *Light in August* in order to suggest how Faulkner might be read in light of Morrison: this is to transpose the direction Morrison criticism has already begun to take in detecting Faulknerian (as well as Twainian, Hawthornian, and Melvillian) influences or traces in Morrison's novels. The usual move—one I have made myself; one that anyone who teaches or writes on Morrison is tempted to make—is to suggest how certain scenes in Morrison's novels intertextually echo, modify, and signify upon those to be found in the canonical predecessor. Thus, to take the single example of *Beloved*, traces of Hawthorne can be found in Morrison's portrait of the perverse schoolteacher; the relation between Denver and Sethe recapitulates and, in terms of race and gender, reverses the relation between Huck and Jim on the river; as Denver and Sethe talk, they reconstruct the past through their conversation and attain a "happy marriage of speaking and hearing" in the manner of Shreve and Quentin in *Absalom, Absalom!*.[1]

While the critical process that elicits these intertextualities may be of value in determining how Morrison revises white writing and plays upon its figures, it has the effect, in part, of re-placing her within a genealogy of writing that the figures of *Beloved* and the hermeneutic of *Playing in the Dark* seek to transform in the terms of genealogy. One of the most disturbing images to be found in *Beloved* is that of the bleeding whipping scars on Sethe's back, which Denver "reads" as forming the shape of a cherry tree. It is possible to view the scar in any number of ways: as a perverse tree of life—the sign of the corrupt Eden of the South under slavery—that attests to both Sethe's agony and survival; as the mark of cruelty and domination that also, somehow, manifests the kinship of blood and suffering in the historical experience of slavery which cannot be abolished and which remains on the body; as the sign of bondage and bonding of the "other nation" under slavery.[2] That the image evokes multiple readings is not in question, but it may also be seen as an anti-genealogical and anti-hermeneutic conceit that protests against the insertion of Sethe's body into any available cultural or textual orders or systems by the "reading" of this wound: after all, the mark is not a stigmata, self-generated, but one inflicted on her body by others. In the terms I have used to discuss the reading of Faulkner through Morrison, Sethe's body might properly be seen neither as multivalent palimpsest—as "background" for the critic's hermeneutic operations—nor as reified object. Implicitly, *Playing in the Dark* offers a parallel protest against reading Morrison "genealogically," that is, either reading Faulkner as the text to be signified upon by Morrison, or reading Morrison as the culmination and radical revision of Faulknerian troping upon race. Either procedure would reinforce the relation that Morrison attempts to reverse in *Playing in the Dark*, an anti-genealogical reversal that takes place between the lines of her readings of black figures in white writing.

This reversal suggests the extent to which—and this is what is truly radical in Morrison's choice to write extensively upon an author such as Hemingway—the writing of white identity has been founded upon black figures. What Morrison wishes to do, in her own writing, is to change the background into the foreground, to transform the body/palimpsest of the black figure in white writing into the sign of both how that figure has been deployed and what may lie beyond its use-value in that deployment. This transformation takes place upon the ground of the intertextual differential to be seen in Morrison's relation to Faulkner which, I have argued, is the relation of indeterminacy to determinacy founded upon the ciphering of black identity. The work of *Playing in the Dark* might be thus viewed as Morrison's mapping out of her intertextual relation to white writing which she inverts, or overwrites, in her fiction.

The playing out of this relation and its reversal necessitates a casting of Morrison before Faulkner—in a sense, as if *she* were the canonical predecessor.[3] One of the reasons that Morrison has little to say about Faulkner in *Playing in the Dark* is that, perhaps, she has already said a great deal about him in her fiction; in other terms, her novels do the work of reversing her relation to Faulkner as the critique of *Playing in the Dark* does for Cather, Twain, and Hemingway. What does it mean, then, to read Faulkner in light of Morrison? I have offered a partial response to this question in my reading of a passage from *Light in August*—a reading that proceeds as if Faulkner, in constructing Joe Christmas's emergence into the headlights, were working under the influence of *Playing in the Dark*. I'll conclude with a scene from *Absalom, Absalom!* in which another racial encounter is highlighted. The scene occurs in the novel's fifth chapter, Rosa's narrative, where Rosa describes the moment in which she encounters Clytie on the stairs of the Sutpen mansion as she attempts to make her way to Judith's room after Bon has been shot. Sutpen's daughter by one of his slaves, misnamed Clytemnestra for Cassandra, blocks Rosa's path by putting her hand on her, and in a passage that plays in slow motion, Rosa responds with outrage and horror:

> *I know that my entire being seemed to run at blind full tilt into something monstrous and immobile, with a shocking impact too soon and too quick to*

> be mere amazement and outrage at the black arresting and untimorous hand
> on my white woman's flesh. Because there is something in the touch of flesh
> with flesh that abrogates, cuts sharp and straight across the devious intricate
> channels of decorous ordering, which enemies as well as lovers know because it
> makes them both . . . let flesh touch with flesh, and watch the fall of all the
> eggshell shibboleth of caste and color too. Yes, I stopped dead—no woman's
> hand, no negro's hand, but bitted bridle-curb to check and guide the furious
> and unbending will—I crying not to her, but to it; speaking to it through the
> negro, the woman, only because of the shock which was not yet outrage because
> it would be terror soon, expecting and receiving no answer because we both
> knew it was not to her I spoke: "Take your hand off me, nigger!" (111–12)

This moment of crisis and blockage has often been read in an ameliorative sense
as one in which "race" is transcended (in Rosa's mind) in the face of a family
tragedy that has the effect of foreclosing the family's exfoliating relations, thus
collapsing those relations into each other. At the same time, this "indecorous"
instant of "abrogation" rapidly moves toward a reinscription of racism and racial
difference (" 'Take your hand off me, nigger' ") precisely because there has been a
momentary cessation in the erection of racial barriers—the "fall" of the "eggshell
shibboleth" (criteria or watchword) of "caste and color"—as black hand meets
white body.

Read through Morrison—that is, read as a scene in which the black figure
of Clytie is the palimpsest upon which Rosa's white identity is inscribed—
this paradoxical moment in which racial boundaries are, however temporarily,
supposedly transgressed begins to look quite different. Rosa is initially outraged
because it is a black woman who presumes to block her path; but her abhorrence
increases with Clytie's touch because she realizes that, by means of that touch,
she is in a different, corporeal relation to Clytie that cannot be described by or
contained within racial binaries. But this different relation is no happy marriage
of speaking and hearing, nor a merging of bodies across boundaries in a corporeal
uniting of equals. Here, Rosa only sees in Clytie (as she says earlier in this
passage) the face of Sutpen. Through Clytie she pits her "furious and unbending
will" against Sutpen's, as if Clytie were merely the mediator of contending
wills, the "bitted bridle-curb." Clytie has thus become in this highly compressed
figure the force of the embodiment against which Rosa must contend in order
to define herself as not Sutpen, not his agent, nor part of the tragic, narrative,
historic sequence that has led to this impasse. Far from being a scene in which
race is "surpassed" as women touch in a moment of crisis, in this moment,
Clytie is erased as a subject in Rosa's narrative, and made over into the historical
restraint that blocks Rosa's desire to see and touch Bon at last, even if he is dead.
And it is precisely through this sublimation of race—through the prosopopeic

conversion of Clytie into a prop in the tortuous dramaturgy of Rosa's subject-formation—that Rosa is able to re-establish her white identity. She does so by talking through Clytie to Sutpen's will, an act that requires her to call Clytie (or, not Clytie, but the abstract "it" into which Clytie has been converted) a "*nigger*." As in the passage depicting Joe Christmas's emergence into the light and the novel for which it serves as an epiphanic moment, the contradictory abrogation and announcement of racial difference we see in Clytie's encounter with Rosa are essential to the determination of a "white" identity that depends upon the erasure of "black" identity relegated to the narrative function of imagistic screen, blocking agent.

In her criticism, Morrison is engaged in the task of showing us how to read such narrative occasions—moments that she refers to as "narrative gearshifts"—where the exploitation of black figures in white writing is revealed in all of its contradiction and complexity (*Playing* x). Understanding this critical project—a task well-commenced in this collection—is crucial to understanding how we should construct Morrison's relation to Faulkner as one of a differential intertextuality wherein Morrison is neither simply "influenced" by Faulkner, nor simply troping upon or trumping the black and white figures to be found in his fiction. In her fiction, Morrison's project is quite different: there, she is intent upon inscribing black figures in other terms than those that apply to the writers she discusses in *Playing in the Dark*; she is committed in her novels to bringing those figures to the historical and narrative foreground. But that is another story, and one that presumes upon the disfigurations of the writing of race that Morrison brings out into the open in *Playing in the Dark*.

Notes

1. See Woidat and Moreland (" 'He Wants' ") for discussions of, respectively, the presence of Hawthorne and Twain in Morrison.
2. See O'Donnell for an examination of the various significances of Sethe's scar.
3. Kiely argues that "postmodernism," since it defies linear and genealogical conceptions of tradition, influence, and intertexuality, allows us to read Hawthorne through Nabokov, or Twain through Borges. I am posing a somewhat similar argument for refiguring the relation between Morrison and Faulkner, but this relation has already been critically inflected with and grounded in the question of race in ways that these other relations, for Kiely, are not.

CONTRIBUTORS

Nancy Ellen Batty teaches at Red Deer College in Alberta, Canada. She is the recipient of the Governor General's Gold Medal and has published articles in *Mississippi Quarterly, Ariel,* and *Canadian Ethnic Studies.* Her essay in this volume was first presented in 1994 at the American Literature Association Conference.

Keith E. Byerman, Professor of English at Indiana State University and Managing Editor of *African American Review,* is the author of *Seizing the Word: History, Art, and Self in the Work of W. E. B. Du Bois* (U of Georgia P, 1994). He has also written *Alice Walker: An Annotated Bibliography, 1968–1986* (Garland, 1989) with Erma Banks and *Fingering the Jagged Grain: Tradition and Form in Recent Black Fiction* (U of Georgia P, 1986).

Carolyn Denard is Associate Professor of Twentieth- Century American Literature at Georgia State University and President of the Toni Morrison Society. Her research and teaching focus on the cultural and ethical uses of literature. Her published works on Morrison include essays in *Critical Essays on Morrison* (Nellie McKay, ed.), in Scribner's *Modern American Women Writers Series,* and in the forthcoming MLA publication, *Approaches to Teaching Toni Morrison.* She is currently finishing a book-length manuscript on myth and heroism in Morrison's fiction.

Andrea Dimino, Associate Professor of Literature at New College of the University of South Florida, has recently completed a study of Faulknerian time. She is the founder and coordinator of the New College Gender Studies program. Her publications on Faulkner include essays on patriarchy and the "counterfamily," on gender and narrative indeterminacy in *Absalom, Absalom!,* and on narrative desire and narrative politics. She is currently at work on a study of women and narrative.

John N. Duvall, Professor of English at the University of Memphis, is the author of *Faulkner's Marginal Couple: Invisible, Outlaw, and Unspeakable Communities* (U of Texas P, 1990). He has published essays on Faulkner and Morrison in the *Arizona Quarterly* and the *Faulkner Journal.*

Doreen Fowler is Professor of English at the University of Mississippi. Her book, *Faulkner: The Return of the Repressed*, is forthcoming from the University Press of Virginia. She has authored a developmental study of Faulkner's canon, *Faulkner's Changing Vision*, and has co-edited eleven collections of essays on Faulkner, the proceedings of the annual Faulkner and Yoknapatawpha conference.

Michael Hogan is a doctoral candidate at the University of North Carolina-Chapel Hill. His special interests include southern and Anglo-Irish literature. He most recently completed a monograph on Seamus Heaney, and he has published on Reynolds Price.

Karla F. C. Holloway is Wm. R. Kenan, Jr., Professor of English and African American Literature and Director of the African and Afro-American Studies program at Duke University. She is the author of numerous essays on literature, linguistics, and cultural theory. She has published four books, which have won national awards, including *Codes of Conduct: Race, Ethics, and the Color of our Character* (Rutgers UP, 1995) and *Moorings and Metaphors: Figures of Culture and Gender in Black Women's Literature* (Rutgers UP, 1992). Her current work in progress is *Passed On: African American Mourning Stories.*

Catherine Gunther Kodat is Assistant Professor of English and American Studies at Hamilton College. Her paper "Beyond the Pale: The Art of Blackness in William Faulkner's 'Carcassone' and 'Black Magic'" was recently presented at the Society for the Study of Multi-Ethnic Literature of the United States. Her article on Hurston's *Their Eyes Were Watching God* is forthcoming in *Haunted Bodies: Gender and Southern Texts.*

Carol A. Kolmerten is Professor of English at Hood College and series editor for "Writing American Women" for Syracuse University Press. Her books include *Women in Utopia* (Indiana UP, 1990) and the 1991 Syracuse University Press reprint of *Unveiling a Parallel*, by Alice Ilgenfritz Jones and Ella Merchant. She is co-editor of *Utopian and Science Fiction by Women: Worlds of Difference* (Syracuse UP, 1993). Currently working on a biography of nineteenth-century women's rights activist Ernestine L. Rose, she began teaching "Faulkner and Morrison" in the mid-1980s.

Lucinda H. MacKethan is the author of *Daughters of Time: Creating Woman's Voice in Southern Story* (U of Georgia P, 1990) and a charter member of the Toni Morrison Society. She is Professor of English at North Carolina State University, recently named as the NCSU Alumni Outstanding Teacher of 1995. Her most recent contributions have been included in *The Oxford Companion to African American Literature*, *CLA Journal*, and *CEA Critic*.

Phillip Novak teaches at Colgate University and is currently working on an examination of the relation between meaning and mourning in twentieth-century literary discourse. The first chapter of this study will appear in an upcoming issue of *The Faulkner Journal*.

Patrick O'Donnell is Professor of English at Purdue University and Editor of *mfs: modern fiction studies*. His publications include *Echo Chambers; Figuring Voice in Modern Narrative* (U of Iowa P, 1992) and the Introduction to the annotated version of F. Scott Fitzgerald's *This Side of Paradise* for Penguin's Twentieth Century Classics Series. Currently he is completing a book on paranoia and history in contemporary American narrative.

Stephen M. Ross is the Director of Challenge Grants at the National Endowment for the Humanities and President of the William Faulkner Society. He was a professor of English at the U.S. Naval Academy, where he taught American literature, African-American literature, and literary theory. He has published on Faulkner and on African-American literature, including *Fiction's Inexhaustible Voice: Speech and Writing in Faulkner* (U of Georgia P, 1989).

Roberta Rubenstein, Professor of Literature at American University, is the author of *The Novelistic Vision of Doris Lessing: Breaking the Forms of Consciousness* (U of Illinois P, 1979) and *Boundaries of the Self: Gender, Culture, Fiction* (U of Illinois P, 1987). She has published a number of essays on modernist and contemporary writers and has served as Contributing Editor to *Belles Letters: A Review of Books by Women* since 1989.

Theresa M. Towner, Senior Lecturer at the University of Texas at Dallas, is the author of "Spirit Scripts" and "It Ain't Funny A'-Tall: The Transfigured Tales of *The Town*," both appearing in *Mississippi Quarterly*, and " 'How Can a Black Man Ask': Race and Self-Representation in Faulkner's Later Fiction" in *The Faulkner Journal*. She is working on a book on race and Faulkner's later novels.

Philip M. Weinstein, Alexander Griswold Cummins Professor of English at Swarthmore College, is the author of *The Semantics of Desire: Changing Models of Identity from Dickens to Joyce* (Princeton UP, 1984) and *Faulkner's Subject; A Cosmos No One Owns* (Cambridge UP, 1992). His most recent book is *What Else But Love? The Ordeal of Race in Faulkner and Morrison* (Columbia UP, 1996).

Judith Bryant Wittenberg is Professor of English at Simmons College. Her articles on Faulkner, Thomas Hardy, Ellen Glasgow, and Sarah Orne Jewett have appeared in books and in journals such as *Novel, Studies in American Fiction, Mississippi Quarterly, Faulkner Studies, Colby Quarterly,* and *Centennial Review.* The author of *Faulkner: The Transfiguration of Biography,* she is a member of the editorial board of the *Faulkner Journal* and served for seven years as President of the William Faulkner Society.

WORKS CITED

Adams, Richard. *Faulkner: Myth and Motion*. New Jersey: Princeton UP, 1968.

Adorno, Theodor W. *Aesthetic Theory*. Trans. C. Lenhart. Ed. Gretel Adorno and Rolf Tiedemann. London: Routledge, 1984.

———. *Negative Dialectics*. Trans. E. B. Ashton. New York: Continuum, 1973.

Aiken, Conrad. "William Faulkner: The Novel as Form." Hoffman and Vickery 135–42.

Alwes, Karla. " 'The Evil of Fulfillment': Women and Violence in *The Bluest Eye*." *Women and Violence in Literature: An Essay Collection*. Ed. Katherine Anne Ackley. New York: Garland, 1990. 89–104.

Atwood, Margaret. "Haunted by Their Nightmares." *New York Times Book Review* 13 Sept. 1987: 1, 49–50.

Awkward, Michael. *Inspiriting Influences: Tradition, Revision, and Afro-American Women's Novels*. New York: Columbia UP, 1989.

———. "Roadblocks and Relatives: Critical Revision in Toni Morrison's *The Bluest Eye*." McKay 57–68.

———. " 'Unruly and Let Loose': Myth, Ideology, and Gender in *Song of Solomon*." *Callaloo* 13 (1990): 482–98.

Bachelard, Gaston. *The Poetics of Space*. Trans. Maria Jolas. 1958; rpt. Boston: Beacon, 1969.

Baker, Houston A., Jr. *Blues, Ideology, and Afro-American Literature: A Vernacular Theory*. Chicago: U of Chicago P, 1984.

———. *Modernism and the Harlem Renaissance*. Chicago: U of Chicago P, 1987.

Batty, Nancy E. "The Riddle of *Absalom, Absalom!*: Looking at the Wrong Black-bird?" *Mississippi Quarterly* 47 (1994): 461–488.

Blake, Susan L. "Toni Morrison." *Dictionary of Literary Biography*. Vol. 33. 1984.

Bleikasten, André. "Fathers in Faulkner." *The Fictional Father: Lacanian Readings of the Text*. Ed. Robert Con Davis. Amherst: U of Massachusetts P, 1981. 115–45.

———. *Faulkner's* As I Lay Dying. Bloomington: Indiana UP, 1973.

———. *The Ink of Melancholy: Faulkner's Novels from* The Sound and the Fury *to* Light in August. Bloomington: Indiana UP, 1990.

Bloom, Harold. *The Anxiety of Influence: A Theory of Poetry.* New York: Oxford UP, 1973.

———, ed. *Toni Morrison.* New York: Chelsea, 1990.

Blotner, Joseph. *Faulkner: A Biography.* 2 vols. New York: Random, 1974. Revised, 1-Volume Edition, 1984.

Brooks, Cleanth. "The Community and the Pariah." *William Faulkner: The Yoknapatawpha Country.* New Haven: Yale UP, 1963. 47–74.

Brooks, Peter. *Reading for the Plot: Design and Intention in Narrative.* Cambridge: Harvard UP, 1984.

Brylowski, Walter. *Faulkner's Olympian Laugh: Myth in the Novels.* Detroit: Wayne State UP, 1968.

Budick, Emily Miller. "Absence, Loss, and the Space of History in Toni Morrison's *Beloved.*" *Arizona Quarterly* 48.2 (Summer 1992): 117–138.

Burke, Kenneth. *The Philosophy of Literary Form.* Baton Rouge: Louisiana State UP, 1941.

Byerman, Keith E. *Fingering the Jagged Grain: Tradition and Form in Recent Black Fiction.* Athens: U of Georgia P, 1985.

———. "Intense Behaviors: The Use of the Grotesque in *The Bluest Eye* and *Eva's Man.*" *CLA Journal* 25 (1982): 447–457.

Cassier, Ernst. *The Philosophy of Symbolic Form, Vol II: Mythical Thought.* Trans. Ralph Manheim. New Haven: Yale UP, 1955.

Chandler, Marilyn R. *Dwelling in the Text: Houses in American Fiction.* Berkeley: U of California P, 1991.

Coffin, Levi. *Reminiscences of Levi Coffin, The Reputed President of the Underground Railroad.* New York: Arno, 1968 [1898].

Cowart, David. "Faulkner and Joyce in Morrison's *Song of Solomon.*" *American Literature* 62 (1990): 86–100.

Crouch, Stanley. "Aunt Medea." *New Republic* 19 Oct. 1987: 38–43.

Davis, Thadious M. "From Jazz Syncopation to Blues Elegy: Faulkner's Development of Black Characterization." *Faulkner and Race: Faulkner and Yoknapatawpha, 1986.* Ed. Doreen Fowler and Ann J. Abadie. Jackson: UP of Mississippi, 1987. 70–92.

———. "The Yoking of 'Abstract Contradictions': Clytie's Meaning in *Absalom, Absalom!.*" *Studies in American Fiction* 7 (1979): 209–219.

Derrida, Jacques. *Dissemination.* Trans. Barbara Johnson. Chicago: U of Chicago P, 1981.

Dickerson, Vanessa. "The Naked Father in Toni Morrison's *The Bluest Eye.*" Yaeger and Kowaleski-Wallace 108–27.

Dimino, Andrea. "Miss Rosa as 'Love's Androgynous Advocate': Gender and Narrative Indeterminacy in Chapter V of *Absalom, Absalom!.*" *Faulkner and Gender* 181–196.

Doughty, Peter. "A Fiction for the Tribe: Toni Morrison's *The Bluest Eye.*" Graham

Clarke, ed. *The New American Writing: Essays on American Literature Since 1970.* New York: St. Martin's P, 1990. 29–50.

Duvall, John N. "Authentic Ghost Stories: *Uncle Tom's Cabin, Absalom, Absalom!,* and *Beloved.*" *Faulkner Journal* 4.1–2 (Fall 1988-Spring 1989): 83–97.

———. "Doe Hunting and Masculinity: *Song of Solomon* and *Go Down, Moses.*" *Arizona Quarterly* 47.1 (Spring 1991): 95–115.

———. "Faulkner's Critics and Women: The Voice of the Community." Fowler and Abadie, *Faulkner and Women* 41–57.

———. *Faulkner's Marginal Couple: Invisible, Outlaw, and Unspeakable Communities.* Austin: U of Texas P, 1990.

Eckard, Paula Gallant. "The Interplay of Music, Language, and Narrative in Toni Morrison's *Jazz.*" *CLA Journal* 38 (1994): 11–19.

Edwards, Thomas R. "Ghost Story." *New York Review of Books* 5 Nov. 1987: 18–19.

Eliade, Mircea. *Myth and Reality.* New York: Harper and Row, 1963.

Eliot, T. S. "Ulysses, Order, and Myth." *Dial* 75 (November 1923): 483.

Ellison, Ralph. *Invisible Man.* New York: Random, 1947; rpt. 1989.

Fadiman, Clifton. "Faulkner, Extra-Special, Double-Distilled." *New Yorker* 31 Oct. 1936: 62–64.

Faulkner, William. *Absalom, Absalom!: The Corrected Text.* New York: Random, Vintage International, 1990 [1936].

———. "Appendix: Compson: 1699–1945." *The Portable Faulkner.* Rev. and expanded edition. Ed. Malcolm Cowley. New York: Penguin, 1977 [1946].

———. *As I Lay Dying: The Corrected Text.* New York: Random, Vintage International, 1990 [1930].

———. "Evangeline." *Uncollected Stories of William Faulkner.* Ed. Joseph Blotner. New York: Random House, 1979. 583–609.

———. *Faulkner in the University: Class Conferences at the University of Virginia, 1957–58.* Ed. Frederick L. Gwynn and Joseph L. Blotner. New York: Random, Vintage, 1959.

———. *Go Down, Moses.* New York: Random, Vintage International, 1990 [1942].

———. *The Hamlet: The Corrected Text.* New York: Random, Vintage International, 1991 [1940].

———. *Intruder in the Dust.* In *Faulkner: Novels, 1942–1954.* New York: Library of America, 1994 [1948].

———. *Light in August: The Corrected Text.* New York: Random, Vintage International, 1990 [1932].

———. *Lion in the Garden: Interviews with William Faulkner.* Ed. James B. Meriwether and Michael Millgate. New York: Random, 1968; rpt. Lincoln: U of Nebraska P, 1980.

———. *New Orleans Sketches.* Ed. Carvel Collins. New York: Random, 1958.

———. *Requiem for a Nun.* New York: Random, 1951.

———. *Sanctuary: The Corrected Text.* New York: Random, Vintage International, 1993 [1931].

———. *Selected Letters.* Ed. Joseph Blotner. New York: Random, 1977.

———. *Soldier's Pay.* New York: Liveright, 1951 [1926].

———. *The Sound and the Fury: The Corrected Text.* New York: Random, Vintage International, 1990 [1929].

———. "That Evening Sun." *Collected Stories of William Faulkner.* New York: Vintage, 1977 [1950]. 289–309.

———. *The Unvanquished.* In *Faulkner: Novels, 1936–1940.* New York: The Library of America, 1990 [1938].

Fick, Thomas H. "Toni Morrison's 'Allegory of the Cave': Movies, Consumption, and Platonic Realism in *The Bluest Eye.*" *Journal of the Midwest Modern Language Association* 22 (1989): 10–22.

Fowler, Doreen, and Ann J. Abadie, eds. *Faulkner and Women: Faulkner and Yoknapatawpha, 1985.* Jackson: UP of Mississippi, 1986.

Frank, Joseph. "Spatial Form in Modern Literature." *The Widening Gyre: Crisis and Mastery in Modern Literature.* New Brunswick: Rutgers UP, 1963. 3–62.

Freud, Sigmund. *The Standard Edition of the Complete Psychological Works of Freud.* Ed. and trans. James Strachey. 24 vols. London: Hogarth, 1961. 1953–74.

Fuss, Diana. *Essentially Speaking: Feminism, Nature and Difference.* New York: Routledge, 1989.

Gallop, Jane. *Feminism and Psychoanalysis: The Daughter's Seduction.* Ithaca: Cornell UP, 1985.

Gates, Henry Louis, Jr. *Figures in Black: Words, Signs, and the "Racial" Self.* New York: Oxford UP, 1987.

———. "Preface to Blackness: Text and Pretext." *Afro-American Literature: The Reconstruction of Instruction.* Ed. Robert Stepto and Dexter Fisher. New York: MLA, 1979. 44–69.

———. *The Signifying Monkey: A Theory of African-American Literary Criticism.* New York: Oxford UP, 1988.

——— and K. A. Appiah, eds. *Toni Morrison: Critical Perspectives Past and Present.* New York: Amistad, 1993.

Gelfant, Blanche H. "Faulkner and Keats: The Ideality of Art in 'The Bear.'" *Southern Literary Journal* 2 (Fall 1969): 43–65.

Gerster, Carole J. "From Film Margin to Novel Center: Toni Morrison's *The Bluest Eye.*" *West Virginia University Philological Papers* 38 (1992): 191–99.

Gibson, Donald B. "Text and Countertext in Toni Morrison's *The Bluest Eye.*" *Literature, Interpretation, Theory* 1 (1989): 19–32.

Gilroy, Paul. *The Black Atlantic.* Cambridge: Harvard UP, 1993.

Godden, Richard. "*Absalom, Absalom!,* Haiti and Labor History: Reading Unreadable Revolutions." *ELH* 61 (1994): 685–720.

Gunn, Daniel. *Psychoanalysis and Fiction: An Exploration of Literary and Psychoanalytic Borders.* Cambridge: Cambridge UP, 1988.

Guth, Deborah. "A Blessing and a Burden: The Relation to the Past in *Sula, Song of Solomon,* and *Beloved.*" *Modern Fiction Studies* 39 (1993): 575–95.

Gwin, Minrose. *Black and White Women of the Old South: The Peculiar Sisterhood in American Literature.* Knoxville: U of Tennessee P, 1985.

———. *The Feminine and Faulkner: Reading (Beyond) Sexual Difference.* Knoxville: U of Tennessee P, 1990.

———. "(Re)Reading Faulkner as Father and Daughter of His Own Text." Yaeger and Kowaleski-Wallace 238–258.

Harper, Michael S. and Robert Stepto, eds. *Chant of Saints: A Gathering of Afro-American Literature, Art, and Scholarship.* Urbana: U of Illinois P, 1979.

Harris, Middleton, with the assistance of Morris Levitt, Roger Furman, and Ernest Smith. *The Black Book.* New York: Random, 1974.

Harris, Trudier. *Fiction and Folklore: The Novels of Toni Morrison.* Knoxville: U of Tennesse P, 1991.

Hartman, Charles O. *Jazz Text: Voice and Improvisation in Poetry, Jazz, and Song.* Princeton: Princeton UP, 1991.

Harvey, Mark S. "Jazz and Modernism: Changing Conceptions of Innovation and Tradition." *Jazz in Mind: Essays on the History and Meanings of Jazz.* Ed. Reginald T. Buckner and Steven Weiland. Detroit: Wayne State UP, 1991. 128–47.

Heinze, Denise. *The Dilemma of "Double-Consciousness": Toni Morrison's Novels.* Athens: U of Georgia P, 1993.

Hirsch, Marianne. "Knowing Their Names: Toni Morrison's *Song of Solomon.*" Smith 69–92.

Hoffman, Frederick J., and Olga W. Vickery, eds. *William Faulkner: Three Decades of Criticism.* Michigan State UP, 1960.

Holloway, Karla F. C. "*Beloved*: A Spiritual." *Black American Literature Forum* 23.1 (Spring 1989): 179–182. Also *Callaloo* 13 (1990): 516–525.

———. *Moorings and Metaphors.* New Brunswick: Rutgers UP, 1992.

———. "Revision and (Re)membrance: A Theory of Literary Structures in Literature by African-American Women Writers." *Black American Literature Forum* 24 (1990): 617–31.

———, and Stephanie Demetrakopoulos. *New Dimensions of Spirituality: A Biracial and Bicultural Reading of the Novels of Toni Morrison.* New York: Greenwood P, 1987.

Homans, Margaret. "Feminist Fictions and Feminist Theories of Narrative." *Narrative* 2 (1994): 3–16.

Horvitz, Deborah. "Nameless Ghosts: Possession and Dispossession in *Beloved.*" *Studies in American Fiction* 17 (1989): 157–67.

House, Elizabeth B. "Toni Morrison's Ghost: The Beloved who is not Beloved." *Studies in American Fiction* 18 (1990): 17–26.

Hutcheon, Linda. *A Poetics of Postmodernism: History, Theory, Fiction.* New York: Routledge, 1988.

Irwin, John. *Doubling and Incest/Repetition and Revenge: A Speculative Reading of Faulkner.* Baltimore: Johns Hopkins UP, 1975.

———. "Horace Benbow and the Myth of Narcissa." Kartiganer and Abadie, *Faulkner and Psychology* 242–71.

Iser, Wolfgang. *The Implied Reader: Patterns in Communication in Prose Fiction from Bunyan to Beckett.* Baltimore: Johns Hopkins UP, 1974.

———. "Towards a Literary Anthropology." *The Future of Literary Theory.* Ed. Ralph Cohen. New York: Routledge, 1989. 208–28.

Jameson, Frederic. *Postmodernism; or, The Cultural Logic of Late Capitalism*. Durham: Duke UP, 1991.

Johnson, Barbara. "'Aesthetic' and 'Rapport' in Toni Morrison's *Sula*." *Textual Practice* 7 (1993): 165–72.

———. *A World of Difference*. Baltimore: Johns Hopkins UP, 1987.

Kartiganer, Donald M. *The Fragile Thread: The Meaning of Form in Faulkner's Novels*. Amherst: U Massachusetts P, 1979.

——— and Ann J. Abadie, eds. *Faulkner and Gender: Faulkner and Yoknapatawpha, 1994*. Jackson: UP of Mississippi, 1996.

———, eds. *Faulkner and Psychology: Faulkner and Yoknapatawpha, 1991*. Jackson: UP of Mississippi, 1994.

Kessler-Harris, Alice, and William McBrien, eds. *Faith of a (Woman) Writer*. New York: Greenwood, 1988.

Kiely, Robert. *Reverse Tradition: Postmodern Fictions and the Nineteenth Century Novel*. Cambridge: Harvard UP, 1993.

Kinney, Arthur F. *Faulkner's Narrative Poetics: Style as Vision*. Amherst: U of Massachusetts P, 1978.

Klotman, Phyllis R. "Dick-and-Jane and the Shirley Temple Sensibility in *The Bluest Eye*." *Black American Literature Forum* 13 (1979): 123–25.

Korenman, Joan S. "Faulkner's Grecian Urn." *Southern Literary Journal* 7 (Fall 1974): 3–23.

Kristeva, Julia. *Revolution in Poetic Language*. Trans. Margaret Waller. New York: Columbia UP, 1984.

Krumholz, Linda. "The Ghosts of Slavery: Historical Recovery in Toni Morrison's *Beloved*." *African American Review* 26 (1992): 395–408.

Kuenz, Jane. "*The Bluest Eye*: Notes on History, Community, and Black Female Subjectivity." *African American Review* 27.3 (1993): 421–431.

Lacan, Jacques. *Ecrits: A Selection*. Trans. Alan Sheridan. New York: Norton, 1977.

———. *The Four Fundamental Concepts of Psycho-Analysis*. Ed. Jacques-Alain Miller. Trans. Alan Sheridan. Hammondsworth: Penguin, 1977.

Leonard, John. "Review of *Jazz*." Gates and Appiah 36–49 [1992].

Lewis, Charles. "The Ironic Romance of New Historicism: *The Scarlet Letter* and *Beloved*." *Arizona Quarterly* 51.1 (Spring 1995): 33–60.

Lincoln, Abraham. *Speeches and Writings 1832–1858*. New York: Library of America, 1989.

Locke, Alain Le Roy, ed. *The New Negro: An Interpretation*. New York: A & C Boni, 1925

Locke, John. *An Essay Concerning the True Original, Extent, and End of Civil Government. The Two Treatises of Government*. Ed. Peter Laslett. Cambridge: Cambridge UP, 1988. 265–428.

Lott, Eric. *Love and Theft: Blackface Minstrelsy and the American Working Class*. New York: Oxford UP, 1993.

Lukács, Georg. *Realism in Our Time: Literature and the Class Struggle*. Trans. John and Necke Mander. Pref. George Steiner. New York: Harper, 1964.

MacKethan, Lucinda. "Names to Bear Witness: The Theme and Tradition of

Naming in Toni Morrison's *Song of Solomon*." *CEA Critic* 49.2–4 (Winter 1986–Spring 1987): 199–208.

Malinoski, Bronislaw. "The Role of Myth in Life." *Sacred Narrative: Readings in the Theory of Myth*. Ed. Alan Dundes. Berkeley: U of California P, 1984. 193–206.

Marshall, Alexander, III. "Faulkner and the Signifying Monkey: *The Sound and the Fury*." American Literature Association Conference. San Diego. 3 June 1994.

Martin, Jay. "Faulkner's 'Male Commedia': The Triumph of Manly Grief." Kartiganer and Abadie, *Faulkner and Psychology* 123–64.

Matthews, John T. "The Elliptical Nature of *Sanctuary*." *Novel* 17 (1984): 246–66.

———. "Faulkner and the Culture Industry." Weinstein, *Cambridge* 51–74.

———. *The Play of Faulkner's Language*. Ithaca: Cornell UP, 1982.

———. "The Rhetoric of Containment in Faulkner." *Faulkner's Discourse: An International Symposium*. Ed. Lothar Hönnighausen. Tübingen: Max Niemeyer Verlag, 1989.

McHale, Brian. *Constructing Postmodernism*. New York: Routledge, 1992.

———. *Postmodernist Fiction*. London: Routledge, 1987.

McKay, Nellie, ed. *Critical Essays on Toni Morrison*. Boston: G. K. Hall, 1988.

McPherson, Karen. "*Absalom, Absalom!*: Telling Scratches." *Modern Fiction Studies* 33 (1987): 431–50.

Mellard, James M. *Using Lacan, Reading Fiction*. Urbana: U of Illinois P, 1991.

Middleton, Joyce Irene. "From Orality to Literacy: Oral Memory in Toni Morrison's *Song of Solomon*." Smith 19–40.

Miller, J. Hillis. "The Two Relativisms: Point of View and Indeterminacy in the Novel *Absalom, Absalom!*" *Relativism in the Arts*. Ed. Betty Jean Craig. Athens: U of Georgia P, 1983: 148–70.

Mobley, Marilyn Sanders. "A Different Remembering: Memory, History, and Meaning in *Beloved*." Bloom, *Toni Morrison* 189–99.

Moreland, Richard C. *Faulkner and Modernism: Rereading and Rewriting*. Madison: U of Wisconsin P, 1990.

———. " 'He wants to put his story next to hers': Putting Twain's Story Next to Hers in Morrison's *Beloved*." *Modern Fiction Studies* 39 (1993): 501–25.

Morrison, Toni. "All That Jazz." Interview with Betty Fussell. Taylor-Guthrie 280–287.

———. "The Art of Fiction CXXXIV." Interview with Elissa Schappell. *Paris Review* 129 (1993): 83–125.

———. *Beloved*. New York: Knopf, 1987.

———. *The Bluest Eye*. New York: Knopf, 1993 [1970].

———. "Faulkner and Women." Fowler and Abadie, *Faulkner and Women* 295–302.

———. "Foreword," *The Harlem Book of the Dead*, by James Van der Zee, Owen Dodson, and Camille Billops. Dobbs Ferry, NY: Morgan & Morgan, 1978.

———. "In the Realm of Responsibility: A Conversation with Toni Morrison." With Marsha Jean Darling. *The Women's Review of Books*. 5 (March 1988): 5–6.

———. Interview with Angels Carabi. *Belles Lettres* 10.2 (1995): 40–43.

———. Interview with Bill Moyers. Taylor-Guthrie 262–274.

————. Interview with Christina Davis. *Présence Africaine* 145 (1988): 141–50.

————. Interview with Gloria Naylor. *The Southern Review* 21 (1985): 567–93.

————. Interview with Melvyn Bragg. *The South Bank Show.* Prod. & dir. Alan Benson. BBC. 1987.

————. Interview with Nellie McKay. *Contemporary Literature* 24 (1983): 413–29; rpt. Taylor-Guthrie 138–155.

————. " 'Intimate Things in Place': A Conversation With Toni Morrison." With Robert Stepto. Harper and Stepto 213–29.

————. *Jazz.* New York: Knopf, 1992.

————. "The Language Must Not Sweat: A Conversation with Toni Morrison." With Thomas LeClair. *New Republic* 21 March 1981: 25–29. Taylor-Guthrie 119–128.

————. "Living Memory: a meeting with Toni Morrison." With Paul Gilroy. *Small Acts: Thoughts on the politics of black cultures.* London: Serpent's Tail, 1993.

————. *The Nobel Lecture in Literature, 1993.* New York: Knopf, 1995.

————. *Playing in the Dark: Whiteness and the Literary Imagination.* Cambridge: Harvard UP, 1992; also Random, Vintage 1993.

————, ed. *Race-ing Justice, En-gendering Power: Essays on Anita Hill, Clarence Thomas, and the Construction of Social Reality.* "Introduction: Friday on the Potomac" vii–xxx. New York: Pantheon, 1992.

————. "Rootedness: The Ancestor as Foundation." *Black Women Writers (1950–1980): A Critical Evaluation.* Ed. Mari Evans. Garden City, NY: Anchor Doubleday, 1984. 339–345.

————. "The Seams Can't Show." Interview with Jane Bakerman. *Black American Literature Forum* 12.2 (1978): 56–60.

————. *Song of Solomon.* New York: Knopf, 1977.

————. *Sula.* New York: Knopf, 1993 [1973].

————. *Tar Baby.* New York: Knopf, 1981.

————. "Toni Morrison, In Her New Novel, Defends Women." Interview with Melvyn Rothstein. *New York Times* 26 August 1987: C17.

————. "Unspeakable Things Unspoken: The Afro-American Presence in American Literature." *Michigan Quarterly Review* 28 (1989): 1–34. Bloom, *Toni Morrison* 201–30.

————[Chloe Wofford]. "Virginia Woolf's and William Faulkner's Treatment of the Alienated." M. A. thesis. Cornell U, 1955.

North, Michael A. *The Dialect of Modernism: Race, Language, and Twentieth-Century Literature.* New York: Oxford UP, 1994.

O'Connor, Flannery. *Mystery and Manners: Occasional Prose.* London: Faber, 1972.

O'Donnell, Patrick. "Remarking Bodies: Divagations of Morrison from Faulkner." *Faulkner, His Contemporaries, and His Posterity.* Ed. Waldemar Zacharasiewicz. Tübingen: Francke Verlag. 322–27.

Otten, Terry. *The Crime of Innocence in the Fiction of Toni Morrison.* Columbia: U of Missouri P, 1989.

Page, Philip. "Circularity in Toni Morrison's *Beloved.*" *African American Review* 26 (1992): 31–39.

Parker, Robert Dale. *Faulkner and the Novelistic Imagination.* Urbana: U of Illinois P, 1985.

Peavy, Charles. *Go Slow Now: Faulkner and the Race Question.* Portland: U of Oregon P, 1971.

Pérez-Torres, Rafael. "Knitting and Knotting the Narrative Thread—*Beloved* as Postmodern Novel." *Modern Fiction Studies* 39 (1993): 689–707.

Pettis, Joyce. "Difficult Survival: Mothers and Daughters in *The Bluest Eye*." *SAGE* 4.2 (1987): 26–29.

Phelan, James. "Toward a Rhetorical Reader-Response Criticism: The Difficult, the Stubborn, and the Ending of *Beloved*." *Modern Fiction Studies* 39 (1993): 709–28.

Polk, Noel. *Faulkner's* Requiem for a Nun: *A Critical Study.* Bloomington: Indiana UP, 1981.

Porter, Carolyn. "Symbolic Fathers and Dead Mothers: A Feminist Approach to Faulkner." Kartiganer and Abadie, *Faulkner and Psychology* 78–122.

———. "(Un)making the Father: *Absalom, Absalom!*" Weinstein, *Cambridge* 168–96.

Rich, Adrienne. "When We Dead Awaken: Writing as Re-Vision." *On Lies, Secrets, and Silence: Selected Prose 1966–1978.* New York: Norton, 1979. 33–49.

Richter, David H., ed. *Falling into Theory: Conflicting Views on Reading Literature.* Boston: St. Martin's, 1994.

Rigney, Barbara Hill. *The Voices of Toni Morrison.* Columbus: Ohio State UP, 1991.

Roberts, Diane. *Faulkner and Southern Womanhood.* Athens: U of Georgia P, 1994.

Rosenblatt, Louise M. *The Reader, The Text, The Poem.* Carbondale: Southern Illinois UP, 1978.

Ross, Stephen M. *Fiction's Inexhaustible Voice: Speech and Writing in Faulkner.* Athens: U of Georgia P, 1989.

Rubenstein, Roberta. *Boundaries of the Self: Gender, Culture, Fiction.* Urbana: U of Illinois P, 1987.

Rushdy, Ashraf H. A. "Daughters Signifyin(g) History: The Example of Toni Morrison's *Beloved*." *American Literature* 64 (1992): 567–97.

———. " 'Rememory': Primal Scenes and Constructions in Toni Morrison's Novels." *Contemporary Literature* 31 (1990): 300–23.

Samuels, Wilfred D., and Clenora Hudson-Weems. *Toni Morrison.* Boston: Twayne, 1990.

Sargent, Robert. "A Way of Ordering Experience: A Study of Toni Morrison's *The Bluest Eye* and *Sula*." Kessler-Harris and McBrien 229–236.

Sartre, Jean-Paul. "Time in Faulkner: *The Sound and the Fury*." Trans. Martine Darmon. Hoffman and Vickery 225–47.

Sarup, Madan. *Jacques Lacan.* Toronto: U of Toronto P, 1992.

Schmudde, Carol E. "The Haunting of 124." *African American Review* 26 (1992): 409–15.

———. "Knowing When to Stop: A Reading of Toni Morrison's *Beloved*." *CLA Journal* 37 (1993): 121–35.

Schwartz, Lawrence H. *Creating Faulkner's Reputation: The Politics of Modern Literary Criticism.* Knoxville: U of Tennessee P, 1988.

Scruggs, Charles. "The Invisible City in Toni Morrison's *Beloved.*" *Arizona Quarterly* 48.3 (Autumn 1992): 95–132.

Silverman, Kaja. *The Acoustic Mirror: The Female Voice in Psychoanalysis and Cinema.* Bloomington: Indiana UP, 1988.

Smith, Valerie, ed. *New Essays on* Song of Solomon. New York: Cambridge UP, 1995.

Snead, James A. *Figures of Division: William Faulkner's Major Novels.* New York: Methuen, 1986.

Spillers, Hortense. "Mama's Baby, Papa's Maybe: An American Grammar Book." *diacritics* 17 (1987): 65–81.

———, ed. *Comparative American Identities: Race, Sex, and Nationality in the Modern Text.* New York: Routledge, 1991.

Stepto, Robert B. *From Behind the Veil: A Study of Afro-American Narrative.* Urbana: U of Illinois P, 1979.

Stockton, Kathryn Bond. "Heaven's Bottom: Anal Economics and the Critical Debasement of Freud in Toni Morrison's *Sula.*" *Cultural Critique* 24 (1993): 81–118.

Strauss, Harold. "Mr. Faulkner is Ambushed in Words." *New York Times* 1 Nov. 1936: 7.

Stryz, Jan. "The Other Ghost in *Beloved*: The Spectre of *The Scarlet Letter.*" *Genre* 24 (1991): 417–34.

Sundquist, Eric J. *Faulkner: The House Divided.* Baltimore: Johns Hopkins UP, 1983.

Tate, Allen. Foreword. Frank vii–x.

Taylor-Guthrie, Danille, ed. *Conversations with Toni Morrison.* Jackson: UP of Mississippi, 1994.

"The Thunder, Perfect Mind." *The Nag Hamadi Library in English.* Ed. James Robinson. 3rd ed. San Francisco: Harper Collins, 1990. 296–303.

Thurman, Judith. "A House Divided." *New Yorker* 2 Nov. 1987: 175–180.

Tirrell, Lynne. "Storytelling and Moral Agency." *Journal of Aesthetics and Art Criticism* 48 (1990): 115–26.

Troy, William. "The Poetry of Doom." *Nation* 31 Oct. 1936: 524–25.

Vickery, Olga W. *The Novels of William Faulkner: A Critical Interpretation.* Baton Rouge: Louisiana State UP, 1959.

Wadlington, Warwick. As I Lay Dying: *Stories Out of Stories.* New York: Twayne, 1992.

———. *Reading Faulknerian Tragedy.* Ithaca: Cornell UP, 1987.

Watson, Jay. *Forensic Fictions: The Lawyer Figure in Faulkner.* Athens: U of Georgia P, 1993.

Weinstein, Arnold. *Nobody's Home: Speech, Self, and Place in American Fiction from Hawthorne to DeLillo.* New York: Oxford UP, 1993.

Weinstein, Philip M., ed. *The Cambridge Companion to William Faulkner.* New York: Cambridge UP, 1995.

———. *Faulkner's Subject: A Cosmos No One Owns.* New York: Cambridge UP, 1992.

———. "Mister: The Drama of Black Manhood in Faulkner and Morrison." Kartiganer and Ann J. Abadie, *Faulkner and Gender* 273–296.

————. *What Else But Love?: The Ordeal of Race in Faulkner and Morrison.* New York: Columbia UP, 1996.

Werner, Craig. "Tell Old Pharoah: The Afro-American Response to Faulkner." *Southern Review* 19 (1983): 711–35.

West, Cornel. *Race Matters.* New York: Random, Vintage, 1994 [1993].

Williamson, Joel. *William Faulkner and Southern History.* New York: Oxford UP, 1993.

Willis, Susan. "Eruptions of Funk: Historicizing Toni Morrison." *Black American Literature Forum* 16 (1982): 34–42. McKay 308–29.

Wittenberg, Judith Bryant. "Race in *Light in August*: Wordsymbols and Obverse Reflections." Weinstein, *Cambridge* 146–167.

Woidat, Caroline M. "Talking Back to Schoolteacher: Morrison's Confrontation with Hawthorne in *Beloved.*" *Modern Fiction Studies* 39 (1993): 527–46.

Woolf, Virginia. "Modern Fiction." *The Common Reader*, First Series [1925]. Ed. Andrew McNeillie. New York: Harcourt, 1984. 146–54.

Wyatt, Jean. "Giving Body to the Word: The Maternal Symbolic in Toni Morrison's *Beloved.*" *PMLA* 108 (1993): 474–88.

Wyatt-Brown, Bertram. *Southern Honor: Ethics and Behavior in the Old South.* New York: Oxford UP, 1982.

Yaeger, Patricia. "The Father's Breasts." Yaeger and Kowaleski-Wallace. 3–21.

————, and Beth Kowaleski-Wallace, eds. *Refiguring the Father: New Feminist Readings of Patriarchy.* Carbondale: Southern Illinois UP, 1989.

Yanuck, Julius. "The Garner Fugitive Slave Case." *Mississippi Valley Historical Review* 40 (1953): 47–66.

INDEX